P   L   E

New York City
from $80 a Day

1st Edition

by Cheryl Farr Leas

with research assistance from Nathaniel R. Leas

IDG Books Worldwide, Inc.
An International Data Group Company
Foster City, CA • Chicago, IL • Indianapolis, IN • New York, NY

ABOUT THE AUTHOR

Cheryl Farr Leas was senior editor at Macmillan Travel before embarking on a freelance writing career. She also authors *Frommer's New York City* and *The Complete Idiot's Travel Guide to Hawaii*, and contributes to numerous other publications. When she's not traveling, she's at home in Park Slope, Brooklyn. Feel free to write her directly at rncleas@yahoo.com.

IDG BOOKS WORLDWIDE, INC.

An International Data Group Company
919 E. Hillsdale Blvd.
Suite 400
Foster City, CA 94404

Find us online at **www.frommers.com**

ISBN 0-02-863446-2
ISSN 1527-3687

Editor: Justin Lapatine
Production Editor: Carol Sheehan
Photo Editor: Richard Fox
Design by Michele Laseau
Staff Cartographers: John Decamillis, Roberta Stockwell
Page Creation by John Bitter and Marie Kristine Parial-Leonardo

Front cover photo: The Lower Manhattan skyline as seen from the Brooklyn Promenade

SPECIAL SALES

For general information on IDG Books Worldwide's books in the U.S., please call our Consumer Customer Service department at 1-800-762-2974. For reseller information, including discounts, bulk sales, customized editions, and premium sales, please call our Reseller Customer Service department at 1-800-434-3422.

Manufactured in the United States of America

5 4 3 2 1

Contents

1   **Planning an Affordable Trip to New York City   1**

   1   35 Money-Saving Tips   2

   2   Visitor Information   11

   3   When to Go   12

   ★   *New York City Calendar of Events*   12

   4   Tips for Travelers with Special Needs   17

   5   Getting There   19

   ★   *Money-Saving Package Deals*   20

   6   For Foreign Visitors   26

2   **Getting to Know New York City   29**

   1   Orientation   29

   ★   *Manhattan's Neighborhoods in Brief*   32

   2   Getting Around   39

   3   Playing It Safe   44

   ★   *Fast Facts: New York City*   45

3   **Accommodations You Can Afford   47**

   1   TriBeCa   48

   2   The Lower East Side   49

   3   Greenwich Village   50

   4   The Flatiron District & Gramercy Park   50

   ★   *Money-Saving Weekend Packages*   54

   5   Chelsea   56

   6   Times Square & Midtown West   57

   ★   *Dealmaking with the Chains*   64

   7   Midtown East & Murray Hill   66

   8   The Upper West Side   69

   9   The Upper East Side   76

  10   Harlem   76

4 **Great Deals on Dining** **78**

1 South Street Seaport & the Financial District 79

2 TriBeCa 82

3 Chinatown 84

4 SoHo & NoLiTa 85

5 The East Village 89

★ *Dining Zone: Little India* 91

★ *The New York Deli News* 92

6 Greenwich Village 94

7 The Flatiron District, Union Square & Gramercy Park 98

8 Chelsea 103

9 Times Square & Midtown West 104

10 Midtown East & Murray Hill 109

★ *Theme Restaurant Thrills!* 110

11 The Upper West Side 114

12 The Upper East Side 117

13 Harlem 118

5 **Exploring New York City** **119**

1 In New York Harbor: Lady Liberty, Ellis Island & the Staten Island Ferry 119

★ *Cheap Thrills: What to See & Do for Free* 122

2 Historic Lower Manhattan's Top Attractions 124

3 The Top Museums 127

4 The Top Skyscrapers & Architectural Marvels 139

5 Affordable Sightseeing Tours 143

★ *Show Me, Show Me, Show Me: Free Walking Tours* 145

6 Central Park 146

★ *Especially for Kids* 153

7 Shopping Highlights for Bargain Hunters 154

★ *Where the Fleas Are* 157

6 New York City After Dark 162

1 All the City's a Stage: The Theater Scene 162

★ *Bargain Alert—How to Save on Theater Tickets* 164

2 The Performing Arts: Concert Halls &
   Companies 165

★ *Last-Minute Discount Ticket-Buying Tips* 168

★ *Park It! Shakespeare & Other Free Fun* 170

3 Live Rock, Jazz, Blues & More 171

★ *Free Music* 174

4 Stand-Up Comedy 175

5 Bars & Cocktail Lounges 176

6 Dance Clubs & Party Scenes 181

7 The Lesbian & Gay Scene 183

Index 185

General Index 185

Accommodations Index 195

Restaurant Index 195

List of Maps

Manhattan Neighborhoods   33

Midtown Accommodations   52

Uptown Accommodations &
    Dining   70

Lower Manhattan, TriBeCa &
    Chinatown   81

The East Village & SoHo
    Area   87

Greenwich Village   95

Midtown Dining   100

Downtown Attractions   121

Midtown Attractions   128

Uptown Attractions   130

Central Park   147

AN INVITATION TO THE READER

In researching this book, we discovered many wonderful places—hotels, restaurants, shops, and more. We're sure you'll find others. Please tell us about them, so we can share the information with your fellow travelers in upcoming editions. If you were disappointed with a recommendation, we'd love to know that, too. Please write to:

Frommer's Portable New York City from $80 a Day, 1st Edition
IDG Travel
1633 Broadway
New York, NY 10019

AN ADDITIONAL NOTE

Please be advised that travel information is subject to change at any time—and this is especially true of prices. The authors, editors, and publisher cannot be held responsible for the experiences of readers while traveling. Your safety is important to us, however, so we encourage you to stay alert and be aware of your surroundings. Keep a close eye on cameras, purses, and wallets, all favorite targets of thieves and pickpockets.

WHAT THE SYMBOLS MEAN
✪ Frommer's Favorites

Our favorite places and experiences—outstanding for quality, value, or both.

The following abbreviations are used for credit cards:

AE	American Express	EU	Eurocard
CB	Carte Blanche	JCB	Japan Credit Bank
DC	Diners Club	MC	MasterCard
DISC	Discover	V	Visa
ER	enRoute		

FIND FROMMER'S ONLINE

Arthur Frommer's Budget Travel Online (www.frommers.com) offers more than 6,000 pages of up-to-the-minute travel information—including the latest bargains and candid, personal articles updated daily by Arthur Frommer himself. No other Web site offers such comprehensive and timely coverage of the world of travel.

Planning an Affordable Trip to New York City

*N*ew York, as everyone knows, is perpetually short on space and overflowing with people. And the city's huge popularity these days means that more people are coming to visit than ever before. It's a situation that turns the economy of supply and demand in the seller's favor, with vendors charging whatever the market will bear for goods and services. The result has been stratospheric prices, generally the highest you'll find in the country.

That's the bad news—but there's plenty of good news to tell, too. Simply put, you *can* stay in New York City comfortably, eat well, and see and do everything you want without blowing your budget. There are plenty of great deals in every category for the intrepid traveler who knows where to look for good value and mine for discounts.

THE NEW YORK–FROM-$80-A-DAY PREMISE

This premise may seem like a pipe dream, but it's not. The idea is this: With good planning and a watchful eye, you can keep your basic daily living costs—accommodations and three meals a day—down to as little as $80. This budget model works best for two adults traveling together who have at least $160 a day to work with and can share a standard room for two. This way, if you aim for accommodations costing around $100 double, you'll be left with about $30 per person per day for food (less drinks and tips).

In defining this basic premise we at Frommer's have assumed that you want to travel comfortably, with your own room rather than a hostel bunk, dining on good food rather than fast food at every meal. This book will also serve you well even if you don't need to keep your two-person budget to a strict $160 a day, but you want to keep the tabs down and get the most for your money at every turn.

Of course, the cost of sightseeing, transportation, and entertainment are all extras. But don't worry—I'll offer plenty of suggestions on how to keep those bills down, too.

1   35 Money-Saving Tips

1. **Buy a money-saving package deal.** In some cases, you'll get airfare, accommodations, transportation to and from the airport, plus extras—maybe a sightseeing tour, or restaurant and shopping discount coupons—for less than the hotel alone would have cost had you booked it yourself. For the lowdown on where and how to get the best package, see the "Money-Saving Package Deals" box, later in this chapter.

2. **Buy a *New York for Less* guidebook.** The primary value in buying this guide ($19.95) is the discount card within, which offers hundreds of discounts of 20% or more at restaurants, attractions, guided tour operators, shops, theaters, and nightlife spots around Manhattan. The card is good for up to four people for up to 8 days. You can order *New York for Less* by calling ☎ **888/ 463-6753** or online at **www.for-less.com**.

WHEN TO GO

3. **Choose your season carefully.** The biggest factor that will affect how much you pay for your hotel room and airfare is the season in which you travel. Prices on hotel rooms, in particular, can vary dramatically—by hundreds of dollars in some cases—depending on what time of year you visit. Winter is the best season for bargains, with summer being second-best. Spring and fall are the busiest and most expensive seasons after Christmas, but negotiating a decent rate is doable, especially in spring. Budget-minded travelers should skip Christmas and New Year's altogether. Thanksgiving, however, is a little-known bargain-hunter's delight.

GETTING TO NEW YORK CITY
AIR TRAVEL

4. **Consider all three airports when you're shopping around.** Fares can be markedly different depending on which airport you fly into—La Guardia, JFK, or Newark, NJ—and none of them are that far from Manhattan. In fact, Newark may often be more convenient to your Manhattan destination than the other two airports, and the public buses that run between the airport and the city are cheap and easy to use.

5. **Try the discount carriers.** When shopping the airlines, don't forget to check with the smaller, no-frills airlines that fly to New York, including Tower Air, ATA, and Spirit Airlines. You may not get the same kind of service or frequent-flyer bonuses that you

will get from the majors, but you may save a lot of dough. See section 5 "Getting There," below.

6. **Check for discounted fares with consolidators.** Also known as bucket shops, consolidators are a good place to find low fares. There's nothing shady about the reliable ones—basically, they're just big travel agents that get discounts for buying in bulk and pass some of the savings on to you. Be aware that consolidator tickets are usually non-refundable or come with stiff cancellation penalties.

   I recommend going with one of these reliable companies: I've gotten many great deals from **Cheap Tickets** (☎ 800/377-1000; www.cheaptickets.com). **Council Travel** (☎ 800/226-8624; www.counciltravel.com) and **STA Travel** (☎ 800/781-4040; www.sta.travel.com) cater especially to young travelers, but their bargain-basement prices are available to travelers of all ages. Other reliable consolidators include **1-800-FLY-4-LESS; Cheap Seats** (☎ 800/451-7200; www.cheapseatstravel.com); **1-800-FLY-CHEAP** (www.1800flycheap.com); or "rebators" such as **Travel Avenue** (☎ 800/333-3335 or 312/876-1116) and **Smart Traveller** (☎ 800/448-3338 or 305/448-3338), which rebate part of their commissions to you.

7. **Search the Internet for cheap advance-purchase fares.** Online booking services can be especially useful because they show you all the options, and some even make lower-priced suggestions on alternatives to your requested itinerary. Keep in mind, though, that it's a good idea to compare your findings with the research of a dedicated travel agent before you buy, especially when you're booking more than just a flight.

   A few of the better-respected virtual travel agents are **Travelocity** (www.travelocity.com) and **Microsoft Expedia** (www.expedia.com). I've also had good luck with the **Internet Travel Network** (www.itn.net). Another good bet is **Arthur Frommer's Budget Travel** (www.frommers.com), which offers detailed information on 200 destinations around the world, plus ways to save on flights, hotels, car reservations, and cruises. The newsletter is updated daily to keep you abreast of the latest ways to save. **Smarter Living** (www.smarterliving.com) is another great site featuring links to hotel, car rental, and other hot travel deals, as well as a low-fare tracker.

8. **Look into courier flights.** They're usually unavailable on domestic flights, but it's worth checking into if you're committed to flying for as little as humanly possible. Companies that hire

couriers use your luggage allowance for their business baggage; in return, you get a deeply discounted ticket. Flights are often offered at the last minute, and you may have to arrange a pretrip interview to make sure you're right for the job. **Now Voyager** (☎ 212/431-1616; www.nowvoyagertravel.com) has cross-country flights for as little as $199 round-trip and also offers non-courier discounted fares, so call the company even if you don't want to fly as a courier.

OTHER TRANSPORTATION OPTIONS

9. **Consider taking a train or bus instead of flying.** It's usually considerably cheaper than flying. And it saves you money upon arrival and departure, since you'll come right into and leave right out of Manhattan (where you want to be). Keep in mind, though, that the bus can eat up a lot of time and be pretty uncomfortable.

10. **Keep an eye out for fare sales.** Go to the "Schedules & Fares" page at **www.amtrak.com** and click on RAIL SALE, where you'll find segments discounted up to 90% on select routes. If you register your e-mail address you'll be notified of rail sale fares as they happen.

    Greyhound advertises fare sales right on their home page at **www.greyhound.com**. This national bus line usually has a number of money-saving deals, ranging from "Friends and Family Ride Free" companion deals to 21-day "Go Anywhere" fares for as little as $99.

GETTING AROUND NEW YORK CITY

11. **Use the subway and bus systems to travel around the city.** The transit system is probably the city's best bargain. It's safe, quick, efficient, and very, very cheap. Use taxis only late at night, when trains and buses can be few and far between, or when traveling a short distance in a group of three or four, when the fare may be less than three or four separate subway fares.

12. **Buy a MetroCard.** With the MetroCard, you can enjoy free transfers between bus and subway for 2 hours. If you're going to be in the city for a few days, buy a $15 pay-per-ride MetroCard, which will get you 11 rides for the price of 10. If you're going to do a lot of running around the city, consider a $4 **daily Fun Pass** or a $17 **Seven-Day MetroCard,** each of which allows unlimited rides for the life of the card.

13. **In the daytime, walk.** No other American city is so rewarding to explore on foot. Walking will save you a bunch of money—and

work off all the fab meals you'll no doubt buy with the savings.

ACCOMMODATIONS

14. **Watch for advertised discounts.** Scan ads in the Travel section of your local Sunday paper, which can be an excellent source for up-to-the-minute hotel deals. Also check the back of the Travel section of the Sunday *New York Times*, where the best weekend discount deals and other hotel bargains are usually on offer.

15. **Don't be afraid to bargain.** Always ask for a lower price than the first one quoted. Most rack rates include commissions of 10% to 25% or more for travel agents, which many hotels will cut if you make your own reservations and haggle a bit. Always ask politely whether a less-expensive room is available than the first one mentioned, or whether any special rates apply to you. You may qualify for corporate, student, military, senior citizen, or other discounts. Be sure to mention membership in AAA, AARP, frequent-flyer programs, corporate or military organizations, or trade unions, which may entitle you to special deals as well. The big chains, such as Sheraton, tend to be good about trying to save you money, but reservation agents often won't volunteer the information—you have to pull it out of them.

16. **Dial direct.** When booking a room in a chain hotel, call the hotel's local line as well as the toll-free number, and see where you get the best deal. The clerk who runs the place is more likely to

How to Save on ATM Charges

New York's Consumer Affairs chief has tried to ward off ATM withdrawal charges for consumers, but it seems to be a losing battle. At press time, the last holdout was **Republic National Bank,** which—thus far, anyway—does not charge for cash withdrawals at their ATM machines. RNB has ATM locations throughout the city, including 1185 Sixth Ave., between 46th and 47th streets; 661 Eighth Ave., at 42nd Street; and on the southeast concourse of the World Trade Center. You'll find a Republic National Bank branch locator online at **www.rnb.com**. At other banks throughout the city, expect to pay $1 or $1.50 each time you withdraw money from an ATM, in addition to what your home bank charges. Try to stay away from commercial machines, like those in hotel lobbies and corner delis, which often charge $2 or more per transaction.

know about booking patterns and will often grant deep discounts in order to fill up.

17. **Call a travel agent.** Certain hotels give travel agents discounts in exchange for steering business their way, so if you're shy about bargaining, an agent may be better equipped to negotiate discounts for you.

18. **Shop online.** New York hotels often offer "Internet-only" deals that can save you 10% to 20% over what you'd pay if you booked by telephone. And consider joining the **Playbill Online Theater Club** (www.playbillclub.com), a free service that offers some excellent members-only rates at select city hotels in addition to discounts on theater tickets.

19. **Investigate reservation services.** These outfits usually work as consolidators, buying up or reserving rooms in bulk, and then dealing them out to customers at a profit. They do garner special deals that range from 10% to 50% off; but remember, these discounts apply to rack rates. You're probably better off dealing directly with a hotel, but if you don't like bargaining, this is certainly a viable option. Most of them offer online services as well.

A few of the more reputable providers are **Accommodations Express** (☎ 800/950-4685; www.accommodationsxpress.com); **Quikbook** (☎ 800/789-9887; www.quikbook.com); and **Room Exchange** (☎ 800/846-7000 in the U.S., 800/486-7000 in Canada). The NYCVB offers a direct link to the **Hotel Reservations Network** (☎ 800/846-7666; www.newyork-hotel.com), which can save you up to 65% on the cost of your room at 140 city hotels ranging from budget to deluxe. **Microsoft Expedia** (www.expedia.com) features an online "Travel Agent" that will also direct you to affordable lodgings.

Another good bet is **Hotel ConXions** (☎ 800/522-9991 or 212/840-8686; www.hotelconxions.com), a consolidator that handles hotels in only a few select destinations, including New York. Also, because Hotel ConXions has guaranteed room blocks in select properties, they can often get you into a hotel that's otherwise sold out.

Important tips: Never just rely on a reservations service. Always check the rate a service offers you with the rate you can get directly from the hotel, which can actually be better on occasion. If you're being offered a stay in a hotel I haven't recommended, do more research to learn about it, especially if it isn't a reliable brand name like Holiday Inn or Best Western. It's not a deal if you end up at a dump.

20. **Be willing to share a bathroom.** For the best bargains in town, do as the Europeans do: Share a hall bath with your fellow travelers. If you can wrap your mind around this idea—it's not much different than sharing with your siblings when you were a kid—you can get a lot of bang for your buck. If you're on a tight budget, you'll be able to stay at a much nicer hotel than if you insist on a private bath. Many rooms even have private sinks, which means you can brush your teeth or wash your face without leaving the room. And, chances are, you'll never even have to wait for the shower anyway.

21. **Consider a suite.** It sounds like the ultimate splurge, but if you're traveling with another couple or your family, a suite can be a terrific bargain. They're always cheaper than two hotel rooms. The living room almost always features a sofa bed, and there's often a kitchenette where you can save money by preparing coffee and light meals for yourself. Remember that some places charge for extra guests beyond two, some don't.

22. **Consider a bed-and-breakfast or homestay.** There are thousands of B&Bs in New York, ranging from Spartan to splendid, and they usually fall on the lower end of the price continuum. A few words of warning, however: Credit cards are often accepted only for the deposit; you may have to pay the balance with a traveler's check, certified check, or cash. We've received complaints about B&Bs and homestays that offer one thing and deliver another, so be sure to get all promises in writing and an exact total up front. And try to pay entirely by credit card if possible, so you can dispute payment if the B&B fails to live up to its promises.

  ✪ **Homestay New York** (☎ 718/434-2071; www. homestayny.com) can book you into a private room with a New York City family that regularly welcomes travelers into their well-kept home. Many homes are in very nice residential neighborhoods in the outer boroughs, but all are within a half-hour of Manhattan via subway or bus. Visitors are matched to hosts by age and interests, and the carefully chosen hosts are more than happy to provide advice and assistance. Rates start at $110 single, $120 double with shared bath; $120 single, $130 double with private bath. A daily breakfast buffet and dinner every other night is included in the rate. Also included is an unlimited-ride MetroCard and a phone card (values depend on the length of your stay), making Homestay New York an excellent value. A 2-night minimum is required, and no credit cards are accepted.

Manhattan Getaways (☎ 212/956-2010; www.
manhattangetaways.com) can book you into a selection of B&B
rooms and private apartments that they have personally inspected,
starting at $95 a night. There's a three-night minimum, monthly
rates are available, and credit cards are accepted.

Manhattan Lodgings (☎ 212/677-7616; www.
manhattanlodgings.com), also provides B&B stays and private
apartments for stays lasting 3 days to 3 months. Rates start at $85
per night. Credit cards are accepted for deposits, but you'll have
to pay the balance with cash, money order, or traveler's checks.
New York Bed and Breakfast Reservation Center (☎ 800/
747-0868 or 212/977-3512) provides a similar service, but they
do not accept credit cards.

23. **If you're on a shoestring budget, book a hostel bed.** You'll have
no privacy whatsoever—you'll share a room with fellow travelers
from all over the world and all facilities are common—but there's
no arguing with the rate. The largest hostel in the **Hostelling
International–American Youth Hostels** system (☎ 800/
444-6111 or 202/783-6161; www.hiayh.org) houses travelers in
bunk-bedded rooms for $22 to $27 per night. Also consider the
dorms at the better-located **Gershwin Hotel,** costing just $22.

24. **Try the Y.** The Y isn't as cheap as hostel living, but the facilities
are much better. The **YMCA of Greater New York,** 333 Seventh
Ave., New York, NY 10001 (☎ 212/630-9600; www.ymcanyc.
org), has eight residences for travelers throughout the city's five
boroughs. You'll have a private room (some have private baths)
and access to the on-site fitness center for absolutely free. A number of Ys also feature a calendar of cultural and other events,
which fosters a warm community spirit. The main Manhattan
branches are reviewed in chapter 3.

25. **Do as little business as possible through the hotel.** Any service
the hotel offers will come with a stiff premium. You can easily
find dry cleaners or other services in most areas of Manhattan.
Find out before you dial whether your hotel imposes a surcharge
on local or long-distance calls; it may be cheaper to use the pay
phone in the lobby instead.

26. **If you're driving into the city and will need to garage your
car, check parking rates with the hotel before you book.** Many
hotels negotiate discounted parking rates at nearby garages.
Choose a hotel that has negotiated a good rate, or you may end
up paying a fortune for parking (thereby negating any savings
you've earned by booking a cheap hotel).

DINING

27. **Book a hotel room with a kitchenette.** Booking a room with a kitchenette allows you to grocery shop and eat some meals in. Even if you only use it to prepare breakfast, you're bound to save money on food this way.

28. **Stay at a place that includes breakfast in the rate.** Always ask what's included, especially if you're used to starting the day with a hearty meal; the offerings will most likely be a limited continental breakfast.

29. **Use any coupons you can get your hands on.** The New York Convention & Visitors Bureau offers a free visitor's guide that includes discount coupons in the back. Even if you order one in advance (see "Visitor Information," below), stop into the local visitor centers while you're in town, where the wall racks sometimes have coupons and ads for freebies, two-for-ones, and other dining discounts. And before you leave home, check the deals offered through the **Playbill Online Theater Club** (**www.playbillclub.com**), which often include a few dining discounts; joining is free. If you're an American Express cardholder, check for online dining coupons at **www.americanexpress.com,** by clicking on "Special Offers" under "Personal," then "Cardmember Special Offers." If you do use a dining discount coupon, remember to tip your waiter based on the full value of the meal; he's on a budget, too.

30. **Eat ethnic.** New York has what's probably the best collection of ethnic restaurants in the country, and the best of them offer first-class eats for low, low prices. For tips on where to go, see chapter 4.

SIGHTSEEING

31. **Buy a CityPass.** Pay one price ($27.50) for admission to six top attractions—the observation deck at the World Trade Center, the Metropolitan Museum of Art, the Museum of Modern Art, the Empire State Building, the American Museum of Natural History, and the *Intrepid* Sea-Air-Space Museum—which would cost you fully twice as much to visit if you paid for each one separately. This just may be New York's best sightseeing deal, especially for newcomers intent on hitting all the big sights. More importantly, CityPass is not a coupon book; it contains actual admission tickets, so you can bypass lengthy ticket lines. CityPass is good for 9 days from the first time you use it. It's sold at all participating attractions, and discounted rates are available for kids and seniors.

If you want to avoid that first line, order your CityPass online at **www.citypass.net** or www.ticketweb.com, or call **Ticketweb** at ☎ **212/269-4TIX.** Call **CityPass** at ☎ **707/256-0490** for further details.

32. **Take advantage of freebies.** Many of the best things to do and see in Manhattan are absolutely free, from walking the Brooklyn Bridge to riding the Staten Island Ferry to exploring Central Park to attending TV show tapings. Additionally, a number of organizations now offer neighborhood walking tours at absolutely no charge. And many museums and attractions that charge admission have free or pay-as-you-wish programs one day or evening a week. For details, see chapter 5.

PERFORMING ARTS & NIGHTLIFE

33. **Buy discounted theater tickets in advance.** Joining the **Playbill Online Theater Club** (**www.playbillclub.com**) can yield substantial savings on theater tickets for select Broadway and off-Broadway shows. Becoming a member is free; all you have to do is register, and you'll have access to discounts that can range from a few dollars to as much as 45% off regular ticket prices.

   If you're visiting between early February and late April, be sure to look into the **Passport to Off Broadway,** which can save you even more money—between 10% and 50%—on more than 200 off- and off-off-Broadway shows. Go online at **www.newyork. sidewalk.com/passport** or call the Visitors Bureau for further information.

34. **Buy discounted same-day theater tickets at the TKTS booth.** If your heart is set on seeing a particular show, you should buy full-price advance tickets before you come to the city. But if you're flexible about what you see, check out TKTS, which sells day-of-show tickets to popular plays both on Broadway and off at 25% to 50% off. Many theater box offices also sell discounted day-of-show tickets directly. See chapter 6.

35. **Eschew high-priced, high-profile performances for lesser-known, lower-priced surprises.** Sure, attending a performance at the New York Philharmonic or a big-name Broadway extravaganza is a must if you can afford it. But you'll save money—and maybe even enjoy yourself more—by looking beyond the obvious to lower-profile options. Some of the city's top cultural organizations offer free outdoor events in summer, from Shakespeare in the Park to the Metropolitan Opera. Comb the

listings in *Time Out New York, New York* magazine, *The New Yorker,* and the *New York Times* at any time of year for free entertainment throughout the city, which may range from free dance performances to book talks at Barnes & Noble.

2 Visitor Information

For information before you leave home, your best source (besides this book, of course) is the **New York Convention & Visitors Bureau** (NYCVB). You can call the bureau's 24-hour hotline at ☎ **800/NYC-VISIT** or 212/397-8222 to order a **Big Apple Visitors Kit,** detailing hotels, restaurants, theaters, attractions, events, and more. The bureau also has a terrific Web site at **www. nycvisit.com**. To speak to a travel counselor who can answer specific questions, call ☎ **212/484-1222** Monday through Friday from 9am to 5pm EST (multilingual counselors are available). If you prefer to write for information, send your request to the NYCVB at 810 Seventh Ave., New York, NY 10019.

For visitor center locations once you arrive, see "Orientation" in chapter 2.

FOR U.K.-BASED VISITORS   In late 1998, an **NYCVB Visitor Information Center** opened in London at 33–34 Carnaby St. (☎ **020/ 7-437-8300**). The new center offers a wealth of information and free one-on-one travel-planning assistance to New York–bound travelers. It's open Monday through Friday from 10am to 4pm.

SITE SEEING: THE BIG APPLE ON THE WEB

The NYCVB's **www.nycvisit.com** is a terrific online resource offering tons of information on the city, from trip-planning basics to tips on where to take the kids. But there's much more to be learned from the web than the official line:

- **www.newyork.citysearch.com**   **Citysearch,** done in cooperation with the *Daily News* and *Time Out* magazine, is an excellent source for up-to-the-minute information on what's happening in the city.
- **www.nytoday.com**   Set up in an easy-access daily calendar format, this *New York Times* site is an expanded version of the paper's coverage. You'll find even more events listings and critics' reviews in this electronic version, including museum schedules and sports events, plus the *Times'* definitive restaurant reviews.

3　When to Go

Summer or winter, rain or shine, there's always great stuff going on in New York City, so there's no real "best" time to go.

If money is your biggest concern, you might want to visit in winter, between the first of the year and early April. Sure, the weather can suck, but hotels are suffering from the post-holiday blues, and rooms often go for a relative song.

Spring and fall are the busiest, and most expensive, seasons after holiday time. From April to June and September to November, temperatures are mild and pleasant, and the light is beautiful. Don't expect hotels to be handing you deals, but you may be able to negotiate a decent rate.

New York's spit-shined image means that the city is drawing more families these days, and they usually visit in the summer. Still, the prospect of heat and humidity keeps some people away, making June, July, and the first half of August a generally cheaper time to visit than later in the year, and very good hotel deals are often available.

At Christmas, all bets are off—expect to pay top dollar for everything. But Thanksgiving can be a great time to come: It's a little-known secret that most hotels away from the Thanksgiving Day Parade route have empty rooms sitting, and they're usually willing to make great deals to fill them.

NEW YORK CITY CALENDAR OF EVENTS

As with any schedule of events, the following information is always subject to change. Always confirm information before you make plans around an event. Call the venue or the NYCVB at ☎ 212/484-1222, or go to www.nycvisit.com for the latest details on these or other events taking place during your trip.

February

- **Chinese New Year.** Every year Chinatown rings in its own New Year (based on a lunar calendar) with 2 weeks of celebrations, including parades with dragon and lion dancers and vivid costumes of all kinds. In 2000 (4698 in the Chinese designation), the Year of the Dragon, the Chinese New Year falls on February 5. Call ☎ **212/484-1222** or the Chinese Center at 212/373-1800.

- ✪ **Westminster Kennel Club Dog Show.** Some 30,000 dog fanciers from the world over congregate at Madison Square Garden for the "World Series of Dogdom." The ultimate purebred pooch fest.

Call ☎ **800/455-3647** for information. Tickets become available after January 1 through **Ticketmaster** (☎ 212/307-7171 or 212/307-1212; www.ticketmaster.com). Mid-February.

March

- **St. Patrick's Day Parade.** More than 150,000 marchers join in the world's largest civilian parade, as Fifth Avenue from 44th to 86th streets rings with the sounds of bands and bagpipes. The parade usually starts at 11am, but go extra-early if you want a good spot. Call ☎ **212/484-1222.** March 17.

- **Ringling Bros. and Barnum & Bailey Circus.** The circus comes to town in grand style as elephants and bears and other performing animals parade down the city streets from the railroad at Twelfth Avenue and 34th Street to Madison Square Garden early on the morning before the first performance (usually well before daybreak). Call ☎ **212/465-6741** for this year's dates, or **Ticketmaster** (☎ **212/307-7171** or 212/307-1212; www.ticketmaster.com) for tickets. Usually late March to early April.

April

✪ **The Easter Parade.** This isn't a traditional parade, per se: There are no marching bands, no baton twirlers, no protesters. Once upon a time, New York's gentry came out to show off their tasteful but discreet toppings. Today, it's more about flamboyant exhibitionism, with hats and costumes that get more outrageous every year—and anybody can join right in for free. The parade generally runs Easter Sunday from about 10:30am to 3pm along Fifth Avenue from 48th to 57th streets. Call ☎ **212/484-1222.**

May

- **Ninth Avenue International Food Festival.** Spend the day sampling sizzling Italian sausages, homemade pierogi, spicy curries, and an assortment of other ethnic dishes at one of the city's best street fairs, stretching along Ninth Avenue from 37th to 57th streets. Call ☎ **212/581-7217.** One weekend in mid-May.

✪ **Fleet Week.** About 10,000 Navy and Coast Guard personnel are "at liberty" in New York for the annual Fleet Week. Usually from 1 to 4pm daily, you can visit the ships and aircraft carriers that dock at the piers on the west side of Manhattan, and watch some dramatic exhibitions by the U.S. Marines. But even if you don't take in any of the events, you'll know it's Fleet Week, since those 10,000 sailors invade midtown in their starched white uniforms. It's simply wonderful—*On the Town* come to life. Call ☎ **212/245-2533,** or visit **www.uss-intrepid.com**. Late May.

June

- **Lesbian and Gay Pride Week and March.** Fifth Avenue goes wild as the gay/lesbian community celebrates the Stonewall Riot of June 27, 1969—which for many marks the beginning of the gay liberation movement—with bands, marching groups, floats, and plenty of panache. The parade starts on upper Fifth around 52nd Street and continues into the Village, where a street festival and a waterfront dance party with fireworks cap the day. Call ☎ 212/807-7433. Mid- to late June.

- ✪ **Shakespeare in the Park.** The Delacorte Theater in **Central Park** is the setting for first-rate free performances under the stars. Be prepared to line up hours in advance for tickets; you're allowed to collect two. Call ☎ **212/539-8750** or 212/539-8500, or point your web browser to **www.publictheater.org**. June through August.

- ✪ **Restaurant Week.** Dine for only $20 at some of New York's finest restaurants. Participating places vary each year, so watch for the full-page ads in the *New York Times* and other publications, or call the visitors bureau, since they usually have a list of restaurants by mid- or late May. Reserve instantly. One week in late June; some restaurants extend their offers through summer to Labor Day.

July

- ✪ **Independence Day Harbor Festival and Fourth of July Fireworks Spectacular.** Start the day amid the patriotic crowds at the Great July Fourth Festival in Lower Manhattan, watch the tall ships sail up the Hudson River in the afternoon, and then catch Macy's great fireworks extravaganza (one of the country's most fantastic) over the East River (the best vantage point is from the FDR Drive, which closes to traffic several hours before sunset). Call ☎ **212/484-1222,** or Macy's Special Events at 212/494-2922. July 4.

August

- **Lincoln Center Out-of-Doors.** This series of free music and dance performances is held outdoors at Lincoln Center. Schedules are available in July. Call ☎ **212/875-5108,** or visit **www.lincolncenter.org**. August to September.

- **New York Fringe Festival.** Held in a variety of tiny Lower East Side venues for a mainly hipster crowd, this ten-day arts festival presents alternative as well as traditional theater, musicals, dance, comedy, and all manner of performance art, including new media. The quality can vary wildly and some performances really push the envelope, but you'd be surprised at how many shows are actually *good.* Call ☎ **888/FRINGENYC** or 212/307-0229, or point your web browser to **www.fringenyc.org**. Mid- to late August.

✪ **U.S. Open Tennis Championships.** The final Grand Slam event of the tennis season is held at the slick new facilities at **Flushing Meadows Park** in Queens. Tickets go on sale in May, and the event sells out far in advance. You can usually scalp tickets outside the complex (an illegal practice, of course). The last few matches of the tournament are most expensive, but you'll see a lot more tennis early on, when your ticket allows you to wander the outside courts and view several different matches. Call ☎ **718/760-6200** or Telecharge at ☎ **800/524-8440** for tickets as far in advance as possible; visit **www.usopen.org** for additional information. Two weeks surrounding Labor Day.

• **Harlem Week.** The world's largest black and Hispanic cultural festival actually spans about two weeks. Expect a whole slate of music, from gospel to hip hop, and lots of other festivities. Call ☎ **212/862-7200** or 212/484-1222 for this year's schedule. Mid-August.

September

✪ **Wigstock.** Come see the Lady Bunny, Lypsinka, and even RuPaul—plus hundreds of other fabulous drag queens—strut their stuff. The crowd is usually wilder than the stage acts. For information on this year's event, visit **www.wigstock.nu** or call ☎ **800/494-TIXS** or the Lesbian and Gay Community Services Center at ☎ 212/620-7310. Labor Day weekend.

• **Broadway on Broadway.** This free afternoon show features the songs and casts from virtually every Broadway production performing on a stage erected in the middle of Times Square. Call ☎ **212/768-1560.** Early or mid-September.

• **Feast of San Gennaro.** An atmospheric and festive Little Italy street fair honoring the patron saint of Naples, with great food, traditional music, carnival rides, games, and vendors set up along Mulberry Street north of Canal Street. Usually mid-September.

✪ **New York Film Festival.** This 2-week festival is a major stop on the film-fest circuit. Screenings are held in various Lincoln Center venues; advance tickets are a good bet always, and a necessity for certain events (especially evening and weekend screenings). Call ☎ **212/875-5610,** or visit **www.filmlinc.com**. Late September to early October (Sept 22–Oct 9 in 2000).

✪ **BAM Next Wave Festival.** One of the city's most important cultural events takes place at the Brooklyn Academy of Music. The months-long festival showcases experimental new dance, theater, and music works by both renowned and lesser-known international artists. Call ☎ **718/636-4100** or visit **www.bam.org**. September through December.

October
• **Ice-Skating.** Show off your skating style in the limelight at the diminutive **Rockefeller Center** rink (☎ 212/332-7654), open from mid-October to mid-March (you'll skate under the magnificent Christmas tree for the month of December) or at the larger **Wollman Rink** in Central Park, at 59th Street and Sixth Avenue (☎ 212/396-1010), which usually closes in early April, depending on the weather.

✪ **Greenwich Village Halloween Parade.** This is Halloween at its most outrageous, with drag queens and assorted other flamboyant types parading through the village in wildly creative costumes. The parade route has changed over the years, but most recently it has started after sunset at Spring Street and marched up Sixth Avenue to 23rd Street or Union Square. Check the papers for the exact route so you can watch—or participate, if you have the threads and the imagination. October 31.

November
✪ **New York City Marathon.** Some 25,000 hopefuls from around the world participate in the largest U.S. marathon, and at least a million fans will cheer them on as they follow a route that touches on all five New York boroughs and finishes in Central Park. Call ☎ **212/860-4455,** or visit **www.nyrrc.org** for the date (most likely to be Nov 4 or 11 in 2000).

• **Radio City Music Hall Christmas Spectacular.** A rather gaudy extravaganza, but lots of fun nonetheless. Starring the Radio City Rockettes and a cast that includes live animals. For information, call ☎ 212/247-4777 or visit **www.radiocity.com**; buy tickets at the box office or via Ticketmaster's **Radio City Hotline** (☎ 212/307-1000). Mid-November to early January.

✪ **Macy's Thanksgiving Day Parade.** The procession from Central Park West and 77th Street down Broadway to Herald Square at 34th Street continues to be a national tradition. Huge hot-air balloons of Rocky and Bullwinkle, Snoopy, Bart Simpson, and other cartoon favorites are the best part of the fun. The night before, you can usually see the big blow-up on Central Park

West at 79th Street; call in advance (☎ **212/494-5432** or 212/494-2922) to see if it will be open to the public again this year. November 23 in 2000.

✪ **Big Apple Circus.** New York City's homegrown, not-for-profit circus is a favorite with children and the young at heart. A tent is pitched in Damrosch Park at Lincoln Center. Call ☎ **212/268-2500.** November to January.

December

✪ **Lighting of the Rockefeller Center Christmas Tree.** The annual lighting ceremony is accompanied by an ice-skating show, singing, entertainment, and a huge crowd. The tree stays lit around the clock until after the new year. Call ☎ **212/632-3975.** Early December.

✪ **Holiday Trimmings.** Stroll down festive Fifth Avenue, and you'll see doormen dressed as wooden soldiers at **FAO Schwarz,** a 27-foot sparkling snowflake floating over the intersection outside **Tiffany's,** the **Cartier** building ribboned and bowed in red, wreaths warming the necks of the **New York Public Library's** lions, and fanciful figurines in the windows of **Saks Fifth Avenue** and **Lord & Taylor.** Throughout December.

✪ **New Year's Eve.** The biggest party of them all happens in **Times Square,** where hundreds of thousands of raucous revelers count down in unison the year's final seconds until the lighted ball drops at midnight at 1 Times Square. Call ☎ **212/354-0003** or 212/484-1222 or visit **www.timessquarebid.org**. December 31.

4 Tips for Travelers with Special Needs

FOR FAMILIES

Many hotels have babysitting services or will provide you with lists of reliable sitters. If this doesn't pan out, there's the **Baby Sitters' Guild** (☎ 212/682-0227) or the **Frances Stewart Agency** (☎ 212/439-9222). The sitters are licensed, insured, and bonded, and can even take your child on outings.

FOR TRAVELERS WITH DISABILITIES

Hospital Audiences, Inc. (☎ 888/424-4685, Mon–Fri 9am–5pm), proves details about accessibility at cultural institutions, hotels, restaurants, and transportation as well as cultural events adapted for people with disabilities. Trained staff members answer specific questions based on your particular needs and the dates of your trip. This nonprofit organization also publishes the *Access for All* guidebook, available by sending a $5 check to **Hospital Audiences, Inc.,** 220 W. 42nd St., 13th floor, New York, NY 10036 (☎ **212/575-7676;** TTY 212/575-7673; www.hospitalaudiences.org).

Another terrific source is **Big Apple Greeter** (☎ **212/669-8159;** TTY: 212/669-8273; www.bigapplegreeter.org). All of their employees are extremely well-versed on accessibility issues. They can provide a resource list of agencies that serve the city's disabled community, and sometimes have special discounts available to theater and music performances. Big Apple Greeter even offers one-to-one tours that pair volunteers with disabled visitors; reserve at least one week ahead.

GETTING AROUND   **Gray Line Air Shuttle** (☎ **800/451-0455** or 212/315-3006) operates minibuses with lifts from JFK, La Guardia, and Newark airports to midtown hotels by reservation; be sure to arrange pick-up three or four days in advance.

Taxis are required to carry people who have folding wheelchairs and seeing-eye or hearing-ear dogs. However, don't be surprised if they don't run each other down trying to get to you; even though you shouldn't have to, you may have to wait a bit for a friendly (or fare-desperate) driver to come along.

Public buses are an inexpensive and easy way to get around New York. All buses' back doors are supposed to be equipped with wheelchair lifts (though the city has had complaints that not all are in working order). Buses also "kneel," lowering their front steps for people who have difficulty boarding. Passengers with disabilities pay half-price fares (75¢). The **subway** isn't yet fully wheelchair accessible, but some stations are. Call the **Accessible Line** at ☎ **718/596-8585** (daily 6am–9pm) for bus and subway transit info, or point your web browser to **www.mta.nyc.ny.us/nyct**.

FOR SENIOR TRAVELERS

One of the benefits of age is that travel often costs less. New York subway and bus fares are half price (75¢) for people 65 and older. Many museums and sights (and some theaters and performance halls) offer discounted entrance and tickets to seniors, so don't be shy about asking. Always bring an ID card, especially if you've kept your youthful glow.

Members of the **American Association of Retired Persons (AARP),** 601 E. St. NW, Washington, DC 20049 (☎ **800/424-3410** or 202/434-2277; www.aarp.org), get discounts not only on hotels but on airfares and car rentals, too. If you're not already a member, do yourself a favor and join.

FOR GAY & LESBIAN TRAVELERS

If you want help planning your trip, the **International Gay & Lesbian Travel Association** (IGLTA) (☎ **800/448-8550** or 954/776-2626; www.iglta.org), can link you up with the appropriate gay-friendly service organization or tour specialist. Members are kept informed of gay and gay-friendly hoteliers, tour operators, and airline and cruise-line representatives.

   The Lesbian and Gay Community Services Center is at 1 Little W. 12th Street, between Ninth Avenue and Hudson Street, one block south of West 13th Street (☎ **212/620-7310;** www.gaycenter.org), and is open daily 9am to 10:30pm. (This is its temporary home for about two years while its headquarters at 208 W. 13th St. is being renovated.) You can call to request the Community Calendar of Events that lists happenings like lectures, dances, concerts, readings, and films.

   Another good source for lesbian and gay events during your visit is *Homo Xtra (HX),* a weekly magazine you can pick up in appropriate bars, clubs, and stores throughout town. Lesbians now have their own version, *HX for Her.* Both mags have information online at **www.hx.com**. In addition, the weekly *Time Out New York* boasts a terrific gay and lesbian section.

FOR STUDENTS

Many attractions and theaters offer reduced admission to students, so don't forget to bring your valid student ID and proof of age.

5 Getting There

BY PLANE

Three major airports serve New York City: **John F. Kennedy International Airport** (JFK) in Queens, about 15 miles (or one hour's driving time) from midtown Manhattan; **La Guardia Airport** also in Queens, about 8 miles (or 30 minutes) from midtown; and **Newark International Airport** in nearby New Jersey, about 16 miles (or 45 minutes) from midtown. Online information on all three airports is available at **www.panynj.gov**.

   Almost every major domestic carrier serves at least one of these airports; most serve two or all three. **America West** (☎ 800/235-9292; www.americawest.com), **American** (☎ 800/433-7300; www.aa.com), **Continental** (☎ 800/525-0280 or 800/523-3273; www.flycontinental.com), **Delta** (☎ 800/221-1212; www.delta-air.com), **Northwest** (☎ 800/225-2525; www.nwa.com), **TWA** (☎ 800/221-2000; www.twa.com), **US Airways** (☎ 800/428-4322;

Money-Saving Package Deals

Before you start your search for the lowest airfare, you may want to consider booking your flight as part of a travel package.

Package tours are not the same as escorted tours. They are simply a way to buy airfare and accommodations (and sometimes extras like sightseeing tours and hard-to-get theater tickets) at the same time. For visiting New York, a package can be a smart way to go. In many cases, a package that includes airfare, hotel, and transportation to and from the airport will cost you less than your hotel bill alone would have had you booked it yourself. That's because packages are sold in bulk to tour operators, who then resell them to the public at a cost that drastically undercuts standard rates.

Packages, however, vary widely. Some offer a better class of hotels than others. Some offer the same hotels for lower prices. With some packagers, your choice of accommodations and travel days may be limited. Which package is right for you depends entirely on what you want.

The best place to start your search for a package deal is the travel section of your local Sunday newspaper. Also check the ads in the back of national travel magazines like *Travel & Leisure, National Geographic Traveler,* and *Condé Nast Traveler.*

One of the biggest packagers in the Northeast, **Liberty Travel** (☎ **888/271-1584;** www.libertytravel.com) boasts a full-page ad in many Sunday papers. You won't get much in the way of service, but you will get a good deal. They offer great-value 2- to

www.usairways.com), and **United** (☎ 800/241-6522; www.ual.com). Most major international carriers also serve New York.

These smaller, sometimes struggling airlines usually offer lower fares, but don't expect the same kind of service you get from the majors: **AirTran** (☎ 800/AIRTRAN; www.airtran.com), **ATA** (☎ 800/I-FLY-ATA; www.ata.com), **Frontier** (☎ 800/432-1359; www.frontierair.com), **Midway** (☎ 800/446-4392; www.midwayair.com), **Midwest Express** (☎ 800/452-2022; www.midwestexpress.com), **Spirit Airlines** (☎ 800/772-7117; www.spiritair.com), **SunJet International** (☎ 800/4-SUNJET; www.sunjet.com), **Sun Country** (☎ 800/752-1218; www.suncountry.com), and **Tower Air** (☎ 800/34-TOWER or 718/553-8500; www.towerair.com). And the nation's leading discount

7-night New York packages that usually include such freebies as a Circle Line cruise and discounts at Planet Hollywood, plus lots of good hotels to choose from.

The major airlines offering good-value packages to New York include **Continental Airlines Vacations** (☎ 800/634-5555; www.coolvacations.com); **Delta Vacations** (☎ 800/872-7786; www.deltavacations.com); **United Vacations** (☎ 800/328-6877; www.unitedvacations.com); **US Airways Vacations** (☎ 800/455-0123; www.usairwaysvacations.com); **American Airlines Vacations** (☎ 800/321-2121; aav3.aavacations.com); and **Northwest WorldVacations** (☎ 800/800-1504; www.nwa.com/vacpkg).

For one-stop shopping on the web, go to **www.vacationpackager.com**, a search engine that will link you to many different package-tour operators offering New York City vacations, often with a company profile summarizing the company's basic booking and cancellation terms.

In New York, many **hotels** also offer package deals, especially for weekend stays. Some of the best deals in town are those that include theater tickets, sometimes for otherwise sold-out shows like *The Lion King*. (Most aren't air/land combos, however; you'll have to book your airfare separately.) I've included tips on hotels that regularly offer them in chapter 3, but always ask about available packages when you call any hotel.

airline, **Southwest** (☎ 800/435-9792; www.iflyswa.com), flies into Long Island's Islip Airport, 40 miles east of Manhattan.

For advice on how to get the best airfare, see "35 Money-Saving Tips," earlier in this chapter.

TRANSPORTATION TO & FROM THE NEW YORK AREA AIRPORTS

For complete transportation information for all three airports (JFK, La Guardia, and Newark), call **Air-Ride** (☎ 800/247-7433); it gives recorded details on bus and shuttle companies and private-car services registered with the New York and New Jersey Port Authority.

On the arrivals level at each airport, the Port Authority also has Ground Transportation Information counters where you can get information and book transport. Most transportation companies also have courtesy phones near the baggage-claim area.

SUBWAYS & PUBLIC BUSES   Taking the MTA to and from the airport can be a hassle, but it's the cheapest way to go—just $1.50 each way. However, keep in mind that the subways and buses that currently serve the airports involve multiple transfers and staircases; count on more hauling to your hotel (or a taxi fare) once you arrive in Manhattan. This won't work for travelers with too much luggage, because you won't have anywhere to store it on the bus or subway train.

For additional subway and bus information, see "Getting Around" in chapter 2.

From/to Kennedy Airport   You can take the **A train** to Kennedy airport, which connects to one of two free **shuttle buses** that serve all the JFK terminals. Plan on 2 hours or more in each direction: The subway ride to midtown takes about 75 minutes, and you'll need another 20 to 30 minutes for the shuttle ride to your terminal; also be sure to factor in waiting time at both ends.

Upon exiting the terminal, pick up the shuttle bus (marked LONG TERM PARKING LOT) out front; it takes you to the Howard Beach station, where you pick up the A train to the west side of Manhattan.

If you're traveling to JFK from Manhattan, be sure to take the A train that says **FAR ROCKAWAY** or **ROCKAWAY PARK**—*not* LEFFERTS BOULEVARD. Get off at the Howard Beach/JFK Airport station and connect to the shuttle bus.

From/to La Guardia   The **M60 bus** serves all La Guardia terminals. Follow the GROUND TRANSPORTATION signs and look for the M60 stop sign at the curb. The bus will take you to Broadway and 116th Street on Manhattan's west side, where you can transfer to a downtown bus or the 1 or 9 subway; you can also pick up the N subway into Manhattan by disembarking at the Astoria Boulevard station in Queens. The bus runs daily between 6am and 1am, leaving at roughly half-hour intervals and taking about 50 minutes. (From Manhattan, you can pick up the bus as early as 4:30am from Broadway and 106th St.) Be sure to allow at least $1^1/4$ hours, however—you never know about traffic. *Money-saving tip:* Use a MetroCard to pay your fare and you'll save the extra $1.50 it usually costs for the transfer. For the complete schedule and other pick-up and drop-off points, visit **www.mta.nyc.ny.us/nyct/service/ m60.htm**.

From/to Newark   Sorry, there's no public transportation; use one of the private bus services listed below.

PRIVATE BUSES & SHUTTLES   Buses and shuttle services are more expensive than using the MTA for airport transfers, but they're more comfortable and less expensive than taxis (but usually more time-consuming).

Gray Line Air Shuttle (☎ 800/451-0455 or 212/315-3006; www.graylinenewyork.com) vans depart JFK, La Guardia, and Newark every 20 minutes 7am to 11:30pm and will drop you off at most hotels between 23rd and 63rd streets in Manhattan, or Port Authority (34th Street and Seventh Avenue) or Grand Central (42nd Street and Park Avenue) terminals if you need to catch a subway to another part of town or a train to the 'burbs. No reservation is required; just go to the ground-transportation desk or use the courtesy phone in the baggage-claim area and ask for Gray Line. Service from most major mid-Manhattan hotels to all three airports operates 5am to 7pm; you must call a day in advance to arrange a hotel pickup. The one-way fare for JFK is $19, for La Guardia $16, and for Newark $19, but you can save a few bucks by prepaying your round-trip at the airport ($28 for JFK and Newark, $26 for La Guardia).

The familiar blue vans of **Super Shuttle** (☎ 800/258-3826 or 718/482-9703; www.supershuttle.com/nyc.htm) serve all three airports, providing door-to-door service to Manhattan and points on Long Island every 15 to 30 minutes around the clock. As with Gray Line, you don't need to reserve your airport-to-Manhattan ride; just go to the ground-transportation desk or use the courtesy phone in the baggage-claim area. Hotel pickups for your return trip require 24 to 48 hours advance booking. Fares are $15 one-way to and from JFK, $14 one-way to and from La Guardia, $17 one-way to and from Newark.

New York Airport Service (☎ 718/706-9658) buses travel from JFK and La Guardia to the Port Authority Bus Terminal (42nd Street and Eighth Avenue), Penn Station (34th Street and Seventh Avenue), Grand Central Terminal (Park Avenue between 41st and 42nd), or your midtown hotel. Follow the GROUND TRANSPORTA-TION signs to the curbside pickup or look for the uniformed agent. Buses depart the airport every 20 to 70 minutes between 6:30am and midnight. Buses to JFK and La Guardia depart the Port Authority and Grand Central Terminal on the Park Avenue side every 15 to 30 minutes, depending on the time of day and day of the week. To request direct shuttle service from your hotel, call at least 24 hours in advance. One-way fare for JFK is $13, $10 for La Guardia; children under 12 ride free with a parent.

If You're Flying into Islip Airport with Southwest

Southwest Airlines, the nation's leading discount carrier, now flies into the New York area via Long Island's Islip Airport, 40 miles east of Manhattan. If you're on one of these flights and you're Manhattan bound, here's the best way to get into the city:

Call **Village Taxi** when you land (☎ **516/563-4611***),* and they'll send over a driver to take you 3 miles to the Ronkonkoma Long Island Rail Road Station, where you can pick up a LIRR (Long Island Rail Road) train to Manhattan. The taxi fare is $8. From Ronkonkoma, it's about a 1^{1}/$_{2}$-hour train ride to Manhattan's Penn Station; the one-way fare is $9.50 at peak hours, $6.50 off-peak. Trains usually leave Ronkonkoma once or twice every hour, depending on the day and time. For more information, call ☎ **718/ 217-5477** or point your web browser to **www.mta.nyc.ny.us/lirr.**

Classic Transportation (☎ **516/567-5100**) and **Legends** (☎ **888/LEGENDS** or 718/788-1234) will pick you up at Islip Airport and deliver you to Manhattan via private sedan, but expect to pay $100 plus tolls and tip for the privilege of door-to-door service. Be sure to arrange for it 24 hours in advance.

Olympia Trails (☎ **888/662-7700** or 212/964-6233; www. olympiabus.com) provides excellent service every 5 to 15 minutes (less frequently during off hours) from Newark Airport to four Manhattan locations: the World Trade Center (on West Street), Penn Station (at 34th Street and Eighth Avenue), the Port Authority (on 42nd Street between Eighth and Ninth avenues), and Grand Central (41st Street between Park and Lexington). Passengers to and from the Grand Central Terminal location can connect to Olympia's midtown shuttle vans, which service most hotels between 30th and 65th streets. From the above departure points in Manhattan, service runs every 15 to 30 minutes depending on your pickup point; call for exact schedule. The one-way fare is $10, $15 if you connect to the hotel shuttle.

If you're traveling to a borough other than Manhattan, call **ETS Air Service** (☎ **888/467-4996** or 718/221-5341) for shared door-to-door service.

TAXIS   Taxis are available at designated taxi stands outside the terminals, with uniformed dispatchers on hand during peak hours (follow the GROUND TRANSPORTATION or TAXI signs). There may be a long line, but it generally moves pretty quickly. Fares, whether

An Airport Warning

Never accept a car ride from the hustlers who hang out in the terminal halls. They're illegal, don't have proper insurance, and aren't safe. Sanctioned city cabs and car services wait outside the terminals.

fixed or metered, don't include bridge and tunnel tolls ($3.50 to $4) or tip (15% to 20% is customary). They do include all passengers in the cab and luggage—never pay more than the metered or flat rate, except for tolls and a tip (from 8pm to 6am a 50¢ surcharge also applies on New York yellow cabs). Taxis have a limit of four passengers. For more on taxis, see "Getting Around" in chapter 2.

- **From JFK:** At press time, the flat rate of $30 to and from Manhattan (plus any tolls and tip) was in place. The meter will not be turned on and the surcharge will not be added.
- **From La Guardia:** $20 to $25, metered.
- **From Newark:** The dispatcher for New Jersey taxis gives you a slip of paper with a flat rate ranging from $30 to $45 (toll and tip extra), depending on where you're going in Manhattan. The yellow-cab fare from Manhattan to Newark is the meter amount plus $10 and tolls (about $40 to $50, perhaps a few dollars more with tip).

PRIVATE-CAR & LIMOUSINE SERVICES   Private-car and limo companies provide convenient 24-hour door-to-door airport transfers, allowing you to arrange your pick-up in advance and avoid the hassles of the taxi line. Call at least 24 hours in advance (even earlier on holidays), and a driver will meet you near baggage claim or at your hotel for a return trip. You'll probably be asked to leave a credit-card number to guarantee your ride, and be offered the choice of indoor or curbside pickup (you'll save a few dollars with an outside pickup). Prices vary slightly by company and the size of car reserved, but expect to pay around the same as you would for a taxi for a basic sedan with one stop; toll and tip policies are the same. (Note that car services are not subject to the flat-rate rule that taxis are for rides to and from JFK.) Ask when booking what the fare will be and whether you can use your credit card to pay for the ride. There may be waiting charges tacked on if the driver has to wait an excessive amount of time for your plane to land when picking you up, but the car companies will usually check on your flight beforehand to get an accurate landing time.

I've had the best luck with **Carmel** (☎ 800/922-7635 or 212/666-6666); **Legends** (☎ 888/LEGENDS or 718/788-1234); and

Allstate (☎ 800/453-4099 or 212/741-7440). All have good cars, responsive dispatchers, and polite drivers.

BY TRAIN

Amtrak (☎ **800/USA-RAIL;** www.amtrak.com) runs frequent service to Penn Station (Seventh Avenue between 31st and 33rd streets). To get the best rates, book early (as much as six months in advance) and travel on weekends.

BY BUS

Buses arrive at the Port Authority Terminal (Eighth Ave. between 40th and 42nd sts.), where you can easily transfer to your hotel by taxi, subway, or bus. For complete schedule and fare information, contact **Greyhound Bus Lines** (☎ **800/231-2222;** www.greyhound.com).

While the bus is likely to be the cheapest option, don't just assume; sometimes, a full-fare bus ticket is no cheaper than the train. If you get lucky, you might even catch an airline fare sale that will make flying the most prudent option.

BY CAR

From the **New Jersey Turnpike** (I-95) and points west, there are three Hudson River crossings into the city's west side: the **Holland Tunnel** (lower Manhattan), the **Lincoln Tunnel** (midtown), and the **George Washington Bridge** (upper Manhattan).

From **upstate New York,** take the **New York State Thruway** (I-87), which becomes the **Major Deegan Expressway** (I-87) through the Bronx. For the east side, continue to the Triborough Bridge and then down the FDR Drive. For the west side, take the Cross Bronx Expressway (I-95) to the Henry Hudson Parkway (9A) or the Saw Mill River Parkway to the Henry Hudson Parkway south.

From **New England,** the **New England Thruway** (I-95) connects with the **Bruckner Expressway** (I-278), which leads to the Triborough Bridge and the FDR on the east side. For the west side, take the Bruckner to the Cross Bronx Expressway (I-95) to the Henry Hudson Parkway south.

6   For Foreign Visitors

ENTRY REQUIREMENTS

The following requirements may have changed somewhat by the time you plan your trip. Check at any U.S. embassy or consulate for current information and requirements, or plug into the U.S. State Department's Web site at **http://travel.state.gov**. Go to **http://travel.state.gov/visa_services.html** for the latest entry requirements, while **http://travel.state.gov/links.html** will provide you with contact information for U.S. embassies and consulates worldwide.

VISAS   The U.S. State Department has a **Visa Waiver Pilot Program** allowing citizens of certain countries to enter the United States without a visa for stays of up to 90 days.

At press time, this visa waiver program applied to citizens of these countries: Andorra, Argentina, Australia, Austria, Belgium, Brunei, Denmark, Finland, France, Germany, Iceland, Ireland, Italy, Japan, Liechtenstein, Luxembourg, Monaco, the Netherlands, New Zealand, Norway, San Marino, Slovenia, Spain, Sweden, Switzerland, and the United Kingdom. Citizens of these countries need only a valid passport and a round-trip air or cruise ticket in their possession upon arrival.

Canadian citizens may enter the United States without visas; they need only proof of residence.

Citizens of all other countries must have: (1) a valid passport that expires at least six months later than the scheduled end of their visit to the United States; and (2) a tourist visa, which may be obtained without charge from any U.S. consulate.

Obtaining a Visa   To obtain a visa, you must submit a completed application form (either in person or by mail) with a $1^1/_2$-inch-square photo, and must demonstrate binding ties to a residence abroad. Usually you can obtain a visa at once or within 24 hours, but it may take longer during the summer rush from June through August. If you cannot go in person, contact the nearest U.S. embassy or consulate for directions on applying by mail. Your travel agent or airline office may also be able to provide you with visa applications and instructions. The U.S. consulate or embassy that issues your visa will determine if you will be issued a multiple- or single-entry visa and any restrictions regarding the length of your stay.

British subjects can obtain up-to-date passport and visa information by calling the **U.S. Embassy Visa Information Line** (☎ 0891/200-290) or the **London Passport Office** (☎ 0990/210-410) for recorded information).

MEDICAL REQUIREMENTS   Unless you're arriving from an area known to be suffering from an epidemic (particularly cholera or yellow fever), inoculations or vaccinations are not required for entry into the United States. If you have a disease that requires treatment with narcotics or syringe-administered medications, carry a valid signed prescription from your physician to allay any suspicions that you may be smuggling narcotics (a serious offense that carries severe penalties in the U.S.).

For up-to-the-minute information concerning HIV-positive travelers, contact the Center for Disease Control's **National Center for HIV** (☎ **404/332-4559;** www.hivatis.org) or the **Gay Men's Health Crisis** (☎ **212/367-1000;** www.gmhc.org).

DRIVER'S LICENSES   Foreign driver's licenses are mostly recognized in the United States, although you may want to get an international driver's license if your home license is not written in English.

MONEY

The U.S. monetary system is simple: The most common bills are the $1 (colloquially, a "buck"), $5, $10, and $20 denominations. There are also $2 bills (seldom encountered), $50 bills, and $100 bills (the last two are usually not welcome as payment for small purchases). There are six denominations of coins: 1¢ (1 cent, or a penny); 5¢ (5 cents, or a nickel); 10¢ (10 cents, or a dime); 25¢ (25 cents, or a quarter); 50¢ (50 cents, or a half dollar); and the rare $1 piece. A new gold $1 piece will be introduced by the year 2000.

The "foreign-exchange bureaus" so common in Europe are rare in the United States. You'll find them in New York's prime tourist areas like Times Square, but expect to get extorted on the exchange rate. **American Express** (☎ **800/AXP-TRIP;** www. americanexpress.com) has many offices throughout the city, including at the New York Hilton, 1335 Sixth Ave. (☎ 212/664-7798); the New York Marriott Marquis, 1535 Broadway (☎ 212/ 575-6580); at Macy's Herald Square, 34th Street and Broadway (☎ 212/695-8075); and 65 Broadway (☎ 212/493-6500). **Thomas Cook Currency Services** (☎ **212/753-0132;** www. thomascook.com) has locations at JFK Airport; 1590 Broadway (☎ 212/265-6049); 317 Madison Ave. (☎ 212/883-0040); and 511 Madison Ave. (☎ 212/753-2398).

2

Getting to Know New York City

This chapter gives you an insider's take on Manhattan's most distinctive neighborhoods and streets, tells you how to get around town, and serves as a handy reference to everything from personal safety to libraries and liquor laws.

1 Orientation

VISITOR INFORMATION

INFORMATION OFFICES The **Times Square Visitors Center,** 1560 Broadway, between 46th and 47th streets (where Broadway meets Seventh Avenue; ☎ 212/768-1560; www. timessquarebid.org), is the city's top info stop. The center features a helpful information desk offering loads of citywide information. There's also a tour desk selling tickets for Gray Line bus tours and Circle Line boat tours; a Metropolitan Transportation Authority (MTA) desk staffed to sell MetroCards, provide free public transit maps, and answer all of your questions on the transit system; a Broadway Ticket Center selling full-price show tickets (although we suggest you get your tickets across the street from the discount TKTS booth or directly at the box office); ATMs and currency exchange machines; computer terminals with free Internet access courtesy of Yahoo; an international newsstand; and more. It's open daily from 8am to 8pm.

The New York Convention and Visitors Bureau's new **NYCVB Visitor Information Center** is at 810 Seventh Ave., between 52nd and 53rd streets (☎ 212/484-1222; www.nycvisit.com). In addition to loads of information on citywide attractions and a multilingual information counselor on hand to answer questions, the center also has interactive terminals that provide free touch-screen access to visitor information via Citysearch and sell advance tickets to major attractions (which can save you from standing in long ticket lines once you arrive). There's also an ATM, a gift shop, and a bank of phones that connect you directly with American Express card-member services. Open Monday through Friday from 8:30am to 5:30pm, Saturday and Sunday from 9am to 5pm.

PUBLICATIONS   For comprehensive listings of films, concerts, performances, sporting events, museum and gallery exhibits, street fairs, and special events, the following publications are your best bets:

- *The New York Times* (**www.nytimes.com**) features terrific arts and entertainment coverage, particularly in the two-part Friday "Weekend" section and the Sunday "Arts & Leisure" section.

- *Time Out New York* (**www.timeoutny.citysearch.com**) is my favorite weekly magazine. *TONY* features excellent coverage in all categories, and it's attractive, well organized, and easy to use. A new issue hits newsstands every Thursday.

- The free weekly *Village Voice* (**www.villagevoice.com**), the city's legendary alterna-paper, is available late Tuesday downtown and early Wednesday in the rest of the city. The arts and entertainment coverage couldn't be more extensive, but I find the paper unwieldy to navigate.

- The "Cue" section in the back of the glossy weekly *New York* magazine (**www.newyorkmag.com**) is an easy-to-use selective guide to city arts and entertainment.

CITY LAYOUT

Open a map and you'll see the city is comprised of five boroughs: **Manhattan;** the **Bronx; Queens; Brooklyn;** and **Staten Island.** But it is Manhattan, the long finger-shaped island pointing southwest off the mainland, that most visitors think of when they envision New York. Despite the fact that it's the city's smallest borough (13^1/$_2$ miles long, 2^1/$_4$ miles wide, 22 square miles), Manhattan contains the city's most famous attractions, buildings, and cultural institutions.

In most of Manhattan, finding your way around is a snap because of the logical, well-executed grid system by which the streets are numbered. If you can discern uptown and downtown, and East Side and West Side, you can find your way around pretty easily.

Avenues run north and south (uptown and downtown). Most are numbered. **Fifth Avenue** divides the East Side from the West Side of town, and serves as the eastern border of Central Park north of 59th Street. **First Avenue** is all the way east and **Twelfth Avenue** is all the way west. The three most important unnumbered avenues on the East Side you should know are between Third and Fifth avenues: **Madison** (east of Fifth), **Park** (east of Madison), and **Lexington** (east of Park, just west of Third). Important unnumbered avenues on the West Side are **Avenue of the Americas,** which all New Yorkers call Sixth Avenue; **Central Park West,** which is what Eighth Avenue north of 59th Street is called as it borders Central Park on the west; **Columbus Avenue,** which is what Ninth Avenue is called north of 59th Street; and **Amsterdam Avenue,** or Tenth Avenue north of 59th.

Broadway is the exception to the rule—the only major avenue that doesn't run uptown–downtown. It cuts a diagonal path across the island, from the northwest tip down to the southeast corner. As it crosses most major avenues, it creates **squares** (Times Square, Herald Square, Madison Square, and Union Square, for example).

Streets run east–west (crosstown) and are numbered consecutively as they proceed uptown from Houston Street. So to go uptown, simply walk north of, or to a higher-numbered street, than where you are. Downtown is south of (or a lower-numbered street than) your current location. Traffic generally runs east on even-numbered streets and west on odd-numbered streets, with a few exceptions, like the major east–west thoroughfares—**14th, 23rd, 34th, 42nd, 57th, 72nd, 79th, 86th,** and so on—which have two-way traffic.

As I've already mentioned, Fifth Avenue is the dividing line between the **East Side** and **West Side** of town (except below Washington Square, where Broadway serves that function). On the East Side of Fifth Avenue, streets are numbered with the distinction East, on the West Side of that avenue they are numbered West. East 51st Street, for example, begins at Fifth Avenue and runs to the East River, and West 51st Street begins at Fifth Avenue and runs to the Hudson River.

Unfortunately, these rules don't apply to neighborhoods in Lower Manhattan, south of 14th Street—like Wall Street, Chinatown, SoHo, TriBeCa, the Village—since they sprang up before engineers devised this brilliant grid scheme. A good map is essential when exploring these areas.

Orientation Tips

When you give a taxi driver an address, always specify the cross streets. New Yorkers, even most cab drivers, probably wouldn't know where to find 994 Second Ave., but they do know where to find 51st and Second. The exact number is given only as a further precision.

MANHATTAN'S NEIGHBORHOODS IN BRIEF

DOWNTOWN

Lower Manhattan: South Street Seaport & the Financial District   Lower Manhattan constitutes everything south of Chambers Street. Battery Park (point of departure for the Statue of Liberty and Ellis Island) is on the very south tip of Manhattan Island, while historic South Street Seaport lies a bit north on the east coast (just south of the Brooklyn Bridge). The rest of the area is considered the Financial District, which is anchored by the World Financial Center, the World Trade Center, and Battery Park City to the west and Wall Street running crosstown to the south. Most of the streets are narrow concrete canyons, with Broadway serving as the main uptown–downtown artery.

Just about all of the major subway lines congregate here before they either end or head to Brooklyn (the Sixth Avenue B, D, F, Q line being the chief exception).

During the week this neighborhood is the heart of capitalism and city politics, and the sidewalks are crowded with the business-suit set. It's fun to be here at the height of the hustle and bustle, between 8am and 6pm on weekdays.

TriBeCa   Bordered by the Hudson River to the west, the area north of Chambers Street, west of Broadway, and south of Canal Street is the *Tri*angle *Be*low *Ca*nal Street, or TriBeCa. Since the 1980s, as SoHo became saturated with chic, the spillover has been quietly transforming TriBeCa into one of the city's hippest residential neighborhoods, where celebrities and families quietly coexist in cast-iron warehouses converted into spacious, expensive loft apartments. Still, historic sidestreets evoke a bygone, more human-scaled New York, as do a few hold-out businesses and old-world pubs.

I love this neighborhood, because it seems to have brought together the old city and the new without bastardizing either. It also happens to be home to one of my favorite budget hotels in the city. The main uptown-downtown drag is West Broadway (2 blocks to the west of Broadway), and the main subway line is the 1/9, which stops at Franklin in the heart of the 'hood. Take your map; the streets are a maze.

Chinatown   The former marshlands northeast of City Hall and below Canal Street, from Broadway to the Bowery, are where Chinese immigrants were forced in the 1870s. This booming neighborhood is now a conglomeration of Asian populations. As such, it offers tasty cheap eats and exotic shops offering strange foods, herbs,

Manhattan Neighborhoods

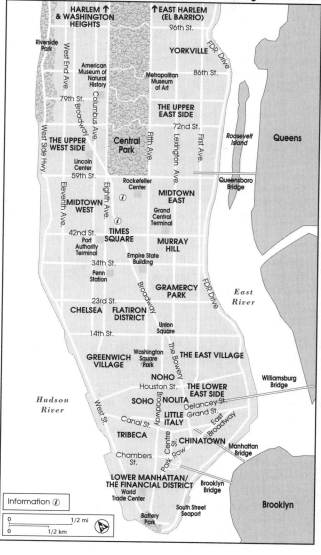

and souvenirs. The area is also home to sweatshops, however, and doesn't have quite the quaint character you'd find in San Francisco. Still, it's a blast to walk down Canal Street, peering into the myriad electronics and luggage stores and watching crabs cut loose from their handlers at the exotic fish markets.

The Grand Street (B, D, Q) and Canal Street (J, M, Z, N, R, 6) stations will get you to the heart of the action. The streets empty out after around 9pm; they remain quite safe, but the neighborhood is more enjoyable during the daytime bustle.

Little Italy   Nearby is Little Italy, just as ethnic if not quite so vibrant, and compelling for its own culinary treats. Traditionally the area east of Broadway between Houston and Canal streets, the community is shrinking today, due to the encroachment of thriving Chinatown. It's now limited mainly to Mulberry Street, where you'll find most restaurants, and just a few offshoots. Walk up Mulberry from the Grand Street Station, or east from the Spring Street station on the no. 6 line.

The Lower East Side   Of all the successive waves of immigrants and refugees who passed through here from the mid-19th century to the 1920s, it was the Eastern European Jews who left the most lasting impression on this neighborhood, which runs between Houston and Canal streets, and east of the Bowery.

Drugs and crime ultimately supplanted the immigrant communities, dragging the Lower East Side into the gutter until recently. While it has been gentrifying nicely over the last few years, the area can still be very dicey in spots. There are some remnants of what was once the largest Jewish population in America along Orchard Street, where you'll find great bargain hunting in its many fabric and clothing stores. The trendy set can be found mostly along Ludlow Street, north of Delancey, with the biggest concentration of action being just south of Houston.

This area is not well served by the subway system, so your best bet is to take the F train to Second Avenue and walk east on Houston; when you see Katz's Deli, you'll know you've arrived.

SoHo & NoLiTa   No relation to the London neighborhood of the same name, **SoHo** got its moniker as an abbreviation of "South of Houston Street" (pronounced HOUSE-ton). This super-fashionable neighborhood extends down to Canal Street, between Sixth Avenue to the west and Lafayette Street (1 block east of Broadway) to the east.

An industrial zone during the 19th century, SoHo is now a prime example of urban gentrification and a major New York attraction thanks to its impeccably restored cast-iron buildings, influential arts scene, and stylish boutiques. On weekends, the cobbled streets are crowded with gallery goers and shoppers, with the prime action being between Broadway and Sullivan Street north of Grand Street. At night, the neighborhood is transformed into a terrific, albeit pricey, dining and bar-hopping neighborhood (although I recommend some appealing affordable options, too; see chapter 4). The neighborhood is easily accessible by subway: Take the B, D, F, or Q train to the Broadway–Lafayette stop; the N, R to the Prince Street Station; or the C, E to Spring Street.

In recent years SoHo has been crawling its way east, taking over Mott and Mulberry streets—and white-hot Elizabeth Street in particular—north of Kenmare Street, an area now known as **NoLiTa** for its *No*rth of *Li*ttle *Ita*ly location. NoLiTa is becoming increasingly well known for its hot shopping prospects, but don't expect bargains. Good, affordable restaurants abound, though, making the neighborhood well worth a browse. The 6 to Spring Street will get you closest by subway, but it's just a short walk east from SoHo proper.

The East Village The East Village, which extends between 14th and Houston streets, from Broadway east to First Avenue and beyond to Avenues A, B, C, and D, is where the city's real Bohemia has gone. It's a fascinating mix of affordable ethnic and trendy restaurants, upstart clothing designers and kitschy boutiques, punk-rock clubs (yep, still) and folk cafes, all of which give the neighborhood a youthful vibe. The gentrification that has swept the city has made a huge impact on this neighborhood, but there's still a seedy element that some of you won't find appealing.

Unless you're traveling along 14th Street (the L line will drop you off at Third and First avenues), your best bet is to take the N, R to 8th Street or the 6 to Astor Place and walk east. Always stay alert in the East Village. The landscape changes from one block to the next, especially the farther east you go. Venture only with care into Alphabet City (avenues A, B, C, and D).

Greenwich Village Tree-lined streets crisscross and wind, each block revealing yet another row of Greek Revival town houses, a well-preserved Federal-style house, or a peaceful courtyard or square. This is "the Village," from Broadway west to the Hudson River, bordered by Houston Street to the south and 14th Street to the north. It defies Manhattan's orderly grid system with streets that predate it, virtually every one choc-a-block with activity, and unless you live here it may be impossible to master the lay of the land—so be sure to have a map on hand as you explore.

The Village changes faces depending on what block you're on. Some of the highest-priced real estate in the city runs along lower Fifth Avenue, which dead-ends at Washington Square Park. Serpentine Bleecker Street stretches through most of the neighborhood, and is emblematic of the area's historical bent. The tolerant, anything-goes attitude in the Village has fostered a large gay community, which is still largely in evidence around Christopher Street and Sheridan Square. The streets west of Seventh Avenue, an area known as the West Village, boast a more relaxed vibe and some of the city's most charming and historic brownstones. Three colleges (New York University, Parsons School of Design, and the New School for Social Research) keep the area thinking young—hence the popularity of Eighth Street, lined with shops selling cheap, hip clothes to bridge-and-tunnel kids and the college crowd.

The Village makes a great base for independent-minded visitors who prefer to avoid more touristy areas in favor of a quirkier, more residential view of the city. The Seventh Avenue line (1, 2, 3, 9) is the area's main subway artery, while the West 4th Street stop (where the A, C, E lines meet the B, D, F, Q lines), serves as its central hub.

MIDTOWN

Chelsea　This neighborhood is coming on strong of late as a hip address, especially for the gay community. A low-rise composite of town houses, tenements, lofts, and factories, Chelsea comprises roughly the area west of Sixth Avenue from 14th to 30th streets. Its main arteries are Seventh and Eighth avenues, and it's primarily served by the C, E and 1, 9 subway lines.

The Chelsea Piers sports complex to the far west and a host of shops, well-priced bistros, and thriving bars along the main drags have contributed to the area's rebirth. You'll find a number of very popular flea markets set up in parking lots along Sixth Avenue, between 24th and 27th streets, on the weekends. The cutting edge of today's New York art scene is on far West 22nd Street, the city's newest "gallery row."

The Flatiron District, Union Square & Gramercy Park　These adjoining and at places overlapping neighborhoods are some of the city's most appealing.

The **Flatiron District** lies south of 23rd Street to 14th Street, between Broadway and Sixth Avenue, and centers around the historic Flatiron Building on 23rd (so named for its triangular shape) and Park Avenue South, which has become a sophisticated new Restaurant Row. Below 23rd Street along Sixth Avenue, mass-market discounters like Filene's Basement and Bed Bath & Beyond have moved in. The shopping gets classier on Fifth Avenue and along Broadway, the city's home-furnishings alley.

Union Square is the hub of the entire area; the N, R, 4, 5, 6, and L trains stop here, making it easy to reach from most other city neighborhoods. Union Square has experienced a major renaissance in the last decade. It's perhaps best known as the setting for New York's premier greenmarket every Monday, Wednesday, Friday, and Saturday, where it's easy to assemble a cheap gourmet picnic. In-line skaters take over the market space in the after-work hours. A number of hip, mostly affordable restaurants rim the square, as do superstores like the city's best Barnes & Noble superstore, a brand-new Virgin Megastore, and an equally infant 14-screen movieplex.

From about 16th to 23rd streets, east from Park Avenue South to about Second Avenue, is the leafy, largely residential district known as **Gramercy Park.**

Times Square & Midtown West   Midtown West, the vast area from 34th to 59th streets west of Fifth Avenue to the Hudson River, is New York's tourism central, where you'll find the bright lights and bustle that draws people from all over the world. As such, this is also the city's biggest hotel neighborhood, with lots of budget and mid-priced choices amidst the famous-name luxury hotels.

The 1, 2, 3, 9 subway line serves the massive neon station at the heart of Times Square, at 42nd Street between Broadway and Seventh Avenue, while the B, D, F, Q line runs up Sixth Avenue to Rockefeller Center. The N, R line cuts diagonally across the neighborhood, following the path of Broadway before heading up Seventh Avenue at 42nd Street. The A, C, E line serves the west side, running along Eighth Avenue.

If you know New York but haven't been here in a few years, you'll be quite surprised by the "new" Times Square. Longtime New Yorkers like to kvetch nostalgic about the glory days of the old peep-show-and-porn-shop Times Square that this cleaned-up, Disney-fied one supplanted, but the truth is that it's a hugely successful regentrification. Most of the great Broadway theaters light up the streets just off Times Square.

Midtown East & Murray Hill   Midtown East, the area including Fifth Avenue and everything east from 34th to 59th streets, is the more upscale side of the midtown map. The stretch of Fifth Avenue from Saks at 49th Street extending to FAO Schwarz at 59th is home to the city's most high-profile haute shopping. This side of town is short of subway trains, served primarily by the Lexington Avenue 4, 5, 6 line.

Claiming the territory east from Madison Avenue, **Murray Hill** begins somewhere north of 23rd Street (the line between it and Gramercy Park is fuzzy), and is most clearly recognizable north of 34th Street to 42nd Street. This is largely a quiet residential neighborhood, most notable for its handful of good budget and mid-priced hotels.

UPTOWN

The Upper West Side   North of 59th Street and encompassing everything west of Central Park, the Upper West Side contains Lincoln Center, arguably the world's premier performing-arts venue; the American Museum of Natural History; and a number of mid-priced hotels whose larger-than-midtown rooms and nice residential location make them particularly good bets for families, or anybody looking for affordable sleeps in an extra-nice neighborhood. Unlike the more stratified Upper East Side, the Upper West Side is home to an egalitarian mix of middle-class yuppiedom, laid-back wealth, and ethnic families who were here before the gentrification. Two major subway lines service the area: the 1, 2, 3, 9 line runs up Broadway, while the B and C trains run up glamorous Central Park West.

The Upper East Side   North of 59th Street and east of Central Park is some of the most expensive residential real estate in the world. This is an area for browsing only, unless you book a room at the 92nd Street Y (see chapter 3). This is New York at its most gentrified: Walk along Fifth and Park avenues, especially between 60th and 80th streets, and you're sure to encounter some of the wizened WASPs and Chanel-suited socialites that make up the most rarefied of the city's population. Madison Avenue to 79th Street is the monied crowd's main shopping strip. The main attraction of this neighborhood is Museum Mile, the stretch of Fifth Avenue fronting Central Park that's home to no fewer than ten terrific cultural institutions, anchored by the mind-boggling Metropolitan Museum of Art. The Upper East Side is served solely by the Lexington Avenue subway line (4, 5, 6 trains).

Harlem   Harlem is really two areas. Harlem proper stretches from river to river, beginning at 125th Street on the West Side and 96th Street on the East Side. Spanish Harlem (El Barrio), an enclave east of Fifth Avenue, runs between East 100th and East 125th streets. Parts of Harlem are benefiting from the same kinds of revitalization that has swept so much of the city, with national-brand retailers moving in and visitors arriving to tour historic sites related to the Golden Age of African-American culture. By all means, come see Harlem—it's one of the city's most vital and historic neighborhoods. Intrepid travelers now even have a place to stay in the neighborhood (see chapter 3). Your best bet is to take a guided tour (see chapter 5). Sights tend to be far apart, and neighborhoods change quickly. Don't wander thoughtlessly through Harlem, especially at night.

2   Getting Around

Frankly, Manhattan's transportation systems are a marvel. It's simply miraculous that so many people can gather on this little island and move around it. For the most part, you can get where you're going pretty quickly and easily using some combination of subways, buses, cabs, and walking.

Forget driving yourself around the city. It's not worth the headache. If you do arrive in New York City by car, park it in a garage (expect to pay in the neighborhood of $20 to $30 per day) and leave it there for the duration of your stay.

As you walk around the city, **never take your walking cues from the locals.** Wait for walk signals, and always use crosswalks—don't cross in the middle of the block, or you could quickly end up with a jaywalking ticket (or worse—as a flattened statistic). And **always pay attention to the traffic flow.** Walk as if you're driving, staying to the right. Pay attention to what's happening in the street, even if you have the right of way. At intersections, keep an eye out for drivers or bicyclists who don't yield, turn without looking, or think a yellow traffic light means "Hurry up!" as you cross.

BY SUBWAY

The much-maligned subway system is actually the best way to travel around New York, especially during rush hours. The subway runs 24 hours a day, seven days a week.

PAYING YOUR WAY   The subway fare is $1.50 (half-price for seniors and those with disabilities), and children under 44 inches tall ride free (up to three per adult). **Tokens** still exist (for now), but most people pay fares these days with the **MetroCard,** a magnetically encoded card that debits the fare when swiped through the turnstile, or the fare box on any city bus. Once you're in the system, you can transfer freely to any subway line that you can reach without exiting your station.

The MetroCard can be purchased in a few different configurations:

Pay-Per-Ride MetroCards, which can be used for up to four people by swiping up to four times (bring the whole family). Every time you put $15 on your Pay-Per-Ride MetroCard, it's automatically credited 10%—that's one free ride for every $15.

Unlimited-Use MetroCards, which can't be used for more than one person at a time or more frequently than 18-minute intervals, are available in three values: the **daily Fun Pass,** which allows you a day's worth of unlimited subway and bus rides for $4; the **7-Day MetroCard,** for $17; and the **30-Day MetroCard,** for $63. These MetroCards cannot be refilled; you throw it out once it's been used up and buy a new one. Note that Fun Passes cannot be purchased at token booths—you can only buy them from a MetroCard merchant or at a station that has a MetroCard vending machine.

To locate the nearest merchant where you can buy the Fun Pass, or for any other MetroCard questions, call ☎ **212/METROCARD.**

USING THE SYSTEM   The subway system basically mimics the lay of the land above ground, with most lines in Manhattan running north and south, like the avenues, and a few lines east and west.

Lines have assigned colors on subway maps and trains—red for the 1, 2, 3, 9 line; green for 4, 5, 6 trains; and so on—but nobody ever refers to them by color. Always refer to them by number or letter when asking questions. Within Manhattan, the distinction between different numbered trains that share the same line is usually that some are express and others local. Express trains often skip about three stops for each one that they make; express stops are indicated on subway maps with a white (rather than solid) circle. Regular stops usually come about nine blocks apart.

Directions are almost always indicated using "Uptown" (northbound) and "Downtown" (southbound), so be sure to know what direction you want to head in. The outsides of some subway entrances are marked UPTOWN ONLY or DOWNTOWN ONLY; read carefully, as it's easy to head in the wrong direction. Once you're on the platform, check the signs overhead to make sure that the train you're waiting for will be traveling in the right direction. If you do make a mistake, it's a good idea to wait for an express station, like

For More Bus & Subway Information

For additional transit information, call the MTA/New York City Transit's **Travel Information Center** at ☎ 718/330-1234. Extensive automated information is available at this number 24 hours a day, and travel agents are on hand to answer your questions and provide directions daily from 6am to 9pm. For online information, visit **www.mta.nyc.ny.us**.

To request free system maps or the *Token Trips Travel Guide* brochure, which gives subway and bus travel directions to more than 120 popular sites, call the **Customer Assistance Line** at ☎ 718/330-3322 (Mon–Fri 9am–5pm). For transit info for riders with disabilities, call the **Accessible Line** at ☎ 718/596-8585 (daily 6am–9pm).

You can get bus and subway maps and additional transit information at most tourist information centers (see "Visitor Information," earlier in this chapter). Maps are sometimes available in subway stations (ask at the token booth), but rarely on buses.

14th Street or 42nd Street, so you can get off and change for the other direction without paying again.

BY BUS

Less expensive than taxis and more pleasant than subways, buses are a good transportation option. Their very big drawback: They can get stuck in traffic, sometimes making it quicker to walk. They also stop every couple of blocks, rather than the eight or nine blocks that local subway traverse between stops. So for long distances, the subway is your best bet; but for short distances or traveling crosstown, try the bus.

PAYING YOUR WAY Like the subway fare, the **bus fare** is $1.50, half-price for seniors and riders with disabilities, free for children under 44 inches (up to three per adult). The fare is payable with a **MetroCard, token** (for now, anyway), or **exact change.** Bus drivers don't make change, and fare boxes don't accept dollar bills or pennies. You can't purchase MetroCards or tokens on the bus, so you'll have to have them before you board; for details, see "Paying Your Way" under "By Subway," above.

USING THE SYSTEM You can't flag a city bus down—you have to meet it at a bus stop. **Bus stops** are located every 2 or 3 blocks on the right-side corner of the street (facing the direction of traffic

---

Money-Saving Transit Tips: Free Transfers

If you pay your subway or bus fare with a MetroCard, you can freely transfer to another bus or to the subway (or from the subway to a bus) for up to 2 hours. You don't need to do anything special: Just swipe your card at the token box or turnstile, and the automated system keeps track.

If you use a token or coins to board a bus and you expect to transfer to another line, you must request a free **transfer slip** that allows you to change to an intersecting bus route only (legal transfer points are listed on the transfer paper) within 1 hour of issue. Transfer slips cannot be used to enter the subway.

---

flow). They're marked by a curb painted yellow and a blue-and-white sign with a bus emblem and the route number or numbers. Guide-A-Ride boxes at most stops display a route map and a hysterically optimistic schedule.

Every major avenue has its own **bus route.** They run either north or south. Additionally, **crosstown buses** run along all major east-westbound streets. Some bus routes, however, are erratic: The M104, for example, starts at the East River, then turns at Eighth Avenue and goes up Broadway. The buses of the Fifth Avenue line go up Madison or Sixth and follow various routes around the city. Most routes operate 24 hours a day, but service is infrequent at night.

To make sure the bus you're boarding goes where you're going, check the maps on the bus signs, get your hands on a route map, or **just ask.** The drivers are helpful, as long as you don't hold up the line too long.

BY TAXI

Cabs can be hailed on any street and will take you right to your destination.

Official New York City taxis, licensed by the Taxi and Limousine Commission, are yellow, with the rates printed on the door and a light with a medallion number on the roof. *Never* accept a ride from any other car except an official city yellow cab (private livery cars are not allowed to pick up fares on the street).

If you're planning to take extensive advantage of taxis, be prepared to pay. The **base fare** on entering the cab is $2 (a surcharge of 50¢ is added 8pm–6am). The cost is 30¢ for every $1/5$ mile or 20¢

per minute in stopped or very slow-moving traffic (or for waiting time). There's no extra charge for each passenger or for luggage. However, you must pay bridge or tunnel tolls. A 15% to 20% tip is customary.

Since it's going to cost you at least $2 just to get in the car, taxis are far more expensive than other forms of public transportation, and can really jack up your expenses quickly. Visitors on a limited travel budget are generally better off relying on subways and buses to get around town, using taxis only late at night (after 11pm or midnight, when buses and subway trains start getting fewer and farther between, and standing at a bus stop or a lonely platform may seem a little daunting), or to reach an out-of-the-way destination on the Lower East Side or in the far East Village. You'll also get your money's worth out of a taxi at night, when there's little traffic to keep them from speeding you to your destination.

The TLC has posted a **Taxi Rider's Bill of Rights** sticker in every cab. Drivers are required by law to take you anywhere in the five boroughs, to Nassau or Westchester counties, or to Newark Airport. They are supposed to know how to get you to any address in Manhattan, and all major points in the outer boroughs. They are also required to provide air-conditioning and turn off the radio on demand, and they cannot smoke while you're in the cab. They are also required to be polite.

You are allowed to dictate the route that is taken. It's a good idea to look at a map before you get in a taxi. Taxi drivers have been known to jack up the fare on visitors who don't know better by taking a circuitous route between point A and point B. On the other hand, listen to drivers who propose an alternate route. A knowledgeable driver will know how to get you to your destination quickly and efficiently.

Taxi-Hailing Tips

- When you're waiting on the street for an available taxi, look at the medallion light on the top of the coming cabs. If the light is out, the taxi is in use. When the center part (the number) is lit, the taxi is available—this is when you raise your hand to flag the cab. If all the lights are on, the driver is off duty.
- A taxi can't take more than four people, so expect to split up if your group is larger.

Always make sure the meter is turned on at the start of the ride. You'll see the red LED read-out register the initial $2 and start calculating the fare as you go. I've witnessed a good number of un-scrupulous drivers buzzing unsuspecting visitors around the city with the meter off, and then overcharging them at drop-off time.

For driver complaints and lost property, call the 24-hour Con-sumer Hotline at ☎ **212/NYC-TAXI.** For further taxi information, point your web browser to **www.ci.nyc.ny.us/taxi**.

3 Playing It Safe

New York has experienced a dramatic drop in crime and is gener-ally safe these days, especially in the neighborhoods visitors tend to frequent. Still, it's important to take precautions. Always remain vigilant, as swindlers and criminals are expert at spotting newcom-ers who appear disoriented or vulnerable.

Men should carry their wallets in their front pockets. Cross cam-era and purse straps over one shoulder, across your front, and un-der the other arm. Never hang a purse on the back of a chair or on a hook in a bathroom stall; keep it in your lap or between your feet with one foot through a strap and up against the purse itself. Avoid carrying large amounts of cash. Keep jewelry and valuables out of sight when you're on the street.

Panhandlers are seldom dangerous but should be ignored (more aggressive pleas should firmly be answered, "Not today"). I hate to be cynical, but experience teaches that if a stranger walks up to you on the street with a long sob story ("I live in the suburbs and was just attacked and don't have the money to get home") it should be ignored—it's a scam. Walk away and don't feel bad. Be wary of an individual who "accidentally" falls in front of you or causes some other commotion, because he or she may be working with someone else who will take your wallet when you try to help. And remember: You *will* lose if you place a bet on a sidewalk card game or shell game.

When using the **subway,** don't wait for trains near the edge of the platform or on extreme ends of a station. During non-rush hours, wait for the train in view of the token booth clerk or under the yel-low DURING OFF HOURS TRAINS STOP HERE signs, and ride in the train operator's or conductor's car (usually in the center of the train; you'll see his or her head stick out when the doors open). Choose crowded cars over empty ones—there's safety in numbers. Splurge on a cab after about 10 or 11pm—it's money well spent to avoid a long wait on a deserted platform. Or take the bus.

The Top Safety Tips: Trust your instincts, because they're usually right. You'll rarely be hassled, but it's always best to walk with a sense of purpose and self-confidence, and don't stop in the middle of the sidewalk to pull out and peruse your map. There's a good police presence on the street, so don't be afraid to stop an officer, or even a friendly looking New Yorker (trust me—you can tell) if you need help getting your bearings.

Anywhere in the city, if you find yourself on a deserted street that feels unsafe, it probably is; leave as quickly as possible. If you do find yourself accosted by someone with or without a weapon, remember to keep your anger in check and that the most reasonable response (maddening though it may be) is not to resist.

FAST FACTS: NEW YORK CITY

American Express   Travel service offices are at many Manhattan locations, including the New York Hilton, 1335 Sixth Ave., at 53rd Street (☎ 212/664-7798); at Macy's Herald Square, 34th Street and Broadway (☎ 212/695-8075); and 65 Broadway, between Exchange Place and Rector Street (☎ 212/493-6500). Call ☎ 800/AXP-TRIP or visit **www.americanexpress.com** for other city locations or general information.

Area Codes   There are four area codes in the city: two in Manhattan, **212** and **646,** and two in the outer boroughs, **718** and (new in late 1999) **347.** At press time, dialing procedures for local calls hadn't been determined; it may always be necessary to dial 11 digits (1, the area code, and the number), even when making a call within the same 212 or 646 or 718 area codes.

Emergencies   Dial ☎ **911** for fire, police, and ambulance.

Hospitals   Downtown: New York Downtown Hospital, 170 William St., at Beekman Street (☎ **212/312-5000**); St. Vincent's Hospital, Seventh Avenue and 11th Street (☎ **212/604-7000**); and Beth Israel Medical Center, First Avenue and 16th Street (☎ **212/420-2000**). **Midtown:** Bellevue Hospital Center, 462 First Ave. and 27th Street (☎ **212/562-4141**); New York University Medical Center, 560 First Ave. and 33rd Street (☎ **212/263-7300**); and Roosevelt Hospital Center, Tenth Avenue and 59th Street (☎ **212/523-4000**). **Upper West Side:** St. Luke's Hospital Center, Amsterdam Avenue and 114th Street (☎ **212/523-4000**). **Upper East Side:** New York Hospital's Emergency Pavilion, York Avenue and 70th Street (☎ **212/746-5050**), and

Lenox Hill Hospital, 77th Street between Park and Lexington avenues (☎ **212/434-2000**). Don't forget your insurance card.

Internet Access The **Times Square Visitors Center,** 1560 Broadway (☎ **212/768-1560**), has computer terminals with free Internet access. The **Internet Cafe,** 82 E. 3rd St. in the East Village (☎ **212/614-0747;** www.bigmagic.com), offers access at $10 per hour; students get a 10% discount with ID. **Cybercafe,** 273 Lafayette St. in SoHo (☎ **212/334-5140;** www.cyber-cafe.com), is $12.80 an hour, but offers much speedier access.

Liquor Laws The minimum legal age to purchase and consume alcoholic beverages in New York is 21. Liquor and wine are sold only in licensed stores, which are closed on Sundays, holidays, and election days while the polls are open. Beer can be purchased in grocery stores and delis 24 hours, except Sundays before noon.

Pharmacies There are two 24-hour **Duane Reade** pharmacies: one at Broadway and 57th Street (☎ **212/541-9708**) and the other at Third Avenue and 74th Street (☎ **212/744-2668**).

Police Dial ☎ **911** in an emergency; otherwise, call ☎ **212/374-5000** for the number of the nearest precinct.

Post Office The main New York City post office is on 421 Eighth Ave., between 31st and 33rd streets and is open 24 hours a day (☎ **212/967-8585**). Call ☎ **800/275-8777** to locate the nearest branch office.

Smoking Smoking is prohibited on all public transportation, in the lobbies of hotels and office buildings, in taxis, and in most shops. Smoking also may be restricted or not permitted in restaurants; for more on this, see chapter 4.

Taxes **Sales tax** is 8.25% on meals, most goods, and some services. **Hotel tax** is 13.25% plus $2 per room per night (including sales tax). **Parking garage tax** is 18.25%.

Weather For the current temperature and next day's forecast, call ☎ **212/976-1212.**

3

Accommodations You Can Afford

*A*s you're probably well aware, New York is more popular than it's been in decades. On one hand, that's terrific: This popularity makes the city feel vital and self-assured; you can practically feel the excitement and energy as you walk down the street. From a more practical standpoint, it has also made the city safer and more visitor friendly than ever.

Now the downside: With increased demand comes higher prices—Econ 101. Occupancy rates are higher than they've been since the pre-war years, and rates have responded accordingly. Average room rates are now hovering around $195, higher than ever before in the city's history, and out of reach of many budget travelers. But don't get discouraged yet—there are still a few remarkable bargains to be had if you know where to look. In the pages that follow, I'll tell you about some truly wonderful places to stay that won't break your bank account.

Nevertheless, keep in mind that this is the land of $200-a-night Holiday Inns and HoJos—so forget about calling up one of the chains and booking a reliable $75 motel room like you could in any other U.S. city. To stay in New York, you must carefully weigh what you're willing to afford versus what you're willing to put up with. If you only want to spend 100 bucks a night—a very budget-basic rate in this city—you're going to have to live with some inconveniences.

First and foremost, don't expect much in the way of **space.** Space is New York's most coveted commodity, and most of it doesn't go to visitors on tight budgets. Don't be surprised if your hotel room isn't much bigger than the bed that's in it, the closet is just a rack screwed to the wall, and/or the bathroom is the smallest you've ever seen.

Also, you may have to stay in a residential district rather than your first-choice **neighborhood.** In general, it's more expensive to stay in the heart of the Theater District than in Murray Hill. But this can be a good thing, especially if you like peace and quiet. Staying in a residential area will also give you better access to affordable restaurants where locals eat rather than at places in tourist-heavy neighborhoods, which tend to jack up their prices.

Last but not least, be aware that many of New York's budget hotel rooms have **shared bathrooms.** There are a few exceptions to the rule, but in general don't count on scoring a double room with a private bathroom for less than $100 a night. If your budget is extra-tight, you may want to seriously consider one of the city's shared-bathroom hotels, some of which are very nice—akin to European-style B&Bs rather than threadbare hotel rooms. I recommend the best of these below.

HOW TO SAVE ON YOUR HOTEL ROOM

The rates quoted in the listings below are the **rack rates**—the maximum rates that a hotel charges for rooms. It's the rate you'd get if you walked in off the street and asked for a room for the night without bargaining. In the listings below, I've also tried to give you an idea of the kind of deals that may be available at particular hotels: which ones have the best discounted packages, which ones offer AAA and other discounts, which ones allow kids to stay with Mom and Dad for free, and so on. But rates in New York can change dramatically depending on demand, and demand is high these days—so be prepared for sticker shock. There's no way of knowing what the market will hold, or what the offers will be when you're booking.

Before you even start calling, be sure to review the **35 Money-Saving Tips** in chapter 1, where you'll find time-tested advice on how to get the most for your accommodations dollar. You'll also find contact information on reservations services and B&B and homestay networks that may be able to book you into a room for better than you could do on your own.

1 TriBeCa

✪ **Cosmopolitan Hotel–Tribeca.** 95 W. Broadway (at Warren St., 1 block south of Chambers St.), New York, NY 10007. ☎ **888/895-9400** or 212/566-1900. Fax 212/566-6909. www.cosmohotel.com. 104 units. A/C TV TEL. $109 double. AE, CB, DC, JCB, MC, V. Parking $20 (with validation) 1 block away. Subway: 1, 2, 3, 9, A, C, E to Chambers St.

Hiding behind a plain-vanilla TriBeCa awning is the best hotel deal in Manhattan for budget travelers who don't want to sacrifice the luxury of a private bathroom. Every room comes with its own small but spotless bathroom, telephone with data port, satellite TV, alarm, and ceiling fan. Everything is strictly budget, but nice: The modern IKEA-ish furniture includes an armoire and a work desk; for a few extra bucks, you can have a loveseat, too. Beds are comfy, and sheets and towels are better-quality than in many more expensive hotels. Rooms are small but well organized, and the whole place is pristine. The two-level mini-lofts have lots of character, but expect to duck on the second level: Downstairs is the bathroom, TV, closet, desk, and club chair, while upstairs is a low-ceilinged bedroom with a second TV and phone. The neighborhood is safe, hip, and subway-convenient, and the Financial District is just a walk away. There's no room service, but a range of great restaurants will deliver. All services are kept at a bare minimum to keep costs down, so you must be a low-maintenance guest to be happy here. If you are, this place is a smokin' deal.

2 The Lower East Side

Off SoHo Suites. 11 Rivington St. (btw. Chrystie St. and the Bowery), New York, NY 10002. ☎ **800/OFF-SOHO** or 212/979-9808. Fax 212/979-9801. www.offsoho.com. 38 units (28 with bathroom). A/C TV TEL. $97.50 economy suite (2 people maximum); $179 deluxe suite (4 people maximum). AE, MC, V. Parking $14, 3 blocks away. Subway: F to Second Ave.; J, M to Bowery.

The good news: Here's a hotel with clean, welcoming rooms with full kitchen facilities at surprisingly low prices. The bad news: When they say "Off SoHo," they mean it. This edge-of-Chinatown neighborhood is primarily industrial, and while close to downtown dining, shopping, and nightlife (trendy Elizabeth Street is just 2 blocks away), it doesn't exactly scream downtown chic. Still, if you're willing to dispense with the old real-estate bromide "location, location, location," you'll get well-rounded if Spartan spaces for a bargain rate. The deluxe suites have a living and dining area with a pullout sofa, fully stocked kitchen (with microwave), private bathroom, and separate bedroom. In the economy suites, a kitchen and bathroom is shared with another room; if four of you are traveling together, you can combine two economy suites into a sizable apartment. Everything is pretty basic and the beds are a bit harder than I like, but the whole place is well kept. Telephones have voice mail and data port, and satellite TV was in the plans at press time. The neighborhood isn't unsafe, just desolate; it's a good idea to take a cab back later in the evening. There's a workout room, a cafe serving breakfast and lunch, and self-service laundry.

3 Greenwich Village

✪ **Larchmont Hotel.** 27 W. 11th St. (btw. Fifth and Sixth aves.), New York, NY 10011. ☎ **212/989-9333.** Fax 212/989-9496. www.citysearch.com/nyc/larchmonthotel. 55 units (none with bathroom). A/C TV TEL. $70–$80 single; $90–$109 double. Rates include continental breakfast. Children under 13 stay free in parents' room. AE, CB, DC, DISC, MC, V. Parking $20 nearby. Subway: 4, 5, 6, N, R, L to Union Square; A, C, E, B, D, F, Q to West 4th St. (use 8th St. exit); F to 14th St.

Excellently located on a beautiful tree-lined block in a quiet residential part of the village, this European-style hotel is simply a gem. If you're willing to put up with the inconvenience of shared bathrooms, you can't do better for the money. The entire place has a wonderful air of warmth and sophistication; the butter-yellow lobby even *smells* good. Each bright guest room is tastefully done in rattan and outfitted with a writing desk, a wash basin, a mini-library of books, an alarm clock, cotton bathrobes, and ceiling fans. Every floor has two shared bathrooms and a small, simple kitchen. The management is constantly renovating, so everything feels clean and fresh. The free continental breakfast, including fresh-baked goods, is the crowning touch that makes the Larchmont an unbeatable deal. And with some of the city's best shopping, dining, and sightseeing, plus your choice of subway lines, just a walk away, you couldn't be better situated. As you might expect, the hotel is always full, so book well in advance (the management suggests 6 to 7 weeks' lead time).

4 The Flatiron District & Gramercy Park

✪ **Gershwin Hotel.** 7 E. 27th St. (btw. Fifth and Madison aves.), New York, NY 10016. ☎ **212/545-8000.** Fax 212/684-5546. www.gershwinhotel.com. 94 doubles, 31 4-person dorms. TV TEL (in doubles only). $109–$139 double; $119–$149 triple; $129–$159 quad, depending on season; $22 per person in dorm. Check Web site for seasonal deals. AE, MC, V. Parking $20 nearby. Subway: N, R, 6 to 28th St.

If you see glowing horns protruding from a lipstick-red facade, you're in the right place. This budget-conscious, youth-oriented hotel caters to up-and-coming artistic types with its bold modern art collection and wild style. The lobby is a colorful, postmodern cartoon of kitschy furniture and pop art by Lichtenstein, Warhol, de Kooning, and others. The standard rooms are clean and saved from the budget doldrums by bright colors, Picasso-style wall murals, Starck-ish takes on motel furnishings, and more modern art. All have private bathrooms; none of the bathrooms are bad, but try to nab a new one. The cheapest accommodations are four- and eight-bedded dorms: They're basic rooms with IKEA bunk beds sharing a bathroom, but better than a hostel, especially if you're traveling with a group and can claim one as your own.

One of the best things about the Gershwin is its great, Factory-esque vibe, sort of like an artsy frat or sorority house. The hotel is more service-oriented than you usually see at this price level, and there's always something going on, whether it's live jazz in the beer and wine bar, a film screening on the rooftop garden, or an opening at the hotel's own art gallery. At press time, a new vendor had just taken over the cafe, and room service was in the works. Air-conditioning was also in the planning stage, but make sure before you book an August stay.

Hotel 17. 225 E. 17th St. (btw. Second and Third aves.), New York, NY 10003. ☎ **212/475-2845.** Fax 212/677-8178. www.citysearch.com/nyc/hotel17. 130 units (all with shared bathroom). AC TV TEL. $75–$85 single; $98–$130 double; $200 3-person suite. Rates include tax. Weekly rates available. No credit cards. Parking $25. Subway: 4, 5, 6 to 14th St.; L to Third Ave.

In the last couple of years, Hotel 17 has managed to garner a reputation as the hippest budget hotel in Manhattan—Madonna, David Bowie, and Maxwell have all been photographed in the eclectic, eccentric rooms. But it's not all hype—Hotel 17 has a lot to recommend it: The neighborhood is great, the block peaceful, and the individually decorated rooms surprisingly attractive. Look beyond the stylish veneer, though, and you'll find rooms that are small, dark, and basic definitely not for travelers looking for creature comforts. Each has its own sink; the shared bathrooms are older but kept very clean. Recent renovation has softened the edge, adding air-conditioning, TVs, hair dryers, and alarm clocks to all rooms. The lobby has a funky streamline, modern feel to it, but the security glass separating you from the front-desk staff detracts. There's a roof garden and self-service laundry. All in all, a good deal for the money, especially if you like some individuality in your hostelry. Expect lots of young and international travelers, who don't mind the inconveniences.

SUPER-CHEAP SLEEPS

Travelers on a shoestring budget should be sure to consider the dorm-style rooms at the **Gershwin Hotel,** above, which go for just $22 per person per night.

Midtown Accommodations

Accommodations

American Inn 13
Belvedere Hotel 27
Best Western Manhattan 11
Best Western President 24
Best Western Woodward 22
Broadway Inn 25
Carlton Arms 5
Chelsea Savoy Hotel 2
Colonial House Inn 1
Comfort Inn Manhattan 12
Comfort Inn Midtown 20
Crowne Plaza at the
   United Nations 14
Gershwin Hotel 6
Gramercy Park Hotel 4
Habitat Hotel 31
Hotel Edison 23
Hotel Grand Union 9
Hotel 17 3
Hotel 31 8
Hotel Wolcott 10
Loews New York 17
Millennium Broadway 21
Park Savoy Hotel 29
Pickwick Arms Hotel 16
Portland Square Hotel 19
Quality Hotel Eastside 7
Quality Hotel & Suites
   Midtown 18
Travel Inn 26
Vanderbilt YMCA 15
Washington Jefferson
   Hotel 28
The Wyndham 30

52

Money-Saving Weekend Packages

Believe it or not, there is a way to stay in New York coddled in the lap of luxury without blowing your middle-class budget: weekend packages. The best weekend deals are available at hotels that cater primarily to a business clientele, in neighborhoods that tend to empty out at the end of Friday's workday. I can't guarantee what the offers will be when you come to town, but if you're visiting New York on a short weekend trip, or you don't mind temporarily moving up to luxury accommodations, see what's being offered at the following hotels:

Without a doubt, the city's best weekend values are available at the **Millenium Hilton,** across from the World Trade Center at 55 Church St. (☎ **800/835-2220** or 212/693-2001; www. hilton.com). This Mobil 4-star, AAA 4-diamond hotel is the top choice in the Financial District for bulls and bears. It also makes a great perch for vacationers on weekends, when its $300-a-night doubles go for just $120 to $199 (depending on the season). The extremely comfortable rooms are light and bright (most have glorious Manhattan or harbor views), and the services and facilities (which include an excellent fitness center with pool) are first rate. Continental breakfast is usually included in weekend packages, and corporate, senior, and other promotions may make the deeply discounted rates even more enticing. This neighborhood goes from bustling to near-desolate on weekends, but multiple subway lines are nearby, ready to whisk you uptown in no time.

You might also check with the **Marriott Financial Center,** 85 West St. (☎ **800/242-8685** or 212/385-4900), and the **Marriott World Trade Center,** 3 World Trade Center (☎ **800/228-9290**

WORTH A SPLURGE

Gramercy Park Hotel. 2 Lexington Ave. (btw. 21st and 22nd sts.), New York, NY 10010. ☎ **800/221-4083** or 212/475-4320. Fax 212/505-0535. 360 units. A/C TV TEL. $165–$170 single; $180 double; from $210 suite. Extra person $10. Children under 12 stay free in parents' room. AE, CB, DC, DISC, EC, JCB, MC, V. Parking $20 nearby. Subway: 6 to 23rd St.

Opened in 1924, this appealing Old World hotel has one of the best settings in the city. It's ideally located on the edge of the private park—restricted to just a few area residents and to hotel guests, who can also get a key—that gives lovely Gramercy Park the air of a quiet London square. The hotel has been plagued by claims of neglect in or 212/938-9100), both excellent branches of the reliable chain that offer similarly discounted weekend rates and promotions. You can find Marriott online at **www.marriott.com**.

If you're intrigued by the promise of weekend discounts but would prefer a midtown location, check with **Crowne Plaza at the United Nations,** 304 E. 42nd St., just east of Second Ave. (☎ **800/227-6963,** 800/879-8836 or 212/986-8800; www.crowneplaza-un.com or www.crowneplaza.com). The lovely neo-Tudor building boasts newly renovated guest rooms with all the creature comforts, plus a surprising amount of individual flair for a chain hotel. It becomes a real steal on most weekends, when U.N. delegates head out of the city. Rack rates are generally $229 to $379 double, but I found rooms going for just $169 on a number of weekends throughout 1999. If you find yourself being offered such a deal, book it—you won't be disappointed.

Finally, if you're Web-savvy, it's worth taking a moment to surf over to the site for the **Millennium Broadway,** 145 W. 44th St. (☎ **800/622-5569** or 212/768-0847; www.millenniumbroadway.com), and click on SPECIAL DEALS. Without question, the Millennium offers the best weekend packages in the Theater District: This terrific luxury high-rise sometimes offers its spacious and comfy art-deco–ish rooms, which normally go for $295–$345 double, to Internet customers for as little as $160 to $179 a night. No doubt pricey for some budget travelers, but an excellent deal if you're splurging. Weekend bunch is often included, and children under 13 stay can free in their parents' room.

recent years, but management seems to be responding well, and the old place is looking really good these days. You'll still have to over-look the finer details—expect a smoky lobby, chipped paint here and there, *Ice Storm*–era carpet in some halls, and ancient TVs—but rooms are huge by city standards, decently furnished, and comfort-able. Standard doubles have a king or two doubles, and some suites have pullout sofas that make them large enough to sleep six; all have big closets, unstocked minifridges, and hair dryers and fluffy towels in the roomy bathrooms. Request a park-facing room, which cost no more but feature great views and small kitchenettes. There's a continental restaurant and a lounge with nightly entertainment off the bustling lobby, plus a beauty salon and newsstand. Dry cleaning, laundry, and limited room service are available.

5 Chelsea

✪ **Chelsea Savoy Hotel.** 204 W. 23rd St. (at Seventh Ave.), New York, NY 10011. ☎ **212/929-9353.** Fax 212/741-6309. www.citysearch.com/nyc/chelseasavoy. 90 units. A/C TV TEL. $99–$115 single; $125–$155 double; $155–$185 quad. Children under 13 stay free in parents' room. Rates include continental breakfast. AE, MC, V. Parking $16 nearby. Subway: 1, 9 to 23rd St.

This newish hotel is our top choice in Chelsea, a neighborhood abloom with art galleries, restaurants, and weekend flea markets. The hallways are attractive and wide, the elevators are swift and silent, and the generic but cheery rooms are good-sized and have big closets and roomy, immaculate bathrooms with tons of counter space. Creature comforts abound: The rooms boast high-quality mattresses, furniture, textiles, and linens, plus hair dryers, minifridges, alarm clocks, irons and boards, in-room safes, and toiletries (VCRs were scheduled to be added at press time). Most rooms are street facing and sunny; corner rooms tend to be brightest and noisiest. Ask for a darker, back-facing room if you crave total silence. There's a plain but pleasant sitting room off the lobby where you can relax and enjoy your morning coffee over a selection of newspapers and magazines. The staff is young and helpful, and the increasingly hip neighborhood makes a good base for exploring both midtown and downtown.

Colonial House Inn. 318 W. 22nd St. (btw. Eighth and Ninth aves.), New York, NY 10011. ☎ **800/689-3779** or 212/243-9669. www.colonialhouseinn.com. 20 rooms (12 with shared bathroom). A/C TV TEL. $80–$99 single or double with shared bathroom; $125–$140 with private bathroom. Rates include continental breakfast. 2-night minimum on weekends. 5% discount for bookings of 7 nights or more. No credit cards. Nearby street parking. Subway: C, E to 23rd St.

This charming 1850 brownstone, on a pretty residential block in the heart of gay-friendly Chelsea, was the first permanent home of the Gay Men's Health Crisis. The four-story walk-up caters to a largely gay and lesbian clientele, but the friendly staff welcomes everybody equally, and straight couples are a common sight. The whole place is beautifully maintained and professionally run. Rooms are small and basic but clean; those that share a hall bathroom (at a ratio of about three rooms per bathroom) have in-room sinks. Both private and shared bathrooms are basic but nice. Rooms with private bathrooms also have minifridges, and a few have fireplaces that accommodate Duraflame logs. A terrific, mostly abstract art collection brightens the public spaces. At parlor level is a cute breakfast room where a continental spread is put out from 8am to noon daily, and coffee and tea is available all day. There's a nice roof deck split by a privacy fence; the area behind the fence is clothing-optional. The neighborhood is chock-full of great restaurants and shopping, and offers easy access to the rest of the city. Book at least a month in advance for weekend stays, as the inn regularly sells out.

6 Times Square & Midtown West

If you're visiting in winter or spring, seriously consider the terrific **Belvedere Hotel** (under "Worth a Splurge," below), where rates can go as low as $125 in these slower seasons. The Belvedere is worth checking out at any time of year if you're a AAA member who can qualify for the 10% discount, or if you catch one of their frequent Internet specials.

Americana Inn. 69 W. 38th St. (at Sixth Ave.), New York, NY 10018. ☎ **888/ HOTEL58** or 212/840-2019. Fax 212/840-1830. www.newyorkhotel.com/ americana. 50 units (all with shared bathroom). A/C TV. $75–$105 double. Extra person $10. AE, DC, DISC, MC, V. Parking $18–$22 nearby. Subway: B, D, F, Q to 42nd St.; N, R to 34th St.

The cheapest hotel from the Empire Hotel Group—the people behind the Belvedere and the Newton among other top-notch properties—is a winner in the budget-basic category. Linoleum floors give the rooms an unfortunate institutional quality, but the hotel is professionally run and immaculately kept. Rooms are mostly spacious, with good-size closets and private sinks, and the beds are the most comfortable I've found at this price. A few can accommodate three guests in two twin beds and a pullout sofa. There's one hall bathroom for every three rooms or so, and all are spacious and spotless. Every floor has a common kitchenette with microwave, stove, and fridge (BYO utensils, or go plastic). The five-story building has an elevator, and four rooms are handicap accessible. The Garment District location couldn't be more convenient for midtown sightseeing and shopping. Ask for a back-facing room away from the street noise.

✪ **Broadway Inn.** 264 W. 46th St. (at Eighth Ave.), New York, NY 10036. ☎ **800/826-6300** or 212/997-9200. Fax 212/768-2807. www. broadwayinn.com. 40 units. A/C TV TEL. $85–$95 single; $115–$170 double; $195 suite. Extra person $10. Rates include continental breakfast. AE, DC, DISC, MC, V. Parking $16 3 blocks away. Subway: 1, 2, 3, 7, 9, S to 42nd St./Times Square; A, C, E to 42nd St.; N, R to 49th St.

More like a San Francisco B&B than a Theater District hotel, this lovely, welcoming inn is a real charmer. The second-floor lobby sets the homey, easy-going tone with stocked bookcases, cushy seating, and cafe tables where breakfast is served. The rooms are basic but comfy, outfitted in an appealing neo-deco style with firm beds. The whole place is impeccably kept. Two rooms have king beds and Jacuzzi tubs, but the standard doubles are just fine. If there's more than two of you, or you're looking to stay awhile, the suites—with pullout sofa, microwave, minifridge, and lots of closet space—are a great deal. The location can be noisy, but double-paned windows keep the peace; still, ask for a back-facing one if you're extra-sensitive.

The inn's biggest asset is its terrific staff, who go above and beyond to make guests happy and at home in New York. And thanks to Mayor Giuliani's quality-of-life campaign, this corner of the Theater District is now porn-free; it makes a great home base, especially for theatergoers. The inn has inspired a loyal following, so reserve early. However, there's no elevator in the four-story building, so overpackers and travelers with limited mobility should book elsewhere.

Comfort Inn Midtown. 129 W. 46th St. (btw. Sixth Ave. and Broadway), New York, NY 10036. ☎ **800/567-7720** or 212/221-2600. Fax 212/790-2760. www.applecorehotels.com. 80 units. A/C TV TEL. $109–$249 double, depending on season. Children under 14 stay free in parents' room. Rates include continental breakfast. Ask about senior, AAA, corporate, and promotional discounts; check www.comfortinn.com for online booking discounts. AE, DC, DISC, MC, V. Parking $20 nearby. Subway: 1, 2, 3, 9 to 42nd St./Times Sq.; N, R to 49th St.; B, D, F, Q to 47–50th sts./Rockefeller Center.

A major 1998 renovation brightened the former Hotel Remington's public spaces and small guest rooms, which now boast nice floral patterns, neo-Shaker furnishings, and marble and tile bathrooms (a few have showers only, so be sure to request a tub if it matters). Everything's fresh, comfortable, and new. In-room extras include hair dryers, coffeemakers, blackout drapes, pay movies, and voice mail. Other plusses include a small fitness center and a business center; a coffee shop was in the works at press time. The location is excellent, steps from Times Square, Rockefeller Center, and the Theater District. We're not thrilled with Apple Core Hotels' (the management company that handles this Comfort Inn franchise) wide-ranging price schedule, but we found that it was relatively easy to get a well-priced room ($150 or less) even around holiday time, and rates drop as low as $79 in the off-season.

☼ Hotel Edison. 228 W. 47th St. (btw. Broadway and Eighth Ave.), New York, NY 10036. ☎ **800/637-7070** or 212/840-5000. Fax 212/596-6850. www.edisonhotelnyc.com. 869 units. A/C TV TEL. $125 single; $140 double; $155–$170 triple or quad; $160–$200 suite. Extra person $15. AE, CB, DC, DISC, MC, V. Valet parking $22. Subway: N, R to 49th St.; 1, 9 to 50th St.

There's no doubt about it—the Edison is one of the Theater District's best hotel bargains, if not the best. No other area hotel is so consistently value-priced. About 90% of the rooms were refurbished in 1998 (the rest should be done by the time you arrive), and they're *much* nicer than what you'd get for just about the same money at the nearby Ramada Inn Milford Plaza (which ain't exactly the "Lullabuy of Broadway!" these days). Don't expect much more than the basics, but you will find a firm bed (flat pillows, though), motel decor that's more attractive than most, a phone with data port, and a clean, perfectly adequate tile bathroom. Most double rooms feature two twins or a full bed, but there are some queens; request one at booking and show up early in the day for your best chance at one. Triple/quad rooms are larger, with two doubles.

Off the attractive deco-ish lobby is Cafe Edison, a hoot of an old-style Polish deli that's a favorite among ladder-climbing theater types and downmarket ladies who lunch; Sofia's, an Italian restaurant; a homey tavern with live entertainment most nights; and a gift shop. Services are kept at a bare minimum to keep rates down, but there is a beauty salon and a guest-services desk where you can arrange tours, theater tickets, and transportation. The hotel fills up with tour groups from the world over, but with nearly 1,000 rooms, you can carve out some space if you call early enough.

Hotel Wolcott. 4 W. 31st St. (at Fifth Ave.), New York, NY 10001. ☎ **212/268-2900.** Fax 212/563-0096. www.wolcott.com. 250 units. A/C TV TEL. $120 double; $140 triple; $170 suite. Discounted AAA, AARP, and promotional rates may be available. AE, JCB, MC, V. Parking $16 next door. Subway: B, D, F, Q, N, R to 34th St.

The Wolcott was one of the grande dames of Manhattan hotels at the start of the 20th century. Somewhat less than that now, it has been reinvented as a good-value option for bargain-hunting travelers. Only the lobby hints at the hotel's former grandeur; these days, the rooms are motel-standard, but they're well kept and quite serviceable. Plusses include spacious bathrooms and voice mail, plus minifridges in most rooms. On the downside, some of the mattresses aren't as firm as I might like, and the closets are small. And some of the triples are poorly configured—the front door to one I saw hit up right against a bed—but they're plenty big enough for three, and come with two TVs to avoid before-bedtime conflicts (as do the suites). All in all, you get your money's worth here. The hotel's has a basement coin-op laundry, a rarity for Manhattan. There's also a tour desk and a snack shop where you can get your morning coffee; an Internet center was in the works at press time.

Park Savoy Hotel. 158 W. 58th St. (btw. Sixth and Seventh aves.), New York, NY 10019. ☎ **212/245-5755.** Fax 212/765-0668. www.neon.net/parksavoy. 70 units. A/C TV TEL. $70 single; $85–$155 double/quad. Rates include tax. AE, MC, V. Parking $20 nearby. Subway: A, B, C, D, 1, 9 to 59th St./Columbus Circle; N, R to 57th St.

The Park Savoy isn't quite as nice as its sister hotel, the Chelsea Savoy (see above), but the lower prices reflect the quality difference, making it a good deal nonetheless. The hotel has been renovated recently so that all rooms have nice new black-and-white–tiled private bathrooms, which are petite (with showers only) but attractive and clean. If your budget is tight, two of you can make do in the smallest rooms; the biggest ones can accommodate three or four in two double beds. Rooms are basic and a few I saw were in need of a fresh coat of paint, but they do the job. All have voice mail on the telephones, most have walk-in closets, and a few have minifridges. Services are kept to a minimum to keep rates low, but there's a good Pasta Lovers restaurant in the building that gives guests 10% off and will deliver to your room. Best of all is the attractive and convenient location—a block from Central Park and a stone's throw from Carnegie Hall, Lincoln Center, and the Columbus Circle subway lines.

Portland Square Hotel. 132 W. 47th St. (btw. Sixth and Seventh aves.), New York, NY 10036. ☎ **800/388-8988** or 212/382-0600. Fax 212/382-0684. www.portlandsquarehotel.com or www.citysearch.com/nyc/portlandsquare. 145 units (30 with shared bathroom). A/C TV TEL. $60–$70 single or double with shared bathroom; $95–$109 single with private bathroom; $109–$119 double with private bathroom; $130–$140 triple or quad (in two double beds). Extra person $10. AE, JCB, MC, V. Parking $24. Subway: B, D, F, Q to Rockefeller Center.

The Portland Square is a good Theater District bet for budget travelers. I like this hotel slightly better than its sister hotel, the Herald Square: The public spaces have been nicely renovated, and everything seems to be in pretty good shape. The rooms are small, simple, and cheaply furnished (think laminated furniture, fluorescent lighting), but clean. Ask for one with an extra-large bathroom; some are almost as big as the bedroom. Avoid the shared bathrooms if you can: The ratio is a high four rooms to a bath, the hall bathrooms I saw were on the crusty side, and most of the shared bathrooms I visited had a smoky odor. But the private bathrooms are a decent deal if money's tight. Every room has its own safe, voice mail on the phone, and air-conditioning year-round (many hotels take window units out in the winter). The staff is friendly and cooperative, but don't expect much in the way of service (that's one way they keep rates low). Luggage lockers are available.

Quality Hotel & Suites Midtown. 59 W. 46th St. (btw. Fifth and Sixth aves.), New York, NY 10036. ☎ **800/567-7720** or 212/719-2300. Fax 212/921-8929. www.applecorehotels.com. 193 units. A/C TV TEL. $109–$249 double; $149–$299 suite, depending on the season. Rates include continental breakfast. Children under 19 stay free in parents' room. Ask about senior, AAA, corporate, and promotional discounts. AE, DC, DISC, MC, V. Parking $20 nearby. Subway: B, D, F, Q to 47th–50th sts./Rockefeller Center.

Here's a fine choice for those looking for your basic, clean, well-outfitted hotel room for not too much money. Nice extras include coffeemaker with free coffee; decent closets with iron, ironing board, and safe; a smallish but fine bathroom with hair dryer; and phone with voice mail, data port, and free local calls (an excellent plus). The suites are great for families, with king bed, pullout sleeper sofa in the living room, and two TVs. The 1902 landmark building, with a beaux-arts facade and an attractive lobby, has been recently renovated to include a nice exercise room with cardio machines, two meeting rooms, and a business center with credit-card–activated Internet access and fax and copy machines, as well as an ATM. The location, in the diamond district between Rockefeller Center and Times Square, is great for both business and pleasure. We're not thrilled with the management's wide-ranging price schedule, but we found that it was relatively easy to negotiate a good rate ($139 or less) even around holiday time, and rates drop as low as $79 in the off-season. (You might even be able to get a suite for 99 bucks if your timing is right.)

Travel Inn. 515 W. 42nd St. (just west of Tenth Ave.). ☎ **888/HOTEL58,** 800/869-4630, or 212/695-7171. Fax 212/265-7778. www.newyorkhotel.com/travel. 160 units. A/C TV TEL. $125–$175 double; $250 executive suite. Extra person $15. Children under 16 stay free. AAA discounts available; check Web site for special Internet deals. AE, DC, DISC, MC, V. Free parking. Subway: A, C, E to 42nd St.–Port Authority Bus Terminal.

This hotel may be a bit on the expensive side for some budget travelers in the high-season or during show time at the nearby Javits Convention Center, but extras like a huge outdoor pool and sundeck, an up-to-date fitness room, and free parking (otherwise unheard of in Manhattan) make Travel Inn well worth the money even in busy seasons. It may not be loaded with personality, but it does offer the clean, bright regularity of a good chain hotel. Rooms are oversized and comfortably furnished, with extra-firm beds, a work desk (no data ports yet, though), alarm clock, full-length mirrors, iron and board, and almost all new bathrooms (ask for one when booking to be on the safe side) with hair dryers. Some of the furnishings are slightly worn at the edges, but everything else is new and fresh. Even the smallest double is sizable and has a roomy bathroom. There's an on-site coffee shop with room service (daily 6am–8pm), a gift shop run by Gray Line that can book tours and airport transfers, a well-equipped conference room, and a lifeguard on duty at that terrific pool in season. The neighborhood has gentrified nicely and isn't as far-flung as you might think: Off-Broadway theaters and great affordable restaurants are at hand, and it's just a 10-minute walk to the Theater District.

Washington Jefferson Hotel. 318 W. 51st St. (just west of Eighth Ave.), New York, NY 10019. ☎ **888/567-7550** or 212/246-7550. Fax 212/246-7622. www.citysearch.com/nyc/washingtonjeff. 150 units (35 with private bathroom). A/C (in summer) TV TEL. $68–$99 double with shared bathroom; $109–$149 double with private bathroom; $129–$169 suite, depending on season. Ask about special deals. AE, MC, V. Parking $15–$20 nearby. Subway: C, E to 50th St.

Here's a good choice in gentrifying Hell's Kitchen, just west of the Theater District. The lobby is warm and welcoming, the old-time staff service oriented, and the leafy, bistro-lined block one of the nicest in the neighborhood. The no-frills, mix-and-match rooms aren't anything special—expect small and K-mart quality and you won't be disappointed—but they do the job. The private bathrooms have tiny tiled bathrooms with shower stalls, while the shared bathrooms have older but larger in-hall bathrooms at a room-to-bathroom ratio of about 3 to 1. All rooms have clock radios, and shared bathrooms have private sinks. Minifridges, microwaves, hair dryers, irons, and coffeemakers are available on request. The hotel has just hired the PR man behind the successful, arts-oriented Gershwin (see above), hoping to appeal to young travelers and up-and-coming actors, so expect a move in that direction.

✪ **The Wyndham.** 42 W. 58th St. (btw. Fifth and Sixth aves.), New York, NY 10019. ☎ **800/257-1111** or 212/753-3500. Fax 212/754-5638. 140 units. AC TV TEL. $125–$140 single; $140–$155 double; $180–$225 1-bedroom suite; $320–$365 2-bedroom suite. AE, DC, MC, V. Parking $35 next door. Subway: N, R to Fifth Ave.; B, Q to 57th St.

This family-owned charmer is one of Midtown's best hotel deals—and it's perfectly located to boot, on a great block steps away from

Fifth Avenue shopping and Central Park. The Wyndham is stuck in the 1970s on all fronts—don't expect so much as an alarm clock or hair dryer in your room, much less a data port—but its guest rooms are enormous by city standards, comfortable, and loaded with character. The entire hotel is papered with a wild collection of wallpaper, from candy stripes to crushed velvets, and some rooms definitely cross the tacky line. But others are downright lovely, with such details as rich oriental carpets and well-worn libraries, and the eclectic art collection that lines the walls boasts some real gems. Most importantly, the Me decade rates mean you get a lot for your money: The rooms all feature huge walk-in closets (the biggest I've ever seen); the surprisingly affordable suites also have full-fledged living rooms, dressing areas, and cold kitchenettes (fridge only). If you're put in a room that's not to your taste, just ask politely to see another one; the loyal staff is usually happy to accommodate. Dry cleaning and laundry service are available, as is limited room service (the restaurant should be in full swing by the time you arrive).

WORTH A SPLURGE

Belvedere Hotel. 319 W. 48th St. (btw. Eighth and Ninth aves.), New York, NY 10036. ☎ **888/HOTEL58** or 212/245-7000. Fax 212/265-7778. www. newyorkhotel.com/belvedere. 350 units. A/C TV TEL. $125–$240 double, depending on season. AAA discounts available; check Web site for special Internet deals. AE, DC, DISC, MC, V. Parking $17 on next block. Subway: C, E to 50th St.

The Belvedere is an excellent hotel from the Empire Hotel Group, the people behind the Americana (above) and the Newton (below). Public spaces, with a sharp retro-modern deco flair, lead to sizable, comfortable, and attractive rooms with smallish but very nice bathrooms with hair dryer and pantry kitchenettes with fridge, sink, and microwave (BYO utensils). Beds are nice and firm, and you'll find voice mail and data ports on the telephones. Ask for a renovated room, where you'll get good-quality cherry-wood furnishings, plus an alarm clock and work desk (in all but a few). Also ask for a high floor (8 and above) for great views; usually they'll cost no more (ask when booking).

On-site extras that make the Belvedere one of the city's top values include dry cleaning and laundry service, a self-serve Laundromat, electronic luggage lockers, fax and Internet-access machines, a brand-new and stylish breakfast room and light-bites cafe for guests, and the terrific Churrascaria Plataforma Brazilian restaurant. The neighborhood is loaded with terrific affordable restaurants along Ninth Avenue, and fancier places two blocks south on Restaurant Row.

Dealmaking with the Chains

As you consider hotels, keep in mind that most—particularly those in the Times Square area, where most visitors want to stay, and particularly ones with recognizable names, like Comfort Inn, Holiday Inn, and Best Western—are highly sensitive to the market, in both directions. Because they hate to see rooms sit empty, they'll often negotiate astounding rates at the last minute and in the off-season.

Also keep in mind that the chains are where you're able to pull out all the stops for discounts, from auto club membership to senior status. AAA or AARP membership is well worth the annual fee for the 10% off it will garner you at most of the chains. And you may be able to take advantage of corporate rates or highly discounted weekend stays (more on that in the box earlier in this chapter). Most chain hotels will let the kids stay with mom and dad for free, and some even offer a special family rate for you and the kids. Always ask for every possible kind of discount; if you find that you get an unhelpful reservation agent at the main number, dial back and you're likely to get a more helpful one. And it's worth calling the hotel direct, where the front-desk staff will wheel and deal to keep their occupancy rate (the badge of honor among city hotels these days) high.

Of course, there's no guarantee what you'll be offered. Even if you're traveling in the off-season, you could stumble on a big convention or some other event that drives rates up. And your chances of getting a deal aren't great if you're visiting in a busy season. But if you're willing to make a few extra phone calls, or spend some time surfing online reservations systems, you may find that you can get a lot for your money at some very comfortable hotels that would otherwise be out of your price range.

Best Western (☎ 800/528-1234; www.bestwestern.com) is one of the most reliable hotel chains in the nation, but the rack rates for their New York City hotels are higher than you'd expect—largely in the $200 range. At the **Best Western Seaport Inn,** 33 Peck Slip at South Street Seaport (☎ **800/HOTEL-NY** or 212/766-6600), doubles go for $169 to $209, but corporate rates and other seasonal discounts can drop to $149. Since rates include continental breakfast, that's a great deal on a very comfortable and well-kept hotel. At Midtown's **Best Western Woodward,** 210 W. 55th St. (☎ **800/336-4110** or 212/247-2000), and the **Best Western President,** 234 W. 48th St. (☎ **800/826-4667** or 212/246-8800), rack rates go well into the $200s, but I've found both hotels to offer rates as low as $119 double ($107 to seniors and AAA members) in slower periods, such as Thanksgiving and just after the New Year.

Frankly, I'm not thrilled with the wide-ranging pricing policy at **Apple Core Hotels** (☎ **800/567-7720;** www.applecorehotels. com) a small management company that handles three chain hotels reviewed in this chapter: the **Comfort Inn Midtown** (p. 58), the **Quality Hotel & Suites Midtown** (p. 61), and the **Quality Hotel Eastside** (p. 68), as well as the **Best Western Manhattan,** 17 W. 32nd St. (☎ **800/551-2303** or 212/736-1600). All have modest but comfortable and well-kept rooms with rack rates ranging from $109 to $249. If you can get a room on the lower end of that scale, it's always a good deal, especially when free continental breakfast and small business and fitness centers sweeten the pie in all but the Quality Hotel Eastside. You may even be able to do better depending on the season in which you visit—I've heard them negotiate rates as low as $79 a night more than once, which is a smokin' deal.

Comfort Inn Manhattan, at 42 W. 35th St. (☎ **800/228-5150** or 212/947-0200; www.comfortinnmanhattan.com), is not run by Apple Core, but it can offer some great deals on comfortable rooms nonetheless. The best time to stay here is between January and July, when standard rates run $129 to $189 double (including a substantial continental breakfast), and you may be able to do better with discounts and a little negotiation.

If you want something a bit on the nicer side, see what's on offer at **Loews New York,** 569 Lexington Ave. (☎ **800/836-6471** or 212/752-7000; www.loewshotels.com/newyork), a very nice chain hotel with business and fitness centers. Rack rates start at $189 here, but you can often do markedly better, especially if you ask for corporate, AAA, or senior discounts. Free cribs and rollaways for the kids can make this hotel a particularly good deal.

7 Midtown East & Murray Hill

Carlton Arms. 160 E. 25th St. (btw. Lexington and Third aves.), New York, NY 10010. ☎ **212/679-0680** (reservations) or 212/684-8337 (guests). 54 units (20 with private bathroom). $57–$90 single–triple with shared bathroom; $68–$101 single–triple with private bathroom. Discounts for students and foreign visitors. 10% discount on 7-night stays paid upon arrival. MC, V. Parking $16 nearby. Subway: 6 to 23rd St.

The motto at the Carlton Arms is "This ain't no Holiday Inn"— and boy, ain't that the truth. The true spirit of bohemianism and artistic freedom reigns in this backpacker's delight of a hotel, where every room is a work of art executed by an edgy artist given full license to go hog wild. Some spaces are sublime, such as Robin Banks' Cartoon Room (#5B), Thias Charbonet's Underwater Room (#1A), the ocean-blue lobby (complete with fish in the TV), and the stunning first-floor mosaic bathroom; others are simply bizarre. Whether you end up with a mermaid mural or a wall of teddy bears, you'll see why this is the most extraordinary hotel in the city.

But if you're looking for creature comforts and modern conveniences, this is *not* the place for you. The cramped rooms are basic— *very* basic. The beds are lumpy, there's no air-conditioning, and everything's old and on the crusty side. Each room has a sink, but you'll most likely end up sharing a hallway bathroom with your fellow travelers: mainly students, foreign travelers, and fellow existentialists. The place is kept clean, but there's no maid service during your stay. On the upside, the staff is super-friendly, and they'll be happy to take phone messages for you in the office (there's a pay phone in the lobby for outgoing calls). Reserve 1 to 2 months in advance, because despite the inconveniences this place is almost always full.

✪ **Habitat Hotel.** 130 E. 57th St. (at Lexington Ave.), New York, NY 10022. ☎ **800/255-0482** or 212/753-8841. Fax 212/829-9605. www.stayinny.com. 300 units (about 60 with private bathroom). A/C TV TEL. $95–$105 single or double with shared bathroom; $110–$120 single or double with semi-private bathroom; $130–$170 single or double with private bathroom. AE, DC, MC, V. Parking $25 nearby. Subway: 4, 5, 6 to 59th St.; E, F to Lexington Ave.

This brand-new hotel is being marketed as "upscale budget," with rooms dressed to appeal to travelers who are short on funds but big on style. They're well designed in a natural palette that's accented with black-and-white photos. Everything is better quality and more attractive than I usually see in this price range, from the firm mattresses to the plush towels to the pedestal sinks in every room. The bathrooms—shared (one for every three to four rooms), semi-private (two rooms sharing an adjacent bathroom), and private—are all brand-new. The only downside—and it may be a big one for romance-seeking couples—are the sleeping accommodations: The double rooms consist of a twin bed with a pullout trundle, which takes up most of the width of the narrow room when it's open. (A few larger doubles with full-size beds and private bathrooms were in the works at press time.) The prices are a tad high on the private bathrooms considering the setup, but they're good for the shared bathrooms; I would definitely choose the Habitat over other similarly accommodated inns.

The neighborhood is excellent, especially for shoppers, since Bloomingdale's is just 2 blocks away. The public spaces were under the renovation when I visited (they should be completed by the time you arrive), but even the temporary lobby was more impressive than most. There's a glass-enclosed veranda looking down Lexington Avenue (where continental breakfast will be served), a bar, and a library lounge. Ask about guests-only deals such as 10% off one item at Bloomie's and reduced-rate access to nearby fitness centers.

Hotel Grand Union. 34 E. 32nd St. (btw. Madison and Park aves.), New York, NY 10016. ☎ **212/683-5890.** Fax 212/689-7397. 95 units. A/C TV TEL. $110 double; $125 twin or triple; $150 quad. Rates increase during the holiday season. AE, DISC, MC, V. Parking $20. Subway: 6 to 33rd St.

This centrally located hotel is big with budget-minded international travelers. The rooms are spacious and clean and come with nice extras like voice mail, minifridges, and free HBO—but bad fluorescent lighting, cheap furniture and textiles, and an utter lack of natural light. The bathrooms vary greatly in quality, from almost-new to disco-era grim. Still, the prices are good, the staff is helpful, the lobby is pleasant, and there's an adjacent coffee shop for convenient meals. If asked to choose, I prefer the nearby Wolcott (see above). I suggest trying there first, and booking here only if you need to save the few dollars' difference.

Hotel 31. 120 E. 31st St. (btw. Park and Lexington aves.), New York, NY 10016. ☎ **212/685-3060.** Fax 212/532-1232. www.citysearch.com/nyc/hotel31. 90 units (about half with private bathroom). A/C TV TEL. $85–$130 double. Rates include tax. No credit cards. Parking about $20 on next block. Subway: 6 to 33rd St.

This sister hotel to trendy Hotel 17 (see above) is situated in a quiet, mostly residential neighborhood that's not quite as lovely as the 17th Street location, but fine nonetheless. The former SRO (the hotel still houses a number of permanent single-room-occupancy tenants) has been reinvented along the same lines as Hotel 17, with quirkily attractive but very basic rooms. They're dark and downright miniscule, but come with air-conditioning, alarm clocks, hair dryers, and voice mail. About half have private bathrooms; if you choose to save a few dollars and share, you'll have access to nice, newish bathrooms. Not all of the no-bathrooms have their own sinks, so be sure to request one when booking. Ask for a recently renovated room, as I spotted a few beginning signs of wear in the older ones. Since the hotel is most popular with—and most suited to—younger travelers and Europeans, there's lots of smoking going on; as a result, the narrow hallways tend to smell like cigarettes. Avid non-smokers may want to book elsewhere.

Pickwick Arms Hotel. 230 E. 51st St. (btw. Second and Third aves.), New York, NY 10022. ☎ **800/PICKWIK** in the U.S., 800/874-0074 in Canada, or 212/355-0300. Fax 212/755-5029. 320 units (200 with bathroom). A/C TV TEL. $70–$99 single; $125–$160 double. AE, CB, DC, MC, V. Parking $28 nearby. Subway: 6 to 51st St.

For a Midtown hotel in prime East Side territory, staying at the Pickwick is like entering an economic time warp. Set in one of the city's most prestigious neighborhoods, the hotel's location couldn't be better. The older, sometimes astoundingly small rooms are spare, some might even say monk-like, but they're well kept, and the entire place is safe and well run. This former SRO has a few doubles and twins with private bathrooms (the larger deluxe twins can accommodate a rollaway for a third person), but the majority of rooms are singles with private, semi-private, or shared-hall bathrooms. Two friends traveling together can take advantage of the semi-private situation: Two singles—each with its own sink, TV, desk, small closet, and telephone—share a bathroom, for the same price as a twin room. All of the bathrooms are worn looking and have showers only, but they're clean. A renovation is spiffing up the halls and some rooms a bit. On site is a rooftop patio with skyline views; Scarabee, a good but pricey French-Mediterranean restaurant; and a wine bar that also serves breakfast.

Quality Hotel Eastside. 161 Lexington Ave. (at 30th St.), New York, NY 10016. ☎ **800/567-7720** or 212/545-1800. Fax 212/790-2760. www. applecorehotels.com. 79 units (59 with private bathroom). A/C TV TEL. $109–$249 double, depending on the season. AE, DISC, MC, V. Parking $17 2 blocks away. Subway: 6 to 33rd St.

This hotel is nothing special—just some small, standard rooms done in a vaguely early-American style with older bathrooms. The property's recommendable features are its location, in a nice, quiet residential neighborhood, and its amenities, which include a business center (with copy and fax machines, plus Internet access) and a fitness room (with treadmill, lifecycle, and nordic track). In-room extras include coffeemaker, iron and board, data port, alarm clock, voice mail, and hair dryer. There's an affordable pasta joint next door, plus an adjacent coffee shop for your morning joe. Though it doesn't exactly excite me, I'm including this place because it can be a real deal—rates have been known to drop to as low as $79 on occasion. Don't bother if rates are higher than $139—you can do better for the money. And skip the shared bathrooms altogether.

Vanderbilt YMCA. 224 E. 47th St. (btw. Second and Third aves.), New York, NY 10017. ☎ **212/756-9600.** Fax 212/752-0210. www.ymcanyc.org. 374 units with shared bathroom, 5 with private bathroom. A/C TV. $65–$75 single; $78–$85 twin; $125–$135 suite. AE, MC, V. Parking about $20 nearby. Subway: S, 4, 5, 6, 7 to Grand Central.

This YMCA boasts a friendly, youthful atmosphere and a fashionable East Side location that's also convenient: It's within walking distance of the United Nations, Rockefeller Center, and Grand Central Terminal, as well as lots of good shopping and restaurants. The rooms are Spartan and tiny—I repeat, tiny—but the beds do somehow fit, as do the TVs, dressers, and desks. The more expensive rooms have sinks, and the suites have private bathrooms. The communal bathrooms and showers are well kept. A state-of-the-art fitness center—with two pools, a sauna, and sundeck, plus a full calendar of classes—is free to Y guests. The sports facilities and reasonably priced meals at the on-site cafe alone make the Y a worthwhile choice; other extras include room service from the cafe, luggage storage, safe-deposit boxes, and a self-service Laundromat. The rooms are booked far in advance, so call well ahead.

8 The Upper West Side

Amsterdam Inn. 340 Amsterdam Ave. (at 76th St.), New York, NY 10023. ☎ **212/579-7500.** Fax 212/579-6127. www.amsterdaminn.com. 20 units (about half with private bathroom). A/C TV TEL. $75–$95 single or double with shared bathroom; $115–$135 single or double with private bathroom. Packages and group discounts may be available. Cash or traveler's checks only. Parking $25 at adjacent lot. Subway: 1, 9 to 79th St.

Housed on the top three floors of a newly renovated five-story walk-up, the Amsterdam Inn offers very basic accommodations for those who want a bit more in terms of amenities and service than they'd get at a hostel. The inn's biggest assets are its prime Upper West Side location and its newness. Accommodations are no-frills: Rooms are small and narrow, with not much more than a bed, a wall rack to hang your clothes on, a cheap set of drawers with a TV on top, a side table with a lamp and a phone that requires a deposit to activate, and

Uptown Accommodations & Dining

Accommodations
Amsterdam Inn 9
De Hirsch Residence at the
  92nd Street YM–YWHA 16
Hostelling International–
  New York 24
Hotel Newton 22
Hotel Riverside 19
Malibu Hotel 23
The Milburn 8
Urban Jem Guest House 26
West Side YMCA 3

Dining
Big Nick's Burger Joint 10
Gabriela's 20
Gray's Papaya 6
Hunan Park 5 21
John's Pizzeria 2 4
Josie's Restaurant & Juice
  Bar 7
Papaya King 15
Pintaile's Pizza 17
Sarabeth's Kitchen 11 12 16
Serendipity 3 1
Sofia Fabulous Pizza 13
Sylvia's 25
Totonno's Pizzeria
  Napolitano 14

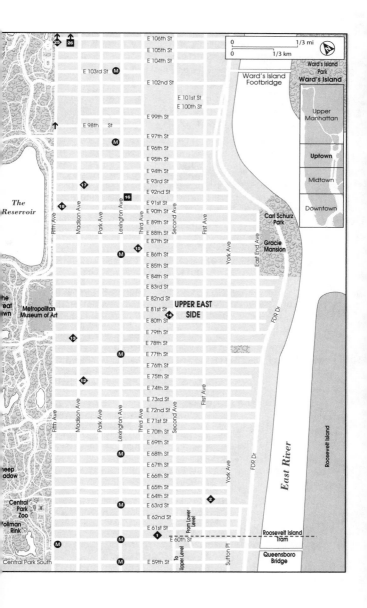

a sink if there's no private bathroom. The Euro-style rooms share the in-hall bathrooms at a ratio of about 2½-to-1. All the bathrooms are brand new and have showers only. Frankly, I think the rates are too high for what you get, but the friendly management seems willing to negotiate, so try to talk them down; if $135 for a double with private bathroom is the best they can do, you can probably do better elsewhere. If you book a double, make sure it's a *real* double, with a double bed, not a single with a trundle. The singles with trundles can accommodate two, but don't expect to have much space left over.

✪ **Hotel Newton.** 2528 Broadway (btw. 94th and 95th sts.), New York, NY 10025. ☎ **888/HOTEL58** or 212/678-6500. Fax 212/678-6758. www. newyorkhotel.com/newton. 120 units (10 with shared bathroom). A/C TV TEL. $85 single or double with shared bathroom; $99–$135 single or double with private bathroom; $150 suite. Extra person $15. Children under 17 stay free. AAA discounts available; check Web site for special Internet deals. AE, DC, DISC, MC, V. Subway: 1, 2, 3, 9 to 96th St.

Finally—a budget hotel that's actually *nice.* Unlike many of its peers, the Newton doesn't scream "budget!" at every turn, or require you to have the carefree attitude of a college student to put up with it. As you enter the pretty lobby, you're greeted by a uniformed staff that's attentive and professional. The rooms are generally large, with good, firm beds, a work desk, and a sizable new bathroom, plus roomy closets in most (a few of the cheapest have wall racks only). About 36 rooms are big enough to accommodate families on a budget in two doubles or two queen beds. The suites feature two queens, a sofa in the sitting room, plus niceties like a microwave, minifridge, iron and board, and hair dryer, making them well worth the few extra dollars. The bigger rooms and suites have been upgraded with cherry-wood furnishings, but even the older laminated furniture is much nicer than I usually see in this price range. Travelers on a shoe-string can opt for one of the few doubles that share a hall bathroom with one other room. The AAA-approved hotel is impeccably kept, and there was lots of sprucing up going on—new drapes here, fresh paint there—during my last visit. The nice neighborhood boasts lots of affordable restaurants, and a cute diner on the same block provides room service from 6am to 1am. The 96th Street express subway stop is just a block away, providing convenient access to the rest of the city. A great bet all the way around.

Hotel Riverside. 350 W. 88th St. (btw. West End Ave. and Riverside Dr.), New York, NY 10024. ☎ **888/HOTEL58** or 212/724-6100. Fax 212/873-5808. www.newyorkhotel.com/riverside. 82 units (37 with shared bathroom). A/C TV TEL. $90–$100 single or double with shared bathroom; $100–$140 single or double with private bathroom. Extra person $10. Children under 16 stay free. Check Web site for special Internet deals. Parking about $29 nearby. Subway: 1, 9 to 86th St.

The Hotel Riverside is another good choice from the Empire Hotel Group, the same people behind the Newton (above). I prefer the Newton over the Riverside for the money, but the Riverside is also nicely kept and boasts a very quiet location, just steps from Riverside Park in one of the city's most desirable residential neighborhoods. Some rooms even have Hudson River views. All have firm beds and work desks, and those with private bathrooms sport fresh tile and new fixtures. The private bathrooms are the best deal here; some of the shared bathrooms (and shared bathrooms themselves) are a tad crusty for the relatively high price tag. Management is friendly and professional, and the public spaces are much finer than what I usually see in hotels in this price range. On-site coin-operated laundry for guests' use is another plus.

Malibu Hotel. 2688 Broadway (at 103rd St.), New York, NY 10025. ☎ **800/ 647-2227** or 212/222-2954. Fax 212/678-6842. www.malibuhotelnyc.com. 150 units (40 with shared bathroom). TV. $39–$69 single or double with shared bathroom; $79–$109 deluxe single or double with private bathroom; $109–$149 quad (2 doubles) with private bathroom. Inquire about discounts for stays of a week or more. MC, V. Parking $20 nearby. Subway: 1, 9 to 103rd St.

If you're committed to finding a private bathroom for less than $100, it's hard to do better than this walk-up hotel. The rooms are small and basic, with little more than a moderately firm bed with a colorful spread (or two in the bigger rooms), an alarm clock on the bedside table, black metal shelving for the TV and your belongings (some rooms also have a wall rack for hanging clothes), and a newish bathroom that's small but slightly roomier than most in the budget category. Those with private bathrooms also have air-conditioning. The shared bathrooms have private sinks and share hall bathrooms at a ratio of one to every three or four rooms. I saw dust along the carpet edges and other maintenance issues here and there,

Money-Saving Tip for Families

Most hotels add a surcharge to the nightly rate—anywhere from $10 to $25 per person, per night—for each extra person beyond two sharing a hotel room. Ten bucks may seem like a drop in the bucket, but it can really add up. So if you're traveling with the kids, choose a hotel that lets kids stay free. Even if the hotel usually charges for kids, they may be willing to drop this extra charge to draw you in, so always ask.

and a hint of cigarette smoke pervaded the halls—but I've seen much worse for more money. (The rooms with private bathrooms seem to be somewhat better maintained.) The clientele is mostly young, with a good number of Europeans in the mix. The neighborhood has really come up in the last few years; it's safe, nice, and filled with lots of affordable restaurants. The front desk can book tours, airline transfers, and Atlantic City bus trips, but don't expect much more in the way of service.

✪ **The Milburn.** 242 W. 76th St. (btw. Broadway and West End Ave.), New York, NY 10023. ☎ **800/833-9622** or 212/362-1006. Fax 212/721-5476. www.milburnhotel.com. 111 units. A/C TV TEL. $119–$145 studio double; $149–$175 1-bedroom suite, depending on season. Extra person $10. Children under 12 stay free in parents' room. AE, CB, DC, MC, V. Parking $16–$20. Subway: 1, 2, 3, 9 to 72nd St.

On a quiet side street a block from the Hotel Beacon, the Milburn also offers rooms with kitchenettes in the same great neighborhood for less. The Milburn may not be quite as nice as the Beacon, but it is arguably better in the less busy seasons, when a double studio goes for just $119. Every room is rife with amenities: dining area, safe, iron and board, hair dryer, two-line phone with data port, alarm, nice newish bathroom, and kitchenette with minifridge, microwave, coffee maker (with free coffee!), hot plate on request, and all the necessary equipment. The one-bedroom suites also boast a pullout queen sofa and a work desk. Don't expect much from the decor, but everything is attractive and in good shape. In fact, the whole place is spotless. But what makes the Milburn a real find is that it's more service oriented than most hotels in this price range. The friendly staff will do everything from providing free copy, fax, and e-mail services to picking up your laundry at the dry cleaners next door. Additional facilities include a self-serve Laundromat, VCR rentals, wheelchair-accessible rooms, discount dining programs at local restaurants, and use of the nearby Equinox health club for a special $15 fee (usually $35). At press time, a small workout room was in the works.

West Side YMCA. 5 W. 63rd St. (btw. Broadway and Central Park West), New York, NY 10023. ☎ **212/875-4100.** Fax 212/875-1334. www.ymcanyc.org. 550 units (25 with private bathroom). A/C TV. $65 single with shared bathroom; $75 double with shared bathroom; $95 single with private bathroom; $110 double with private bathroom. AE, MC, V. Parking about $25 nearby. Subway: 1, 9, A, B, C, D to Columbus Circle.

Another Y with a stellar location (see the Vanderbilt YMCA, above, and the 92nd Street Y, below), this one is housed in a National

Historic Landmark building just steps from Lincoln Center and Central Park. A multimillion-dollar renovation of the public areas and guest rooms has made it more attractive and modern than the typical Y—but it's still a Y, so don't expect more than basic. The rooms are small and most share bathrooms down the hall, but they're well kept and outfitted like a real hotel room. Frankly, the Y is no cheaper than staying at a private hotel, but what makes it worth the money are the excellent health and fitness facilities, which include two pools, gyms, an indoor running track, handball and racquetball courts, exercise classes, and much more. There's also a cafe, luggage storage, and use of safe-deposit boxes. While not the equal of the 92nd Street Y, the West Side Y does offer a busy slate of arts and cultural programs. It's also a good bet for older travelers since the fitness center gives exercise and aqua-therapy classes for seniors, and hosts an extensive Elderhostel Program from September through May. The location and price keep the Y filled to capacity virtually every night, so book well in advance.

SUPER-CHEAP SLEEPS

Hostelling International–New York. 891 Amsterdam Ave. (at 103rd St.), New York, NY 10025. ☎ **800/909-4776, code 01** or 212/932-2300. Fax 212/932-2574. www.hinewyork.org. 624 beds, 4 units with private bathroom. A/C. $22–$24 AYH members, $3 extra nonmembers; private rooms $100 for up to 4 guests. Stays limited to 7 days (length of stay may be negotiable). Individual travelers must be 18 or older. JCB, MC, V. Parking $20 nearby. Subway: 1, 9 to 103rd St.

This landmark building is home to American Youth Hostels' largest hostel. Staying here is like going back to college—a very international college, with clocks set for six different time zones behind the front desk and a young, backpack-toting clientele from around the globe. Beds are incredibly cheap, but expect to bunk it (upper or lower?) with people you don't know in rooms of 4, 6, 8, or 12. Everything is extremely basic, but the mattresses are firm and the shared bathrooms are nicely kept. There are also four rooms with one double and two bunk beds that have private bathrooms. The well-managed hostel feels like a student union, with bulletin boards and listings of events posted; a coffee bar with an ample menu and pleasant seating; two TV rooms; a sundries shop; a game room; and a smoky library with bill- and credit-card–operated computers with Internet access. (An ATM and electronic luggage lockers were to be added during the renovation of the public spaces, which was ongoing at press time.) There's also a common kitchen, vending machines on each floor, a nice coin-op laundry, a second-floor terrace, and a really nice, big yard with picnic tables and barbecues in summer. There's a nice school spirit to the place. The neighborhood has improved over the years, but it's still a little sketchy over here on Amsterdam Avenue; one block over is much nicer Broadway, lined with affordable restaurants and shops.

9 The Upper East Side

De Hirsch Residence at the 92nd Street YM–YWCA. 1395 Lexington Ave. (at 92nd St.), New York, NY 10128. ☎ **888/699-6884,** or 212/415-5650. Fax 212/415-5578. www.92ndsty.org. 372 units (all with shared bathroom). A/C. $69 single; $90 double; long-term stays (2 months or more) $795/month single; $1,100–$1,300/month double. Must be at least 18 and no older than 30 for long-term stays. AE, MC, V. Parking $20 nearby. Subway: 4, 5, 6 to 86th St.; 6 to 96th St.

Contact the 92nd Street Y well in advance, because its good value and its unparalleled cultural programs mean it's always booked up. The de Hirsch Residence offers basic but comfortable rooms, each with either one or two single beds, a dresser, and bookshelves. Each floor has a large communal bathroom, a fully equipped kitchen/dining room with microwave, and laundry facilities. The building is rather institutional-looking, but it's well kept and secure, the staff is friendly, and the location is terrific. This high-rent Upper East Side neighborhood is just blocks from Central Park and Museum Mile, and there's plenty of cheap eats and markets within a few blocks. Daily maid service and use of the Y's state-of-the-art fitness facility (pool, weights, racquetball, aerobics) is included in the daily rates. This is a great bet for lone travelers in particular, since the 92nd Street Y is a community center in a true sense of the word, offering a real sense of kinship and a mind-boggling slate of top-rated cultural happenings.

10 Harlem

Urban Jem Guest House. 2005 Fifth Ave. (btw. 124th and 125th sts.). ☎ **212/831-6029.** Fax 212/831-6940. www.urbanjem.com. 4 units (2 with shared bathroom that can be combined into a suite). A/C TV TEL. $105 double with shared bathroom; $120 double with private bathroom; $200 suite. 2-night minimum. Rates include continental breakfast upon request. Extra person $15. Rates $15 less for single travelers. 10% off 7–13 nights, 15% off 14 days or more. AE, DISC, MC, V. Parking $15 nearby. Subway: 2, 3 or 4, 5, 6 to 125th St.

This B&B is Harlem's best place to stay. It's run by Jane Alex Mendelson, a refugee from the corporate world who has successfully reinvented herself as an innkeeper. Located in the Mount Morris Historic District, her renovated 1878 brownstone is graced with fine woodwork and beautiful original (nonworking) fireplaces. The house is a work in progress, so don't expect perfection—there's still plenty to be done, and the furnishings are largely an odds-and-ends mismatch. But the accommodations offer good value. The second floor has two guest rooms with firm queen beds, new private bathrooms, and spacious kitchenettes with stove, minifridge, and the basic tools for preparing and serving a meal. On the third floor are two nice rooms that share a hall bathroom and kitchen: one a pretty bedroom with a queen bed, the other a spacious room with two foldout futon sofabeds. They can also be combined into a two-bedroom suite, which gives you a whole floor to yourself.

You can pay an extra $7.50 for daily maid service (the trash is taken out daily); otherwise, sheets and towels are changed weekly. There's also a washer-dryer for use ($3). Jane is friendly and helpful, and can provide lots of neighborhood information. The predominately African-American community isn't a regular home base for tourists, but the bustling urban neighborhood has welcomed the inn, and it makes a good starting point for exploring jazz-, gospel-, and history-rich Harlem. Midtown is about a half-hour subway ride away, but Jane recommends taking a cab back after 11pm or so.

4

Great Deals on Dining

*A*ttention foodies: Welcome to Mecca. Without a doubt, New York is the best restaurant town in the country, perhaps tops in the world.

But eating in New York just ain't cheap. The primary cause? The high cost of real estate, which is reflected in what you're charged. Wherever you're from, particularly if you're from the reasonably priced American heartland, New York's restaurants will seem *expensive.* Yet, as you peruse the chapter that follows, you'll see that good value abounds—especially if you're willing to eat ethnic, and venture beyond tourist zones into the neighborhoods where budget-challenged real New Yorkers eat, like Chinatown, the Upper West Side, and the East Village, which is particularly good for getting a lot of bang for your buck. But even if you have no intention of venturing beyond Times Square, don't worry: I've included inexpensive restaurants in every neighborhood in the list below—including some of the city's best-kept secrets.

RESERVATIONS Reservations are always a good idea in New York, and a virtual necessity if your party is bigger than two. Do yourself a favor and make them so you won't be disappointed. If you're booking dinner on a weekend night, it's a good idea to call a few days to a week in advance if you can. In some cases—you want to score a bargain prix-fixe lunch, say, or dinner at TV chef Mario Batali's perennial hotspot Pó—calling a month ahead isn't too soon.

But What If They Don't *Take* Reservations? Lots of city restaurants, especially at the affordable end of the price continuum, don't take reservations at all. One of the ways they're able to keep prices down is by packing people in as quickly as possible. This means that the best cheap and mid-priced restaurants often have a wait. Again, your best bet is to go early. Often, you can get in more quickly on a weeknight. Or just go knowing that you'll have to wait if you head to a popular spot like Boca Chica. There are worse ways to wait than sipping a margarita at the festive bar.

THE LOWDOWN ON SMOKING Following the national trend, New York City enacted strict no-smoking laws a few years back that made the majority of the city's dining rooms blessedly smoke-free. However, that doesn't mean that smokers are completely prohibited from lighting up. Here's the deal: Restaurants with more than 35 seats cannot allow smoking in their dining rooms. They can, however, allow smoking in their bar or lounge areas, and most do.

Restaurants with fewer than 35 seats—and there are more of those in the city than you'd think, especially in the budget category—can allow or prohibit smoking as they see fit. This ruling has turned some of the city's restaurants (like NoLiTa's Cafe Gitane, for instance) into particularly smoker-friendly establishments, which might be a turn-off for non-smokers.

Whether you're a smoker or non-smoker, your best bet is to call ahead and ask if it matters to you. If you're hell-bent on enjoying an after-dinner cigarette indoors, make sure that the restaurant has a bar or lounge that allows smoking. Some restaurants even offer dinner tables in their bar areas, such as Bar Pitti, where you can puff away during the meal if you so choose. And smoking is usually allowed in alfresco dining areas, but never assume—always ask. If you're a non-smoker who doesn't want to be bothered by second-hand smoke, make sure your seat is well away from the bar.

TIPPING   Tipping is easy in New York. The way to do it: Double the $8^{1}/_{4}$% sales tax and voilà! Happy waitperson. In fancier venues, another 5% is appropriate for the captain. If the wine steward helps, hand him or her 10% of the bottle's price.

1 South Street Seaport & the Financial District

If you're want to rub elbows with Wall Street's after-work crowd, head to the **Wall Street Kitchen & Bar,** which, like its sister restaurant **SoHo Kitchen & Bar** (p. 88), serves up affordably priced bar food along with 50 beers on tap and "flight" of wines and microbrews for tasting. Housed in a spectacular former bank building in the heart of the Financial District at 70 Broad St. (☎ **212/ 797-7070**), it's worth a stop for a beer and a burger.

Mangia. 40 Wall St. (btw. Nassau and William sts.). ☎ **212/425-4040** or 212/363-9536. Main courses $5.95–$9.95. AE, DC, MC, V. Mon–Fri 7am–8pm. Subway: 4, 5 to Wall St.; J, M, Z to Broad St. GOURMET DELI.

This big, bustling gourmet cafeteria is an ideal place to take a break during your day of Financial District sightseeing. Between the giant salad and soup bars, the sandwich and hot entrée counters, and an

expansive cappuccino-and-pastry counter at the front of the cavernous room, even the most finicky eater will have a hard time deciding what to eat. Everything is prepared fresh and beautifully presented. The soups and stews are particularly good (there are always
a number of daily choices), and a cup goes well with a fresh-baked
pizzette (a mini-pizza). Pay-by-the-pound salad bars don't get any
better than this, hot meal choices (such as grilled mahi-mahi or
cumin-marinated lamb kabob) are cooked to order, and sandwiches
are made to order. This place is packed with Wall Streeters between
noon and 2pm, but things move quickly and there's enough seating that usually no one has to wait. Come in for a late breakfast or
an afternoon snack, and you'll virtually have the place to yourself.

In addition to the Wall Street location, Mangia also has two
cafeteria-style cafes in Midtown that offer similar, if not so
expansive, menus: at 50 W. 57th St., between Fifth and Sixth
avenues (☎ **212/582-5882**); and at 16 E. 48th St., just east of Fifth
Avenue (☎ **212/754-7600**).

North Star Pub. At South Street Seaport, 93 South St. (at Fulton St.). ☎ **212/
509-6757.** Main courses $7.50–$12.95. AE, CB, DC, MC, V. 11:30am–
10:30pm. Subway: 2, 3, 4, 5 to Fulton St. BRITISH.

This friendly place right at the entrance to the seaport is a refreshing bit of authenticity in this mallified, almost theme park–like historic district. It's the spitting image of a British pub, down to the
chalkboard menus boasting daily specials like kidney pie and the
Guinness, Harp, and Fullers ESB on tap. I love the ale-battered fish
'n' chips (not too greasy); the excellent golden-browned shepherd's
pie (just like grandma used to make); the bangers 'n' mash, made
with grilled Cumberland sausage; and the traditional Ploughman's,
including very good pâté, a sizable hunk of cheddar or stilton, fresh
bread, and all the accompaniments (even Branston pickle!). All in
all, a fun, relaxing place to hang out and eat and drink heartily (and
cheap). In keeping with the theme, there's also an expansive menu
of single-malt scotches and Irish whiskeys.

QUICK BITES

The Twin Towers and environs abound with places to nosh.
After all, those on-the-go bankers and traders have to eat lunch,
don't they? But with so many options at hand, the trick is knowing
where to go.

Sbarro Pizza, Menchenko-Tei for authentic Japanese, and **Fine
& Shapiro** are on the main concourse of the World Trade Center
(WTC), right in a row between Borders and the center of the

Lower Manhattan, TriBeCa & Chinatown

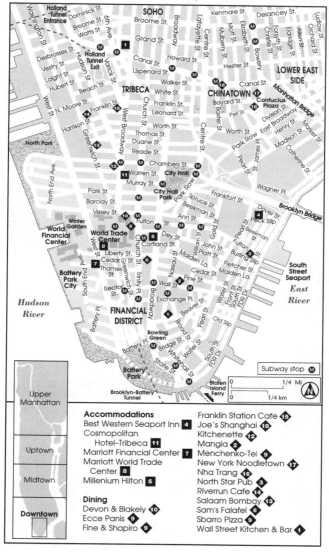

Accommodations

Best Western Seaport Inn 4
Cosmopolitan
    Hotel–Tribeca 11
Marriott Financial Center 7
Marriott World Trade
    Center 8
Millenium Hilton 5

Dining

Devon & Blakely 10
Ecce Panis 9
Fine & Shapiro 9

Franklin Station Cafe 15
Joe's Shanghai 18
Kitchenette 12
Mangia 2
Menchenko-Tei 9
New York Noodletown 17
Nha Trang 16
North Star Pub 3
Riverrun Cafe 14
Salaam Bombay 13
Sam's Falafel 6
Sbarro Pizza 9
Wall Street Kitchen & Bar 1

concourse (where the escalators to the PATH trains are). Menchenko-Tei is actually two restaurants in one: in front they sell Japanese bento box lunches with teriyakis and relatively cheap sushi, which are perfect for taking outdoors in warm weather; in the back are steam tables with Chinese food as well as a counter where you can order hearty udon and soba noodle bowls, which you can dine on at tables in back and upstairs. Fine & Shapiro has two entrances, one for full table-service and one for the "only-to-go" deli.

Across the hall from those three is **Ecce Panis,** an excellent bakery with a small selection of sandwiches, focaccias, breakfast and sweet treats, two daily soups, and tons of variations on the staff of life, including an amazing little creation: the ham and cheese brioche, which is sort of like a filled popover.

Just outside the WTC, between the north concourse entrance and Borders Books & Music, is **Devon & Blakely.** This appealing gourmet shop features lots of yuppie sandwiches (ham and camembert; smoked chicken with roasted tomatoes, spinach, and Caesar dressing), a few daily soups, a good chili with fixins and cornbread, British candy bars, pastries, and an espresso bar. The wide sidewalk just out front is lined with tables when the weather's nice.

Last but not least, there's **Sam's Falafel,** the best falafel cart in town, at the southwest corner of Broadway and Liberty Street. Sam's a well-known name in these parts, so the line can be long at lunchtime, but it always moves quickly. Nearby Liberty Plaza or Trinity Churchyard, two blocks south at Wall Street, both make great spots to enjoy your pita-wrapped lunch on a lovely day.

2 TriBeCa

Franklin Station Cafe. 222 W. Broadway (at Franklin St.). ☎ **212/ 274-8525.** Sandwiches and noodle bowls $6–$9; house specials $10.50–$16.50. AE, DC, MC, V. Daily 8am–11pm. Subway: 1, 9 to Franklin St. FRENCH-MALAYSIAN.

This charming brick-walled cafe is a winner for affordable Malaysian noodle bowls and French-inspired sandwiches. All the dishes on the cute-as-a-button handwritten and illustrated menu are prepared by the health-minded kitchen with all-natural ingredients. Sandwiches are simple but satisfying creations like home-baked ham with honey mustard, lettuce, and tomato; fresh mozzarella with leafy basil, vine-ripened tomato, and extra-virgin olive oil; and smoked salmon with mascarpone and chives. For warm and cozy, you can't do better than one of Franklin Station's noodle bowls, such as tom yum shrimp, with sprouts, pineapple, and cucumber in a pleasingly hot-and-sour broth; or seafood udon, with generous helpings of squid, shrimp, and salmon in a milder vegetable broth. For a more substantial meal, check the blackboard for such house specials as Chilean sea bass in cardamom sauce. Service is friendly and efficient, wine and beer is available, and the desserts are well priced and pleasing.

Kitchenette. 80 W. Broadway (at Warren St.). ☎ **212/267-6740.** Main courses $3.75–$6.50 at breakfast; $5.75–$7.50 at lunch and brunch; $8.50–$16 at dinner. AE ($20 minimum). Mon–Fri 7:30am–10pm; Sat–Sun 9am–10pm (soups and desserts only 4–5pm). Subway: 1, 2, 3, 9 to Chambers St. AMERICAN.

This unpretentious TriBeCa luncheonette has become a prime contender on the comfort-food circuit thanks to Hungry Man–sized breakfasts and just-like-home cooking. The little room has the feel of a New England country diner, with rough-edged folk art on the walls and mismatched country-rustic chairs at the tables. Expect high-cholesterol farmhouse breakfasts and hearty salads and sandwiches during the day. Weekly lunchtime blue-plate specials include excellent shepherd's pie with mashed potato crust on Tuesday, and gooey and delicious four-cheese mac and cheese on Friday (specials are always subject to change). In addition to salads and burgers, the nighttime menu features more sophisticated entrees like chicken pot pie with a cheddar biscuit crust, grilled pork chops (with Kitchenette's secret herb rub), and roast turkey with cornbread stuffing and sweet potato mashies. Everything is well prepared and filling (skip the prepackaged sandwiches at lunch, though). Service is sit-down at breakfast and dinner, but lunch is more cafeteria style, with orders taken at the counter. No wine or beer is served, but your welcome to BYO.

Riverrun Cafe. 176 Franklin St. (btw. Greenwich Ave. and Hudson St.). ☎ **212/996-3894.** Most main courses $7.25–$14.25. AE, DC, DISC, MC, V. Daily 11:30am–midnight. Subway: 1, 9 to Franklin St. AMERICAN.

Down-to-earth as ever, this neighborhood pioneer is now a refreshing find in an increasingly haute 'hood. Before Nobu, before

---

TriBeCa Meal Deal

At attractive **Salaam Bombay,** 317 Greenwich St., between Duane and Reade streets (☎ 212/226-9400), the pan-Indian food is a cut above the standard fare, and the $10.95 all-you-can-eat lunch buffet, offered weekdays from noon to 3pm, is a steal.

Miramax, before Sean Lennon grew up and moved downtown, there was quiet, unpretentious, unassuming Riverrun, trying hard to feed the few savvy pioneers who thought it would be cool to live in a section of town known only for its egg merchants. Like a lot of vintage joints, the decor is more clutter than clean lines, but the menu is dependable: good burgers and salads, great sandwiches, plus a few satisfying entries like chicken pot pie. There's gratis chips for the bar crowd, a sensible wine list, a good selection of beers on tap, and a respectable single-malt selection. Not necessarily worth a special trip from uptown, but a relaxing stop for those tired of New York's high prices and lofty pretensions.

3 Chinatown

✪ **Joe's Shanghai.** 9 Pell St. (btw. Bowery and Mott sts.). ☎ **212/233-8888.** Reservations recommended for 10 or more. Main courses $4.25–$12.95. No credit cards. Sun–Thurs 11am–10pm; Fri–Sat 11am–10:30pm. Subway: N, R, 6 to Canal St.; B, D, Q to Grand St. SHANGHAI CHINESE.

Tucked away on a little elbow of a side street just off the Bowery, this Chinatown institution serves up authentic cuisine to enthusiastic crowds nightly. The stars of the huge menu are the signature soup dumplings, quivering steamed pockets filled with hot broth and your choice of pork or crab, accompanied by a side of seasoned soy. Listed on the menu as "steamed buns" (item numbers 1 and 2), these culinary marvels never disappoint. Neither does the rest of the authentic Shanghai-inspired menu, which boasts such main courses as whole yellowfish bathed in spicy sauce; excellent "mock duck", a saucy bean-curd dish similar to Japanese yuba that's a hit with vegetarians and carnivores alike; and lots of well-prepared staples. The room is set mostly with round tables of ten or so, and you'll be asked if you're willing to share. I encourage you to do so; it's a great way to watch and learn from your neighbors (many of whom are Chinese), who are usually more than happy to tell you what they're eating. If you want a private table, expect a wait.

Joe's Shanghai now has a second Manhattan location, in Midtown at 24 W. 56th St., just west of Fifth Avenue (☎ **212/333-3868**). The Chinatown location remains the better bargain, however; dishes are $2 to $5 more at the Midtown branch, which accepts reservations.

✪ **New York Noodletown.** 28$^1/_2$ Bowery (at Bayard St.). ☎ **212/349-0923.** Main courses $3.95–$10.95. No credit cards. Daily 9am–4am. Subway: N, R, 6 to Canal St. SEAFOOD/CHINESE.

This just may be the best Chinese food in New York City. Among its fans are Ruth Reichl, former restaurant critic for *The New York Times* and now editor-in-chief for *Gourmet* magazine, who constantly puts it at the top of the heap. But don't expect fancy—this is two-star food served in no-star ambiance. So what if the room is reminiscent of a school cafeteria? The food is fabulous. The mushroom soup is a lunch in itself, with earthy chunks of shiitakes, vegetables, and thin noodles. The kitchen excels at seafood, so be sure to try at least one: Looking like a snow-dusted plate of meaty fish, the salt-baked squid is sublime. The Chinese broccoli or the crisp sautéed baby bok choy make great accompaniments. Unlike most of its neighbors, New York Noodletown keeps very long hours, which makes it the best late-night bet in the neighborhood, too.

Nha Trang. 87 Baxter St. (btw. Canal and Bayard sts.). ☎ **212/233-5948.** Reservations recommended for large parties. Main courses $4–$12.50. No credit cards. Daily 10:30am–9:30pm. Subway: N, R, 6 to Canal St. VIETNAMESE.

The decor may be standard-issue, no-atmosphere Chinatown (glass-topped tables, linoleum floors, mirrored walls), but this friendly, bustling place serves up the best Vietnamese in Chinatown. A plate of crispy, finger-sized spring rolls is a nice way to start, as the slightly spicy pork-and-shrimp filling is nicely offset by the wrapping of lettuce, cucumber, and mint. The pho noodle soup comes in a quart-sized bowl brimming with bright vegetables and various meats and seafood. But my favorite dish is the simple barbecued pork chops—sliced paper-thin, soaked in a soy/sugar-cane marinade, and grilled to utter perfection. Everything is well prepared, though, and your waiter will be glad to help you design a meal to suit your tastes. If there's a line, stick around; it won't take long to get a table.

4 SoHo & NoLiTa

Cafe Gitane. 242 Mott St. (at Prince St.). ☎ **212/334-9552.** Reservations not accepted. Main courses $4.50–$6 at breakfast; $7.50–$9.25 at lunch and dinner. AE, MC, V. Daily 9am–midnight. Subway: B, D, F, Q to Broadway–Lafayette St.; 6 to Spring St. FRENCH CAFE.

This NoLiTa cafe feels like it came straight out of the Latin Quarter, complete with lithe French-accented waiters, black-clad bohemian hipsters, and clouds of imported cigarette smoke. It's quite an affected place, alright, but somehow the attitude is the appeal—not to mention the good, cheap eats. The short, internationally accented menu is mainly comprised of sandwiches and noodle bowls. Appealing choices include baked eggs with baguette; noodles with shrimp and white beans in curried coconut milk; and—my favorite—roasted chicken with chipotle mayo, fresh Parmesan, and anchovies on a toasted baguette. In true French style, all the breads are admirable and ultra-fresh. Meals are well worth the money but on the small side; big appetites will have plenty of room for dessert. Beverage choices include strong coffee drinks and French wines by the glass or bottle. The servers may not have found their true calling yet, but they're polite and helpful.

۞ Cafe Habana. 17 Prince St. (at Elizabeth St.). ☎ **212/625-2001.** Reservations not accepted. Main courses $4.95–$12.50. AE, DISC, MC, V. Daily 9am–midnight. Subway: B, D, F, Q to Broadway–Lafayette St.; 6 to Spring St. LATIN AMERICAN.

Lots of new low-priced restaurants have taken root over the past year, but I've enjoyed none more than this sleek update on a typical Latin American luncheonette. It manages to be hip without being the least bit pretentious, and what the food may lack in authenticity it more than makes up for in quality and flavor: shrimp are big and hearty, pork is moist and flavorful, and cilantro and other spices are fresh and aromatic. Winning starters include the hugely popular Mexican corn on the cob, which is coated with lime juice and grated cheese, sprinkled with chili powder, and grilled into a messy but sweet treat. Top-notch mains include the ultra-moist roast pork (perfect with a squeeze of lime) and *camarones al Ajillo,* shrimp in spicy garlic sauce. Most everything comes with your choice of red or black beans and rice; go with the yellow rice. Wine and a handful of Mexican beers are served, but I really enjoyed the not-too-sweet red Hibiscus tea. The room is narrow and tables are petite (especially those for two), but a middle aisle keeps the place from feeling too crowded, and service is easy-going and friendly. Don't be surprised if there's a wait for a table.

Lombardi's. 32 Spring St. (btw. Mott and Mulberry sts.). ☎ **212/941-7994.** Reservations accepted for parties of 6 or more. Small pies (6 slices) $10.50–$16; large pies (8 slices) $12.50–$20. No credit cards. Mon–Thurs 11:30am–11pm; Fri–Sat 11:30am–midnight; Sun 11:30am–10pm. Subway: 6 to Spring St.; N, R to Prince St. PIZZA.

Lombardi's is a living gem in the annals of the city's culinary history. First opened in 1905, "America's first licensed pizzeria" still cooks some of New York's best pizza in its original coal brick oven. The wonderful, crispy-thin crust (a generations-old family recipe) is topped with fresh mozzarella, basil, and tomatoes; Pecorino romano cheese; and virgin olive oil—from there, the choice is yours. Toppings are suitably old-world (pancetta, calamata olives, Italian

The East Village & SoHo Area

Accommodations
Off SoHo Suites 7

Dining

Acme Bar & Grill 10
Angelica Kitchen 21
Boca Chica 6
Bombay Dining 13
Cafe Gitane 5
Cafe Habana 6
Cucina di Pesce 11
Gandhi 14

Haveli 12
Housing Works Used
  Books Cafe 4
Katz's Delicatessen 8
Lombardi's 1
Mitali East 14
Moustache 16
Passage to India 13

Pisces 15
Sapporo East 17
Second Avenue Deli 19
Soho Kitchen & Bar 3
Spring Street Natural
  Restaurant 2
Veselka 18
Village Yokocho 20

sausage, and the like), but Lombardi's specialty is the fresh clam pie, with hand-shucked clams, oregano, garlic, romano, and pepper (no sauce). The main dining room is narrow but pleasant, with the usual checkered tablecloths and exposed brick walls. A big draw is the garden out back, where tables sport Cinzano umbrellas and a flowering tree shoots up through the concrete. Another plus: In a city where rudeness is a badge of honor, Lombardi's waitstaff is extremely affable.

SoHo Kitchen & Bar. 103 Greene St. (btw. Spring and Prince sts.). ☎ **212/ 925-1866.** Reservations are accepted for parties of 6 or more. Main courses $7.75–$18.50. AE, MC, V. Mon–Thurs 11:30am–midnight; Fri–Sat 11:30am–2am; Sun 12:30–11pm. Subway: N, R to Prince St.; C, E to Spring St. AMERICAN.

Even though the food is nothing special, the fun, easy-going atmosphere makes SoHo Kitchen a regular stop for me. This large, lofty space attracts an animated after-work and late-night crowd to its central bar, which dispenses more than 21 beers on tap, a whole slew of microbrews by the bottle, and more than 100 wines by the glass, either individually or in "flights" for comparative tastings. The menu offers predictable but affordable bar fare: buffalo wings, oversize salads, good burgers, and a variety of sandwiches and thin-crust pizzas. You won't spend more than 12 bucks or so on your main meal unless you graduate to entrees like the New York sirloin, which makes this a great bet for wallet-watchers.

If you're in lower Manhattan and you're looking for similar fare, head to the **Wall Street Kitchen & Bar,** housed in a spectacular former bank building in the heart of the Financial District at 70 Broad St. (☎ **212/797-7070**).

Spring Street Natural Restaurant. 62 Spring St. (at Lafayette St.) ☎ **212/ 966-0290.** Main courses $7–$16. AE, DC, MC, V. Sun–Thurs 11:30am– midnight; Fri–Sat 11:30am–1am. Subway: 6 to Spring St. HEALTH-CONSCIOUS.

This 25-year-old spot is as comfortable and easy-going as your old college hangout—and just about as affordable, too. The large brick-walled room is filled with leafy greenery and anchored by an old oak bar. This is the kind of place that you can set yourself down at a table and camp awhile, poring over a good book while you nosh on a farm-fresh entree-sized salad or a terrific tempeh burger; the staff will happily refill your coffee mug as you relax. But while the cuisine is all-natural, it's not strictly vegetarian: there's fresh-off-the-boat seafood and free-range chicken and turkey as well as creative and organic vegetarian dishes. And unlike many other health-minded restaurants, the menu isn't restricted to soups, sand-wiches, and salads; you can come for a full meal, dining on such entrees as broiled New England bluefish with shiitake mushrooms, roasted chicken with pommery mustard glaze, or any number of pastas and stir-frys. Everything is well prepared and satisfying. The kitchen can also satisfy sugar, dairy, and other dietary restrictions. Brunch is served on weekends until 4pm, and there's pleasant out-door seating in the good weather.

QUICK BITES

If you need a coffee break, skip Starbuck's and head instead to **Housing Works Used Books Cafe,** 126 Crosby St. (one block east of Broadway), just south of Houston Street (☎ 212/334-3324). This attractive and airy used-book shop (whose proceeds support AIDS charities) has an appealing cafe in back that serves up coffee and tea, sandwiches, sweets, and other light bites. There are plenty of tables to pull up a chair at, and you're welcome to pull anything off the shelves to peruse as you snack.

5 The East Village

Another great choice for wallet-friendly Middle Eastern fare is **Moustache** (p. 97), at 265 E. 10th St., between First Avenue and Avenue A (☎ 212/228-2022). There's also an East Village branch of **Sapporo** (p. 107) at 245 E. 10th St., at First Avenue (☎ 212/260-1330), for cheap Japanese eats.

Acme Bar & Grill. 9 Great Jones St. (at Lafayette St.). ☎ **212/420-1934.** Reservations not taken. Main courses $5.95–$13.50 at lunch; $9.95 at weekend brunch (including one cocktail, juice, and coffee or tea); $6.95–$15.95 at dinner. DC, DISC, MC, V. Sun–Thurs 11:30am–midnight; Fri–Sat 11:30am–12:30am. Subway: 6 to Bleecker St.; B, D, F, Q to Broadway–Lafayette St. SOUTHERN/BARBECUE.

Acme's motto is "An okay place to eat"—a witty bit of clear-eyed candor in this best-obsessed town. This easygoing NoHo joint is divey in a pleasing way, with a good-natured staff, a Louisiana road-house theme, and the comfortable vibe of a well-worn neighborhood favorite. Acme serves up heaping platters of Southern home cook-ing and barbecue: po-boys, jambalaya, seafood gumbo, thick-cut pork chops, chicken-fried steak, baby-back ribs—not gourmet grub, but good, cheap, filling eats. The restaurant is a hot-sauce lover's delight, with dozens of bottles lining the walls so you can douse your dish with the perfect measure of heat. Yummy fresh-baked cornbread starts the meal, and a range of beers are available.

✪ **Angelica Kitchen.** 300 E. 12th St. (just east of Second Ave.). ☎ **212/228-2909.** Reservations accepted for six or more Mon–Thurs. Main courses $5.95–$14.25; lunch deal (Mon–Fri 11:30am–5pm) $6.75. No credit cards. Daily 11:30am–10:30pm. Subway: L, N, R, 4, 5, 6, to 14th St./Union Sq. ORGANIC VEGETARIAN.

If you like to eat healthy, take note: This cheerful restaurant is serious about vegan cuisine. The kitchen prepares everything fresh daily; they guarantee that at least 95% of all ingredients are organically grown, with sustainable agriculture and responsible business practices additionally required. But good-for-you (and good-for-the-environment) doesn't have to mean boring—this is flavorful, beautifully prepared cuisine served in a lovely country kitchen–style setting. Salads spill over with sprouts and crisp veggies and are crowned with homemade dressings. The Dragon Bowls are heaping portions of rice, beans, tofu, and steamed vegetables. The daily specials feature the best of what's fresh and in season, and may include fiery three-bean chili; baked tempeh nestled in a sourdough baguette and dressed in mushroom gravy; and lemon-herb baked tofu layered with roasted vegetables and fresh pesto on mixed-grain bread. Breads and desserts are fresh baked and similarly wholesome (and made without eggs, of course).

Boca Chica. 13 First Ave. (at 1st St.). ☎ **212/473-0108.** Reservations accepted for parties of 6 or more Mon–Thurs only. Main dishes $7.50–$19.75 (most less than $13). AE, MC, V. Sun–Thurs 6–11pm; Fri–Sat 6pm–midnight. Subway: F to Second Ave. SOUTH AMERICAN.

This lively, colorful joint is always packed with a gleefully mixed crowd working its way through a round of margaritas or a few pitchers of beer. The cuisine is a downmarket version of the pan-Latino favorites that have captivated palates farther Uptown. The food at Boca Chica is a little closer to its hearty South American roots: well-prepared pork, beef, fish, and vegetarian dishes, pleasingly heavy on the sauce and spice, and accompanied by plantains, rice, and beans. There's also a bevy of interesting appetizers, including black bean soup, well seasoned with lime juice, and terrific coconut-fried shrimp. While this approach to cooking now tends to be well out of reach of the under-$25 crowd, Boca Chica keeps things at an affordable level. *Be forewarned:* The place is packed on weekends.

Cucina di Pesce. 87 E. 4th St. (at Second Ave.). ☎ **212/260-6800.** Main dishes $6.95–$10.95 (specials may be slightly higher); 3-course early-bird dinner (offered daily 3:30–6:30pm) $9.95. No credit cards. Daily 4pm–midnight. Subway: F to Second Ave. ITALIAN.

Dining Zone: Little India

The stretch of East Sixth Street between First and Second avenues in the East Village is known as "Little India" thanks to the dozen or more Indian restaurants that line the block (subway: F to Second Avenue). Dining here isn't exactly high style, but Little India's restaurants do offer decent Indian food at discount prices, sometimes accompanied by live sitar music. It's loads of fun to grab a bottle of wine or a six pack from one of the corner stores on Second Avenue (many of Little India's restaurants don't serve alcohol, but even those who do will often let you bring in your own) and cruise the strip, deciding which one most appeals to you. In the warm weather, each usually stations a hawker out front to help convince you that theirs is *so* much better than the competition.

Some people speculate that there's one big kitchen in the alley behind East 6th, but a few of Little India's restaurants deserve special attention. **Bombay Dining,** at 320 E. 6th St. (☎ 212/260-8229), is a standout, serving excellent *samosa* (crisp vegetable-and-meat patties), *pakora* (banana fritters), and *papadum* (crispy bean wafers with coarse peppercorns). Also satisfying are **Gandhi,** 344 E. 6th St. (☎ 212/614-9718), for a touch of low-light romance; **Mitali East,** 336 E. 6th St. (☎ 212/533-2508), the king of curry; and **Passage to India,** 308 E. 6th St. (☎ 212/529-5770), for North Indian tandoori.

Around the corner—and a giant step up in quality—from Little India is ♥ **Haveli,** 100 Second Ave. (☎ 212/982-0533), where the authentically prepared dishes, setting, and service are far superior to what you'll find on East 6th Street. Prices are a little steeper—solidly in the $10 to $16 range—but the Haveli experience is worth the extra dough if you can afford the tab.

This crowded East Village Italian is legendary for its good value—and it's surprisingly charming, too, if a little on the loud side. The focus is on Old World basics like hearty beef lasagna, marinara-topped pasta, shrimp scampi, and veal marsala. Every once in a while somebody in the kitchen goes too far with a shellfish-and-mollusk combo, but by and large the offerings really satisfy. The wide selection of basic pastas (fettuccine primavera, linguine with clam sauce—you get the picture) are always fresh and properly sauced, the veal nicely tender, and the fried calamari well seasoned and perfectly

The New York Deli News

There's simply nothing more Noo Yawk than hunkering down over a mammoth pastrami sandwich or a lox-and-bagel plate at an authentic Jewish deli, where anything you order comes with a bowl of lip-smacking sour dills and a side of attitude.

Opened in 1937, the **Stage Deli,** 834 Seventh Ave., between 53rd and 54th streets (☎ 212/245-7850), may be New York's oldest continuously run deli. The Stage is noisy and crowded and packed with tourists, but it's still as authentic as they come. Connoisseurs line up to sample the 36 famous specialty sandwiches named after many of the stars whose photos adorn the walls: The Tom Hanks is roast beef, chopped liver, onion, and chicken fat, while the Dolly Parton is—drumroll, please—twin rolls of corned beef and pastrami.

For the quintessential New York experience, head to the **Carnegie Deli,** 854 Seventh Ave., at 55th Street (☎ 212/757-2245), where it's worth subjecting yourself to surly service, tourist-targeted pricing, and elbow-to-elbow seating for the best pastrami and corned beef in town. Even big eaters may be challenged by mammoth sandwiches with names like "fifty ways to love your liver" (chopped liver, hard-boiled egg, lettuce, tomato, onion). Cheesecake can't get more divine, so save room!

crisp. The great meal/low price combo means that the place can be a mob scene, but free mussels marinara at the bar makes the sometimes-long wait easier to take. The only disappointment is the wine list, which leaves a lot to be desired; your best bet is to stick with the house red, or opt for beer instead.

✪ **Pisces.** 95 Ave. A (at 6th St.). ☎ **212/260-6660.** Reservations recommended. Main courses $8.95–$19.95; 2-course prix-fixe dinner (Mon–Thurs 5:30–7pm; Fri–Sun 5:30–6:30pm) $14.95. AE, CB, DC, MC, V. Mon–Thurs 5:30–11:30pm; Fri 5:30pm–1am; Sat 11:30am–3:30pm and 5:30pm–1am; Sun 11:30am–3:30pm and 5:30–11:30pm. Subway: 6 to Astor Place. SEAFOOD.

This excellent fish house serves up the best moderately priced seafood in the city. All fish is top-quality and fresh daily, and all smoked items are prepared in the restaurant's own smoker. But it's the creative kitchen, which shows surprising skill with vegetables as well as fish, that makes Pisces a real winner. The mesquite-smoked whole trout in sherry oyster sauce is sublime, better than trout I've

The ✪ **Second Avenue Deli,** 156 Second Ave., at 10th Street (☎ 212/677-0606), is the best kosher choice in town (for all you goyem out there, that means no milk, butter, or cheese is served). There's no bowing to tourism here—this is old-school. The service is brusque, the decor is nondescript, and the sandwiches don't have cute names, but the dishes served here are true New York classics: gefilte fish, matzoh ball soup, chicken livers, potato knishes, nova lox and eggs. And for $11 to $13—several bucks cheaper than Midtown's Carnegie—you get a monster triple-decker sandwich (try wrapping your gums around the corned beef, tongue, and salami) with a side of fries. The crunchy dills are to die for. Keep an ear tuned to the Catskills-quality banter among the crusty waitstaff. It don't get more Noo Yawk than this.

✪ **Katz's Delicatessen,** 205 E. Houston St., at Ludlow Street on the Lower East Side (☎ 212/254-2246), is another first-rate deli choice, beloved for their all-beef hot dogs. Their mammoth deli sandwiches are even less expensive than the Second Avenue Deli—in the $6–$10 range—and the proprietors dare you to even try to finish one. Lest you think that lower prices mean poorer quality, forget it: Katz's has been slicing pastrami on the Lower East Side since 1888, and they're the only ones who still do it by hand.

had for twice the price. There are daily specials in addition to the menu; last time we dined here, I feasted on an excellent grilled mako shark with chard in cockle stew. The wine list is appealing and very well priced, the decor suitably nautical without being kitschy, and the service friendly and attentive. For wallet-watchers, the early-bird prix-fixe can't be beat. The Alphabet City locale attracts a cool crowd, but it's laid-back enough that even grandma will be comfortable here. Tables spill out onto the sidewalk on warm evenings, giving you a ringside seat for the funky East Village show.

Veselka. 144 Second Ave. (at 9th St.). ☎ **212/228-9682.** Sandwiches $1.95–$6.50; main courses $5–$12. AE, MC, V. Daily 24 hours. Subway: 6 to Astor Place. UKRAINIAN DINER.

Whenever the craving hits for substantial Eastern European fare at old-world prices, Veselka fits the bill with *pierogi* (small doughy envelopes filled with potatoes, cheese, or sauerkraut), *kasha varnishkes* (cracked buckwheat and noodles with mushroom sauce), stuffed cabbage, grilled polish kielbasa, fresh-made potato pancakes, and classic soups like borscht, voted best in the city by the *New York Times* and *New York* magazine. Try the buckwheat pancakes for a perfect breakfast or brunch. The diner is comfortable and appealing, with an artsy slant. Thanks to Veselka's we-never-close policy, it's a favorite after-hours hangout for club kids and other night owls.

✪ **Village Yokocho.** 8 Stuyvesant St. (at Third Ave. and E. 9th St.), 2nd floor. ☎ **212/598-3041.** Reservations not taken. Main courses $3.75–$11.50. AE, MC, V. Sun–Wed 5pm–3am; Thurs–Sat 5pm–4am. JAPANESE/KOREAN BBQ.

Village Yokocho is about as authentic as Japanese restaurants get. Entering this casual second-floor spot feels just like stepping into a Tokyo yakitori bar, complete with a hip, young clientele that's a mix of Japanese and in-the-know Westerners. Between the regular menu and the many handwritten sheets taped to the wall advertising the current specials, the choices are vast. Dishes run the gamut from familiar dumplings and yakisoba noodles to exoticalike deep-fried squid eggs. The generous broiled eel bowl is finer quality than eel you'll get at many sushi restaurants, and a deal at $8. The barbecued yakitori skewers, both meat and veggie choices grilled over an open flame just behind the counter, are excellent. Korean dishes include flavorful oxtail soup and bibinbop, a hearty rice bowl topped with veggies, ground beef, and a fried egg. The specials change depending on what's in season and available, but you might find soft-shell crab in ponzu sauce, broiled yellowtail with teriyaki sauce, and any number of sashimi appetizers. There's a big, affordable sake menu as well as a choice of beers. At press time, late-nighters benefited from 50% off Korean barbecue Sunday through Wednesday between midnight and 3am; call to see if this or any other after-hours specials are on while you're in town (they're also posted on the street-level front door).

6 Greenwich Village

Aggie's. 146 W. Houston St. (at MacDougal St.). ☎ **212/673-8994.** Main courses $7–$12.95. MC V. Mon–Wed 8am–10pm; Thurs–Fri 8am–11pm; Sat 10am–11pm; Sun 10am–4pm. Subway: A, B, C, D, E, F, Q to W. 4th St. ECLECTIC.

This funky diner on the southern outskirts of the Village dishes up sandwiches, pastas, and simple American comfort food with a healthful gourmet bent—crab cakes, meat loaf, grilled portabellos, and duck stroganoff with black pepper sauce are favorites. Some complain that portions are not as generous as they were before Aggie's became hip, but they're still plenty big. The hearty breakfasts are especially pleasing; go early or expect a line on weekends.

Greenwich Village

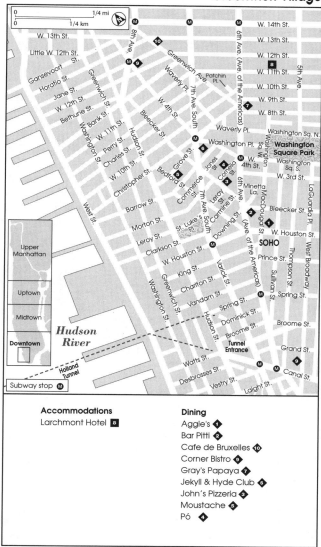

Accommodations

Larchmont Hotel 8

Dining

Aggie's 1

Bar Pitti 2

Cafe de Bruxelles 10

Corner Bistro 9

Gray's Papaya 7

Jekyll & Hyde Club 6

John's Pizzeria 3

Moustache 5

Pó 4

⭕ **Bar Pitti.** 268 Sixth Ave. (btw. Bleecker and Houston sts.). ☎ **212/ 982-3300.** Reservations accepted only for 4 or more. Main courses $5.50– $12.50 (some specials may be higher). No credit cards. Daily noon–midnight. Subway: A, B, C, D, E, F, Q to W. 4th St. (use 3rd St. exit). TUSCAN ITALIAN.

This indoor/outdoor Tuscan-style trattoria is a perennially hip side- walk scene, and one of downtown's best dining bargains. Waiting for a table can be a chore (the wait list never seems very organized), but all is soon forgiven thanks to authentic, affordably priced cui- sine and some of the friendliest waiters in town. Despite the tightly packed seating, Bar Pitti wins you over with its rustic Italian charm. Peruse the menu, but don't get your heart set on anything until you see the well-worn board, which boasts the best of what the kitchen has to offer; last time we dined here, they wowed us with a fabulous veal meatball special. Winners off the regular menu, which focuses heavily on pastas and panini, include excellent rare beef carpaccio; grilled country bread with prosciutto, garlic, and olive oil; and spin- ach and ricotta ravioli in a creamy sage and Parmesan sauce. The all- Italian wine list is high-priced compared to the menu, but you'll find a few good value choices.

Cafe de Bruxelles. 118 Greenwich Ave. (at Horatio St.). ☎ **212/206-1830.** Reservations recommended. Main courses $10.95–$19.50. AE, DC, MC, V. Tues–Thurs noon–11:30pm; Friday and Sat noon–midnight; Sun and Mon noon–10:30pm. Subway: A, C, E, 1, 2, 3, 9 to 14th St. BELGIAN.

This wonderfully low-key, lace-curtained restaurant is the city's top stop for Belgian-style mussels, frites, and beers. Yummy starters in- clude wild mushrooms in puff pastry, thick-cut country pate, and escargot in rich Roquefort sauce. You might want to follow with the *carbonade flamande,* beef stew made with dark Belgian beer; boudin blanc with apples and onions; or one of eight varieties of mussels, the best of which is the simple mariniere—nothing more than a large bowl of the mollusks cooked in onion, garlic, and white wine. No matter what you choose, your order is accompanied by a metal cone of excellent crispy fries with the traditional accompaniment, mayonnaise. There's an excellent selection of Trappist ales and lambics, too, making this a great choice for dark beer lovers.

Corner Bistro. 331 W. 4th St. (at Jane St., near Eighth Ave.). ☎ **212/ 242-9502.** Reservations not taken. Burgers and sandwiches $2.50–$5. No credit cards. Daily 11am–3:30am. Subway: A, C, E to 14th St. (go 2 blocks south on Eighth Ave.). BURGERS.

This unpretentious, old-time neighborhood bar serves up what some people (including Jon Stewart) consider the best burger in the city. I don't know if I can stand by that claim (I really *love* the burgers at the Old Town), but the Corner Bistro's well-charred, beefy burgers are deservedly famous—and you'd be hard-pressed to dine so well for so little anywhere else in the city. The top of the line is the bistro burger, with bacon, cheese, lettuce, and tomato, for all of five bucks. The thin, crispy fries, served up on a crimped paper plate, are an appropriate accompaniment. Head elsewhere if you want anything else, because the other offerings are limited to a grilled chicken sandwich, grilled cheese, a BLT, and some chunky chili—all half-hearted at best, except for the chili. Beers on tap include Sam Adams, local McSorley's, and good ol' Bud. Service can be slow, but who's ever in a rush at a neighborhood local like this?

Moustache. 90 Bedford St. (btw. Barrow and Grove sts.). ☎ **212/229-2220.** Reservations not taken. Main dishes $5–$12. No credit cards. Daily noon–11:30pm. Subway: 1, 9 to Christopher St. MIDDLE EASTERN.

Moustache is the sort of exotic neighborhood spot that's just right. On a quiet side street in the West Village, this charming hole-in-the-wall boasts a cozy Middle Eastern vibe and authentic fare that's both palate-pleasing and wallet-friendly. Delicately seasoned dishes bear little resemblance to the food at your average falafel joint. Expect subtly flavored hummus, tabbouleh, and spinach-chickpea-tomato salad; excellent oven-roasted "pitzas", thin, matzoh-like pita crusts topped with spicy minced lamb and other savory ingredients; and—best of all—fluffy, hot-from-the-oven homemade pita bread, which puts any of those store-bought Frisbees to shame. Moustache is hugely and justifiably popular, so don't be surprised if there's a line—but it's well worth the wait. Also in the East Village at 265 E. 10th St., between First Avenue and Avenue A (☎ **212/228-2022**).

✪ **Pó.** 31 Cornelia St. (btw. Bleecker and W. 4th sts.). ☎ **212/645-2189.** Reservations recommended well in advance. Main courses $8–$10 at lunch, $12–$15 at dinner; tasting menu $35. Tues–Sat 11am–2pm and 5–11pm; Sun 11am–2pm and 5–10pm. AE. Subway: A, B, C, D, E, F, Q to W. 4th St. (use W. 3rd St. exit). ITALIAN.

He may not be Emeril (yet), but chef Mario Batali has become quite the entrepreneur. His zesty Italian food has attracted a lot of attention since he began appearing on TV's Food Network. Well, kudos to Mario for keeping Pó real despite his burgeoning fame; it's well priced and justifiably popular. Batali's pastas are unparalleled; even a simple white-bean ravioli in balsamic vinegar and browned butter takes on new, remarkable life in his kitchen. Other winning entrees include cavatelli with sage and three mushrooms (including stellar porcinis), and beautifully tender veal picatta with baby

---

Pizza! Pizza!

In the mood for a slice or two . . . or three? The village is the perfect place to be. The original location of **John's Pizzeria** (p. 105), 278 Bleecker St. between Sixth and Seventh avenues (☎ **212/243-1680**), is a New York original and still one of the city's best. The pies are thin-crusted, properly sauced, and served up piping hot in an authentic old-world setting. Sorry, no slices.

---

artichokes. The wine list is surprisingly affordable, and the service appealingly old world despite the hip address. The only downsides are that the pretty, narrow room is too tightly packed and smoking is allowed at the bar (a little too close to some dining tables in my view). Call well ahead—a month if you can—because Pó is perpetually booked.

QUICK BITES

Ask any New Yorker—one of the cheapest, most satisfying meals to be had in the city is the $1.95 two-dogs-and-drink deal from **Gray's Papaya,** 402 Sixth Ave., at 8th Street (☎ **212/260-3532**). This legendary storefront hot dog stand hawks nothing but all-beef dogs (50¢ each), crispy thin fries, and your choice of tropical-flavored fruit drinks ranging from piña colada to Orange Julius–style OJ. Best of all, you can indulge in a Gray's frank and juice at any hour, since they never close.

---

7   The Flatiron District, Union Square & Gramercy Park

Chat 'n' Chew. 10 E. 16th St. (btw. Fifth Ave. and Union Sq. W.). ☎ **212/243-1616.** Reservations not taken. Sandwiches $5.75–$10.50; main courses $6.95–$12.50. AE, MC, V. Mon–Thurs 11:30am–11pm; Fri 11:30am–11:30pm; Sat 10am–11:30pm; Sun 10am–10pm. Subway: L, N, R, 4, 5, 6 to Union Sq. AMERICAN.

This cute little hole-in-the-wall excels at down-home American cooking. In fact, the space is so down-homey that it's on the brink of becoming a theme restaurant, but the chow's the real thing. Look for honey-dipped fried chicken, roast turkey with all the fixin's, BBQ pork chops with skin-on mashed potatoes, and mac 'n' cheese that's as crispy on the outside and gooey on the inside as it should be. There are a few unnecessary nods to contemporary tastes— if you're looking for grilled tuna, you don't belong here!—but the only real misstep I can see is the meatloaf, which was a bready disappointment. Weekend brunch sees such standards as hot oatmeal with brown sugar and hearty three-egg omelettes with honey-baked ham on the side. Portions are all hungry man–sized, service is snappy, and beer's available to wash it all down. Desserts are of the Duncan Hines layer-cake variety, and the soda fountain serves up everything from egg creams to Häagen-Dazs shakes. The crowd is mainly comprised of the very young and hip (the kind that can afford to throw caution to the wind when it comes to calories), but everyone will fill perfectly welcome.

Coffee Shop. 29 Union Sq. W. (at 16th St.). ☎ **212/243-7969.** Reservations accepted for 6 or more. Main courses $7.95–$16.95. AE, DC, MC, V. Wed–Fri 6:30am–5:30am; Sat 8am–5:30am; Sun 8am–2am; Mon 6:30am–2am; Tues 6:30am–4am. Subway: L, N, R, 4, 5, 6 to 14th St.–Union Sq. AMERICAN/ BRAZILIAN.

There are worse ways to spend a sunny afternoon than sitting at a sidewalk table at the Coffee Shop, watching the world go by while chowing down on Brazilian feijoada (pork and bean stew), a Sonia Braga sandwich (chicken salad in a flour tortilla with papaya and cashews), or a good old burger (beef, turkey, or veggie—your choice) with a side of excellently crisped fries. The barbecued chicken sandwich with nonfat cilantro-lime mayonnaise will keep you trim and satisfied. The just-fine food isn't anything special, but it's not hard to see why this spirited perch, situated just across the street from super-popular Union Square Park, is a magnet for models and club kids. Of course, its own celebrity can make it hard to get a seat here on a balmy summer day. But the inside space is pleasant as well, with funky 1950s lamps and sleek chrome touches. The service can be a roll of the dice, so come with a nonchalant attitude and just enjoy the affordable food and the pretty scene. Also inside is the **World Room,** which serves up exotic cocktails and becomes quite a party scene in the wee hours.

✪ **Old Town Bar & Restaurant.** 45 E. 18th St. (btw. Broadway and Park Ave. South). ☎ **212/529-6732.** Main courses $6–$15. AE, MC, V. Mon–Sun 10am–midnight. Subway: 4, 5, 6, L, N, R to 14th St./Union Sq. MOSTLY BURGERS.

If you've watched TV at all over the last couple of decades, this place should look familiar: It was featured nightly in the old *Late Night with David Letterman* intro, starred as Riff's Bar in *Mad About You*, and appeared in too many commercials to count. But this is no stage set—it's a genuine tin-ceilinged 19th-century bar serving up good pub grub, lots of beers on tap, and a real sense of New York history. Sure, there are healthy salads on the menu, but everybody comes for

Midtown Dining

Amy's Bread 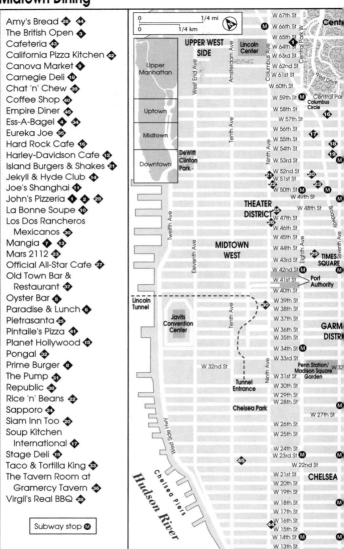 20 44
The British Open 3
Cafeteria 43
California Pizza Kitchen 42
Canova Market 9
Carnegie Deli 18
Chat 'n' Chew 39
Coffee Shop 40
Empire Diner 46
Ess-A-Bagel 4 24
Eureka Joe 35
Hard Rock Cafe 16
Harley-Davidson Cafe 12
Island Burgers & Shakes 21
Jekyll & Hyde Club 14
Joe's Shanghai 11
John's Pizzeria 1 2 29
La Bonne Soupe 10
Los Dos Rancheros
  Mexicanos 36
Mangia 7 13
Mars 2112 27
Official All-Star Cafe 42
Old Town Bar &
  Restaurant 37
Oyster Bar 5
Paradise & Lunch 6
Pietrasanta 25
Pintaile's Pizza 41
Planet Hollywood 15
Pongal 32
Prime Burger 8
The Pump 31
Republic 38
Rice 'n' Beans 22
Sapporo 26
Siam Inn Too 20
Soup Kitchen
  International 17
Stage Deli 19
Taco & Tortilla King 33
The Tavern Room at
  Gramercy Tavern 34
Virgil's Real BBQ 28

Subway stop M

100

the burgers. Whether you go low-fat turkey or bacon-chili-cheddar, they're perfect every time. Other good choices include spicy Buffalo wings with blue cheese, fiery bowls of chili sprinkled with cheddar cheese and dolopped with sour cream, and a Herculean Caesar salad slathered with mayo and topped with anchovies. Food comes up from the basement kitchen courtesy of ancient dumbwaiters behind the bar, where equally crusty bartenders would rather *not* make you a Cosmopolitan, thank you very much. If you want to escape the cigarettes and the predatory singles scene that pulls in on weekends, head upstairs to the blissfully smoke-free dining room.

Republic. 37 Union Sq. W. (btw. 16th and 17th sts.). ☎ **212/627-7172.** Reservations not accepted. Main courses $6–$9. AE, DC, MC, V. Sun–Wed noon–11pm; Thurs–Sat noon–midnight. Subway: L, N, R, 4, 5, 6 to 14th St./ Union Sq. PAN-ASIAN NOODLES.

Proving once and for all that you don't have to sacrifice high style for wallet-friendly prices, this ultra-chic, minimalist noodle joint serves up affordable fast food in an area where it's getting harder and harder to find a deal. Customers slurp up the Chinese-, Vietnamese-, and Thai-inspired noodle dishes while sitting on cushionless, backless benches pulled up to pine-and-steel refectory tables that don't encourage lingering: This is the kind of place that knows how to make you feel hip and happy while getting you out the door efficiently. For a one-bowl meal, try the spicy coconut chicken (chicken slices in coconut milk, lime juice, lemongrass, and galangal) or spicy beef (rare beef and wheat noodles spiced with chilies, garlic, and lemongrass). The long curving bar is perfect for solitary diners.

Pizza! Pizza!

Pintaile's Pizza, 124 Fourth Ave., between 12th and 13th sts. (☎ 212/475-4977), dresses its daintily crisp organic crusts with layers of plum tomatoes, extra virgin olive oil, and other fabulously fresh ingredients. This new Union Square–area sibling of the Upper East Side favorite even has lots of seating for in-house eating.

Also in the Union Square neighborhood is **California Pizza Oven,** at 122 University Place, between 13th and 14th streets (☎ 212/ 989-4225), which cooks their thin-crust brick-oven pizzas over hickory and cherry wood, imbuing them with a rich, smoky flavor. A line of tables near the hearth make a cozy spot to enjoy a quick slice.

QUICK BITES

A great choice for a yummy pastry (I just love the tea cake) or a well-made salad or sandwich is **Eureka Joe,** 168 Fifth Ave., at 22nd Street (☎ **212/741-7500**). One of my favorite coffeehouses in the city, Eureka Joe boasts comfy sofa nooks and a loungey, stay-as-long-as you want vibe, plus a wine and beer bar and live music or readings in the evenings.

WORTH A SPLURGE

The Tavern Room at Gramercy Tavern. 42 E. 20th St. (btw. Broadway and Park Ave. South). ☎ **212/477-0777.** Reservations not taken. Starters $6–$9.50; main courses $12.50–$18. AE, DC, MC, V. Mon–Thurs and Sun noon–11pm; Fri–Sat noon–midnight. Subway: 6, N, R to 23rd St. CONTEMPORARY AMERICAN.

Unquestionably, Gramercy Tavern's main dining room is one of the finest in town. However, dining there requires reservations weeks in advance, and deep, deep pockets. Not so in the front Tavern Room, a friendly, informal bistro-style alternative where you can decide to eat at the last minute and still dine on some of the best food in town—without breaking the bank in the process. The compact but immensely appealing menu offers a lighter, more casual take on chef Tom Colicchio's excellent, creative American fare. I love the perfectly roasted baby chicken with butternut squash succotash—nobody in town does chicken better. And where else are you going to get a filet mignon this good for less than $20? There's a good selection of salads and a handful of fish dishes and sandwiches for lighter eaters, plus the restaurant's signature selection of cheeses and desserts. The room is very comfortable, with well-spaced tables and a pleasant energy that still allows for conversation; and owner Danny Meyer has a blanket no-smoking policy. Service is top-notch, too. All in all, one of the best dining values in town.

8 Chelsea

Cafeteria. 119 Seventh Ave. (at 17th St.). ☎ **212/414-1717.** Reservations recommended. Sandwiches $7.50–$12.95; main courses $10.95–$18.95. AE, DISC, MC, V. Open 24 hours. Subway: 1, 9 to 18th St. AMERICAN.

The greasy spoon goes glam at this round-the-clock Chelsea hotspot. More über-diner than automat, Cafeteria is all about high style, from the white-leather banquettes to the waifish waitstaff. Luckily, there's follow-through: Both the food and the service are better than they have to be in this veneer-happy town. The menu features modern takes on blue-plate classics—meatloaf, chicken pot pie, fried chicken and waffles, and killer mac and cheese made with both cheddar and fontina (yum!)—as well as surprisingly successful neo-American fare, including a well-seared, thick cut tuna loin. On the downside, seating is tight. A great choice for those who want a dose of downtown cool; just put on your best basic black and you'll fit right in. Cafeteria is at its best after 10pm or so, but be sure to call ahead or you may be turned away at the door.

Empire Diner. 210 Tenth Ave. (at 22nd St.). ☎ **212/243-2736.** Reservations not accepted. Main courses $9.95–$16.95. AE, CB, DC, DISC, MC, V. Daily 24 hours. Subway: C, E to 23rd St. AMERICAN DINER.

Used to be that the Empire was the only thing doing this far west in Chelsea, but the emergence of an alternative-to-SoHo gallery scene in the west 20s has raised the neighborhood's profile a notch. Not that it matters in this throwback shrine to the slicked-up all-American diner. This classic joint, which looks suspiciously like an Airstream camper plunked down on the corner, boasts a timeless Art Deco vibe, honest coffee, and supreme mashed potatoes, Manhattan's best. The food is all basic and good: eggs, omelets, burgers, overstuffed sandwiches, and a very nice turkey platter. There's live piano music courtesy every day at lunch and dinner, and at weekend brunch. If you want quiet, go early. If you want an eyeful, wait for the after-hours crowd; the hours between 1 and 3am offer the best people-watching, when Prada and Gucci meld with Phat Farm and Levi's. When the weather's warm, a sidewalk cafe appears, and the limited traffic this far over—mostly aiming for the Lincoln Tunnel—keeps the soot-and-fumes factor down.

9 Times Square & Midtown West

✪ **Island Burgers & Shakes.** 766 Ninth Ave. (btw. 51st and 52nd sts.). ☎ 212/307-7934. Main courses $5.50–$8.75. No credit cards. Sat–Thurs noon–10:30pm; Fri noon–11:15pm. Subway: C, E to 50th St. GOURMET BURGERS/SANDWICHES.

This excellent aisle-sized diner glows with the wild colors of a California surf shop. A small selection of sandwiches and salads are on hand, but as the name implies, folks come here for the Goliath-sized burgers—either beef hamburgers or, the specialty of the house, churascos (flattened grilled chicken breasts). Innovation strikes with the more than 40 topping combinations: choose anything from the horseradish, sour cream, and black pepper burger to the Hobie's (with black-pepper sauce, bleu cheese, onion, and bacon). Pick your bread from a wide selection, ranging from soft sourdough to crusty ciabatta. Though Island Burgers serves fries now, you're meant to eat these fellows with their tasty dirty potato chips. Terrifically thick shakes and cookies are also available for those with a sweet tooth.

✪ **John's Pizzeria.** 260 W. 44th St. (btw. Broadway and Eighth Ave.). ☎ **212/391-7560.** Reservations accepted for ten or more. Pizzas $9–$12.50 (plus toppings); pastas $6–$8. AE, MC, V. Mon–Thurs 11:30am–11:30pm; Fri–Sat 11:30–1am; Sun noon–12:30am. Subway: A, C, E to 42nd St.–Port Authority; 1, 2, 3, 9, N, R, S, 7 to 42nd St.–Times Sq.. PIZZA.

Thin-crusted, properly sauced, and fresh, the pizza at John's has long been one of New York's best—some even consider it the best pie New York has to offer. Housed in the century-old Gospel Tabernacle Church, the split-level dining room is vast and pretty, with a gorgeous stained-glass ceiling and chefs working at classic brick ovens right in the room. More importantly, it's big enough to hold pre-theater crowds, so there's never too long of a wait despite the place's popularity. Unlike most pizzerias, whole pies are made to order, so come with friends or family. There's also a good selection of traditional pastas to choose from, such as baked ziti, and well-stuffed calzones. This Theater District location is my favorite, but the original Bleecker Street location, at 278 Bleecker St., between Sixth and Seventh avenues (☎ **212/243-1680**), is loaded with old-world atmosphere. The locations near Lincoln Center, 48 W. 65th St. (☎ **212/721-7001**), and on the Upper East Side, 408 E. 64th St. (☎ **212/935-2895**), are also worth checking out.

La Bonne Soupe. 48 W. 55th St. (btw. Fifth and Sixth aves.). ☎ **212/586-7650.** Reservations recommended. Main courses $8.95–$18.25; "les bonnes soupes" prix fixe $12.95; lunch and dinner prix-fixe $19.95. AE, DC, MC, V. Mon–Sat 11:30am–midnight; Sun 11:30am–11pm. Subway: E, F to Fifth Ave.; B, Q to 57th St. FRENCH BISTRO.

This little slice of Paris has been around forever; I remember discovering the magic of fondue here on a high school French Club field trip that took place more years ago than I care to think about. But for gourmet at good prices, it's still hard to beat this authentic bistro, where you'll even see French natives seated elbow-to-elbow in the newly renovated dining room. "Les bonnes soupes" are satisfying noontime meals of salad, bread, a big bowl of soup (mushroom and barley with lamb is a favorite), dessert (chocolate mousse, crème caramel, or ice cream), and wine or coffee—a great bargain at just $12.95. The menu also features entree-sized salads (including a good niçoise), high-quality steak burgers, and traditional bistro fare like omelets, quiche Lorraine, croque monsieur, and steak frites. Rounding out the menu are those very French fondues: emmethal cheese, beef, and yummy, creamy chocolate. Bon appetit!

Los Dos Rancheros Mexicanos. 507 Ninth Ave. (at 38th St.). ☎ **212/ 868-7780.** Reservations not taken. Breakfast $1–$3; tacos $2; soups and sandwiches $3.50–$6; platters $7–$12. No credit cards. Daily 10:30am–11pm. Subway: A, C, E to 42nd St. MEXICAN.

This big, bright place is probably the most authentic Mexican restaurant in New York City. The decor is no-frills on every front—expect fluorescent lighting, tables with paper menus beneath the glass, plastic cups, and cheap dishes—but a neon-bright Wurlitzer jukebox pumping out Spanish-language pop adds genuine charm. The hearty Pueblo-style food is isn't for the faint of heart: the justifiably famous moles are extra-rich; the housemade salsas are hot, hot, hot; and barbecued goat, tripe soup, and tongue tacos are among the specialties. But even the less adventurous will dig into the enchiladas (don't pass up the beef), burritos with your choice of fillings, and other, more familiar choices with gusto. Everything is extremely affordable and excellently prepared, and warm, soft, freshly made corn tortillas are served with just about every dish. Service is attentive, and Mexican beers are available. A few blocks south of gentrified Ninth Avenue, the neighborhood isn't unsafe but can be desolate at night, so I suggest going earlier rather than later.

Pietrasanta. 683 Ninth Ave. (at 47th St.). ☎ **212/265-9471.** Reservations recommended. Main courses $8.95–$14.95. AE, MC, V. Sun–Mon noon–10:30pm, Tues–Thurs noon–11pm, Fri noon–midnight, Sat 11:30am–midnight. Subway: C, E to 50th St. TUSCAN ITALIAN.

This charming trattoria is an excellent choice for an affordable pre-theater meal. The well-priced pastas are far superior to what you'll get for the same money—or even more—at countless other pasta houses around town. The chef has a deft hand and a fondness for bold flavors, so the dishes are at once refined and appealingly robust. Look for such winning starters as grilled calamari seasoned with fresh basil, white wine, and the perfect squirt of lemon juice; asparagus spears wrapped in imported prosciutto and dressed in a divine lemon-butter sauce; and *fagioli con pancetta,* an unassuming white-bean dish that springs to life with the first bite thanks to flavorful pancetta, rosemary, and lemon. Pasta mains worth seeking out include *agnolotti di Angello,* hand-formed half-moon pasta filled with hearty lamb in a rosemary, basil, and red-wine sauce; and *trenette con calamari,* a simple but gorgeous tri-color dish of black squid-ink pasta, white calamari rings, and roasted red peppers. The kitchen also has an excellent reputation for its time-honored fish, chicken, veal and pasta preparations. A new waiter made the service a bit awkward on my last visit, but the staff is efficient and well-known for keeping an eye on curtain time.

Rice 'n' Beans. 744 Ninth Ave. (btw. 50th and 51st sts.) ☎ **212/265-4444.** Reservations not taken. Full plates $5.95–$14.95. MC, V. Mon–Thurs 11am–10pm; Fri–Sat 11am–11pm; Sun 1–9pm. Subway: C, E to 50th St. BRAZILIAN.

This cool, dark, hallway-sized restaurant dishes up kick-ass, stick-to-your-ribs fare. Between the bold flavors and the bargain-basement prices, you'll want to stand up and samba. Among the Brazilian specialties they whip up here are *feijoada*—the national dish of Brazil—a hearty, brackish-looking stew of black beans, pork ribs, and linguiça (Portuguese sausage); and a lovely roasted chicken seasoned with tomato and cilantro. The best bargain is the eponymous dish: For a mere $9.25 you get a large oval plate mounded with rice, beans, mixed vegetables, collard greens, and sweet plantains—a vegetarian's delight. Portions are monstrous across the board. The weekday lunch specials—full meals with rice, beans, plantains, and your choice of roasted or sauteed chicken, beef stew, thin-cut sauteed pork chops, or the day's fried fish—are a steal. Service can be slow at times and don't expect much in the way of ambiance—but at these prices, who cares?

✪ **Sapporo.** 152 W. 49th St. (btw. Sixth and Seventh aves.). ☎ **212/869-8972.** Reservations not taken. Main courses $6–$9. No credit cards. Subway: N, R to 49th St. JAPANESE.

In my world, comfort food doesn't get any better than a big ramen or fried rice bowl from Sapporo. This bustling, no-frills restaurant serves up good and cheap Japanese eats, and the mostly Japanese crowd is testimony to the food's authenticity. Sapporo is famous for their excellent *gyoza*, pork-filled dumplings that are pan fried and served with a soy, rice vinegar, and chili oil dipping sauce. Other winning choices include *chahan*, lightly fried Japanese rice with veggies, egg, fish cake, and your choice of pork or chicken; appealingly sweet beef and tofu sukiyaki; cleanly fried pork cutlets; and any of the gargantuan noodle bowls. Frankly, you can't really go wrong with anything—I've eaten here more times that I can count, and I've never been disappointed by a dish. Some of the servers speak little English, so feel free to just point to your choice, and don't hesitate to ask for silverware if you prefer it over chopsticks. Beer and sake are served in addition to soft drinks.

If you're in the East Village, you'll find **Sapporo East** at 245 E. 10th St., at First Avenue (☎ **212/260-1330**).

Siam Inn Too. 854 Eighth Ave. (btw. 51st and 52nd sts.). ☎ **212/757-4006.** Reservations accepted. Main courses $7.95–$15.95. AE, DC, MC, V. Mon–Fri noon–11:30pm; Sat 4–11:30pm; Sun 5–11pm. Subway: C, E to 50th St. THAI.

Situated on an unremarkable stretch of Eighth Avenue, Siam Inn is an attractive outpost of very good Thai food. All of your Thai favorites are here, well prepared and served by a brightly attired waitstaff. Tom kah gai soup (with chicken, mushrooms, and coconut milk), chicken satay with yummy peanut sauce, and light, flaky curry puffs all make good starters. Among noteworthy entrees are the masaman and red curries (the former rich and peanuty, the latter quite spicy), spicy sauteed squid with fresh basil and chilies, and perfect pad thai. And unlike many of the drab restaurants in this neighborhood, there's a semblance of decor—black deco tables and chairs, cushy rugs underfoot, and soft lighting.

Virgil's Real BBQ. 152 W. 44th St. (btw. Sixth and Seventh aves.). ☎ **212/921-9494.** Reservations recommended. Main courses $5.95–$24.95 (barbecue platters $12.95–$19.95). AE, DC, MC, V. Tues–Sat 11:30am–midnight; Sun–Mon 11:30am–11pm. Subway: 1, 2, 3, 7, 9, N, R to 42nd St./Times Sq. SOUTHERN/BARBECUE.

Virgil's may look like a comfy theme-park version of a down-home barbecue joint, but this place takes its barbecue seriously. The meat is house-smoked with a blend of hickory, oak, and fruitwood chips, and most every regional school is represented, from Carolina pulled pork to Texas beef brisket to Memphis ribs. You may not consider this contest-winning chow if you're from barbecue country, but we less-savvy Yankees are thrilled to have Virgil's in the 'hood. The ribs are lip-smackin' good, and the chicken is moist and tender—go for a combo if you just can't choose. Burgers, sandwiches, and other entrees (chicken-fried steak, anyone?) are also available. And cast that cornbread aside for a full order of buttermilk biscuits, which come with maple butter so good it's like dessert. So hunker down, pig out, and don't worry about making a mess; when you're through eating, you get a hot towel for washing up. The bar offers a huge selection of on-tap and bottled brews.

QUICK BITES

Canova Market, 134 W. 51st St., between Sixth and Seventh avenues (☎ **212/969-9200**), is a sprawling gourmet deli where your choices are only limited by your imagination (or your stomach). There's a fresh salad bar, an expansive deli counter, a soup bar, a sushi bar, and—my favorite—a pay-per-pound Mongolian grill, where you assemble your own concoction of fresh veggies, meats, seafood, rice, noodles, and seasonings to be grilled, and then watch the chefs do their stuff. There's a large dining area in the back where you can eat once you've paid. This place really bustles at lunch, but lines move fast.

Over on Ninth Avenue, **Amy's Bread,** at no. 672, between 46th and 47th streets (☎ **212/977-2670**), makes a great daytime stop. The cute, brick-walled bakery/cafe serves up fresh-baked breakfast pastries, sandwiches made on some of the city's best homemade bread, and excellent sweets as well as cappuccino.

Mangia (p. 79) also has a cafeteria-style cafe that's much smaller than the Wall Street location, but pleasing nonetheless: It's at 50 W. 57th St., between Fifth and Sixth avenues (☎ **212/582-5882**). **Paradise & Lunch,** at 55 W. 44th St., between Fifth and Sixth avenues (☎ **212/944-5544**), serves similar gourmet lunch fare in their sleek cafeteria-style cafe.

It's not hard to find Al Yeganeh, the famously dour soup vendor parodied on *Seinfeld*—just head for 55th Street, and walk to the end of the very long line at **Soup Kitchen International,** 259A W. 55th St., at Eighth Avenue (☎ **212/757-7730**). Many wait for the novelty, and even hope to be yelled at. Here's the thing: It's ridiculously expensive for takeout soup—$6 to $16—but it's really that good. Yeganeh labors fiercely, coddling the Hungarian goulash, mushroom barley, and mulligatawny, all subtly spiced and wonderful. I once found an entire lobster claw in my seafood bisque. The 12 or so soups offered change daily, but don't call because he'll hang up on you. "Whatever soup you want, I have!" he snaps. Come after 2pm to minimize waiting; yes, have your money ready; and no, don't ask to take his picture, as he finds that insulting.

10 Midtown East & Murray Hill

The British Open. 320 E. 59th St. (btw. First and Second aves.). ☎ **212/355-8467.** Main courses $7.50–$19.75 (most under $13). AE, DC, DISC, MC, V. Mon–Sat noon–midnight; Sun noon–10pm. Subway: 4, 5, 6 to 59th St. BRITISH.

Here's the perfect pub for golf lovers, or anybody who pines for a pint and some good English grub. This charmer of an alehouse is more sophisticated than most, with a polished mahogany bar, a pretty dining room in back, and friendly, attentive service. Tartan carpet completes the theme and little blue lights create a romantic glow. This isn't a copy of a Brit pub—it's the real thing, bartender, malt vinegar, and all. The North Star at South Street Seaport is equally genuine, but it's more after-work local than Sunday dinner, if you know what I mean. The extensive menu serves well-prepared versions of the pub staples, plus steaks, chops, and the like. But go for the standards: light, well-battered fish with crispy chips; excellent cottage pie with veggies and perfectly browned mash; plus steak

Theme Restaurant Thrills!

There's no doubt about it—New York's theme restaurant trend is on the wane. Sure, the Hard Rock, Planet Hollywood, and the All-Star Cafe are still going strong, but you won't see the legendary lines of the 80s forming outside these days. And we've already lost the weakest of the bunch, the trouble-plagued Fashion Cafe and the stand-up–themed Comedy Nation. This biz will prove to be Darwinist yet.

There are some good ideas in the works. The best is **ESPN Zone,** which should be open at 42nd Street and Broadway by the time you read this. With 42,000 square feet of space slated to house a grill with set replicas from ESPN's hit shows, a lounge with 13 massive TV screens and reclining leather chairs with speakers in the headrests, and a floor of sports-related arcade games, this upscale sports bar and restaurant should prove to be a sports fan's dream come true. (All-Star Cafe? What All-Star Cafe?)

In addition, the World Wrestling Federation has the **Raw Restaurant** in the works for Times Square (Stone Cold Steve cheeseburger, anyone?), and the **Rainforest Cafe** is planning to put down roots in the neighborhood. But until then:

Always the perennial favorite, New York's ✪ **Hard Rock Cafe,** 221 W. 57th St., between Broadway and Seventh Avenue (☎ 212/459-9320), is one of the originals of the chain, and a terrific realization of the concept. The memorabilia collection is excellent, with lots of great Lennon collectibles. The menu boasts all the Hard Rock standards, and the comfortable bar mixes up great cocktails.

Harley-Davidson Cafe, 1370 Sixth Ave., at 56th Street (☎ 212/245-6000), brings out the Hell's Angel in all of us. The just-fine munchies do the trick, and memorabilia documents 90 years of Hog history.

and kidney pie, bangers and mash, and so on. You'll find Guinness, Bass, Fullers ESB, and other British imports on tap, and golf and other sports on the telly at any hour.

✪ **Ess-A-Bagel.** 831 Third Ave. (at 51st St.). ☎ **212/980-1010.** Sandwiches $1.35–$8.35. AE, DC, DISC, MC, V. Mon–Fri 6:30am–10pm; Sat–Sun 8am–5pm. Subway: 6 to 51st St.; E, F to Lexington Ave. BAGEL SANDWICHES.

Ess-A-Bagel turns out the city's best bagel, edging out rival H&H, who won't make you a sandwich. Baked daily on-site, the giant

Something new to scare you with, my dear? The **Jekyll & Hyde Club,** 1409 Sixth Ave., between 57th and 58th streets (☎ **212/ 541-9505**), has five floors of bone-chilling bizarro. Kids love it. There's a second, more pub-like location at 91 Seventh Ave. South, between Barrow and Grove streets, in Greenwich Village (☎ **212/ 989-7701**).

The subterranean red planet–themed restaurant, ✪ **Mars 2112,** 1633 Broadway, at 51st Street (☎ **212/582-2112**), is a hoot, from the simulated red-rock rooms to the Martian-costumed waitstaff to the silly "Man Eats on Mars!" newspaper-style menu. The eclectic food is better than you might expect, but skip the Star Tours–style simulated spacecraft ride at the entrance if you don't want to lose your appetite before you get to your table. The kids won't mind, though—they'll love it, along with the video arcade.

Superstar athletes Andre Agassi, Wayne Gretzky, Ken Griffey, Jr., Joe Montana, Shaquille O'Neal, Monica Seles, and Tiger Woods are the names behind the successful **Official All-Star Cafe,** 1540 Broadway, at 45th Street (☎ **212/840-8326**). The food is straight from the ballpark—hot dogs and hamburgers, St. Louis ribs, Philly cheese steak sandwiches, and the like.

Bruce Willis, Sly Stallone, and Ah-nuld are the moneymongers behind **Planet Hollywood.** 140 W. 57th St., between Sixth and Seventh avenues (☎ **212/333-7827**). Frankly, the movie memorabilia doesn't hold the same excitement as the genuine rock 'n' roll goods over at the Hard Rock (didn't I see the R2D2 and C3PO robots at three *other* PHs?), but it's still plenty of fun for film buffs nonetheless. Watch for a 2000 move to Times Square.

hand-rolled delicacies come in 12 flavors and are so plump, chewy, and satisfying it's hard to believe they contain no fat, cholesterol, or preservatives. Head to the back counter for a baker's dozen or line up for an overstuffed sandwich. Fillings can range from a generous schmear of cream cheese to smoked Nova salmon or chopped herring salad (both have received national acclaim) to sun-dried tomato tofu spread. There are also lots of deli-style meats to choose from, plus a wide range of cheeses and salads (egg, chicken, light tuna, and so on). The cheerful dining room has plenty of bistro-style tables.

There's a second, smaller location at 359 First Ave., at 21st St. (☎ **212/260-2252**).

✪ **Pongal.** 110 Lexington Ave. (btw. 27th and 28th sts.). ☎ **212/696-9458.** Reservations accepted. Main courses $4.95–$9.25. DC, DISC, MC, V. Mon–Fri noon–3pm and 5–10pm, Sat–Sun noon–10pm. Subway: 6 to 28th St. VEGETARIAN INDIAN.

One of my favorite finds of the year is this Indian spot, a real standout on Curry Hill, the stretch of Lexington in the high 20s that's home to a number of Indian restaurants. Pongal specializes in the vegetarian cuisine of southern India, and also happens to be kosher (only in New York!). Trust me—you don't have to be a vegetarian to love this place. The hearty dishes are always freshly prepared to order by the conscientious kitchen (no vats of saag paneer sitting around this joint). Ingredients are always top-quality, vegetables and legume dishes are never overcooked, and the well-spiced sauces are particularly divine. The specialty of the house is *dosai,* a large golden crepe filled with onions, potatoes, and other goodies, accompanied by coconut chutney and flavorful sauce. The food is very cheap, with nothing priced over $9, but that doesn't mean you have to put up with a crusty cafeteria to get such a bargain: The restaurant is low-lit and attractive, with professional service and a pleasing ambiance, making it a nice choice for a special night on the town.

Prime Burger. 5 E. 51st St. (btw. Fifth and Madison aves.). ☎ **212/759-4729.** Main courses $3.25–$7.95. No credit cards. Mon–Fri 5am–7pm; Sat 6am–5pm. Subway: 6 to 51st St.; E, F to Lexington/Third aves. and 53rd St. BURGERS.

Just across the street from St. Patrick's Cathedral, this coffee shop is a heavenly find. The burgers and sandwiches are tasty, the fries crispy and generous. The front seats, which might remind you (if you're old enough) of old wooden grammar-school desks, are great fun—especially when ever-so-serious suited-up New Yorkers quietly take their places at these oddities. A great quickie stop during a day of Fifth Avenue shopping.

Taco & Tortilla King. 285 Third Ave. (btw. 22nd and 23rd sts.). ☎ **212/679-8882** or 212/481-3930. Tacos, burritos, and sandwiches $1–$6.79; fajitas $12.99–$13.99. No credit cards. Daily 11am–11:30pm. Subway: 6 to 23rd St. MEXICAN.

This place may be slightly off the tourist track, but if you're jonesing for some good, cheap Mexican, it's well worth the walk. This low-profile sleeper is little more than a lunch counter with a few tables and chairs, but the authentic Mexican food can't be beat. Sit down to a couple of tacos and you'll think you've been temporarily transported to one of those super-cheap, gourmet Mexican joints your friends in southern California keep raving about. The kitchen won me over with the basics: Chunky fresh-made guacamole infused with lime, and flour tortillas made from scratch and baked on premises. All the Mexican staples, from well-stuffed burritos to sizzling fajitas, are authentically prepared, hearty, and satisfying; a good portion of the offerings can be prepared meatless for vegetarians. An all-around winner for a fast meal at an unbeatable price.

QUICK BITES

Mangia (p. 79) has a third cafeteria-style cafe that's much smaller than the Wall Street location, but pleasing nonetheless: at 16 E. 48th St., just east of Fifth Avenue (☎ 212/754-7600).

The Pump. 113 E. 31st St. (btw. Park and Lexington aves.). ☎ **212/ 213-5733.** Breakfast $2.50–$7; sandwiches and salads $3–$7; full plates $6.50–$12. AE, MC, V. Mon–Thurs 9:30am–9:30pm; Fri 9:30am–6:30pm; Sat 11am–7pm. Subway: 6 to 33rd St. HEALTH-CONSCIOUS.

This little storefront is a terrific stop for diners who are watching their figures as well as their wallets. Everything on the menu is low in fat and high in protein, but doesn't sacrifice flavor for healthfulness. This is casual food made with all-natural ingredients: salads, sandwiches, "supercharged" combo platters, fresh juices, high-protein and health shakes. Although they serve up a great nature burger (a pleasing blend of brown rice, sunflower seeds, herbs, and veggies), the Pump isn't a vegetarian restaurant—lean beef, turkey, and chicken are served. And since they cater to a big workout crowd that needs energy, portions are substantial. Salad dressings are all fat-free creations, like tahini and honey mustard, and guilt-free pizzas are prepared with non-fat mozzarella, low sodium tomato sauce, and whole wheat crust. At breakfast, eggs, pancakes, and potatoes are all baked, never fried—which is precisely why you can indulge in the steak and eggs sandwich (served on a whole wheat pita) and feel not the least bit sinful.

WORTH A SPLURGE

Oyster Bar. In Grand Central Terminal, lower level (btw. Vanderbilt and Lexington aves.). ☎ 212/490-6650. Reservations recommended. Main courses $9.45–$34.95. AE, CB, DC, DISC, JCB, MC, V. Mon–Fri 11:30am–9:30pm (last seating). Subway: 4, 5, 6, 7, S to 42nd St./Grand Central. SEAFOOD.

Here's one New York institution housed within another: the city's most famous seafood joint in the world's greatest train station, newly renovated Grand Central Terminal. Fully recovered from a 1997 fire, the restaurant is looking spiffy, too, with a main dining room sitting under an impressive curved and tiled ceiling, a more casual luncheonette-style section for walk-ins, and a wood-paneled saloon-style room for smokers. If you love seafood, don't miss this place. A new menu is prepared every day, featuring only the freshest fish. The oysters are irresistible: Kumomoto, Bluepoint, Malepeque, Belon—the list goes on and on. The list of daily catches, which can range from arctic char to mako shark to ono (Hawaiian wahoo), is equally impressive. Most dinners go for between $19.95 and $24.95, and it's easy to jack up the tab by ordering live Maine lobster or one of the rarer daily specialties. But it's just as easy to keep the tab down by sticking with hearty fare like one of the excellent stews and pan roasts, or by pairing the New England clam chowder (at $4.50, an unbeatable lunch) with a smoked starter to make a great meal.

11 The Upper West Side

Near Lincoln Center, at 48 W. 65th St. between Columbus Avenue and Central Park West, **John's Pizzeria** (☎ **212/721-7001**) serves up one of the city's best pies (p. 105).

Big Nick's Burger Joint. 2175 Broadway (at 77th St.). ☎ **212/362-9238.** Main courses $3.50–$11. No credit cards. Open 24 hours. Subway: 1, 9 to 79th St. AMERICAN.

A neighborhood legend since 1962, Big Nick's is one of the best spots in the city for a midnight snack. They offer a full menu 24 hours a day, which includes everything from killer French toast and pancakes to Nick's infamous gourmet beefburgers. The classic char-broiled burgers come in a whole host of varieties, from your all-American cheeseburger to the Mediterranean, stuffed with herbs, spices, and onions and topped with anchovies, feta, and tomato. There's also a good selection of Big Nick–style pizzas, like the Gyromania, topped with well-seasoned gyro meat and onions. As the name suggests, Nick's is a real joint, specializing in homegrown Noo Yawk fare; however, the kitchen gets kudos for developing a diet-watchers menu, with pizzas prepared with skim cheese and lean-ground veal and turkey burgers. The atmosphere is suitably lively, with waiters and busboys scrambling about, cooks calling out orders, and crowded tables happily chowing down.

✪ **Gabriela's.** 685 Amsterdam Ave. (at 93rd St.). ☎ **212/961-0574.** Reservations accepted. Main courses $5–$12.95. AE, MC, V. Mon–Thurs 11:30am–11pm; Fri–Sat 11:30am–midnight; Sun noon–10pm. Subway: 1, 2, 3, 9 to 96th St. MEXICAN.

If you love roast chicken, trust me: it's well worth the trip uptown for Gabriela's. A blend of Yucatan spices and a slow-roasting rotisserie results in some of the most tender, juiciest chicken in town—and at $6.95 for a half-chicken with two sides (plenty for all but the biggest eaters) and $12.95 for a whole, it's one of the city's best bargains, too. All of the Mexican specialties on the extensive menu are well prepared, generously portioned, and satisfying, from the monster tacos to the well-sauced enchiladas. The fresh, chunky, perfectly limed guacamole should please even Southwest natives. The dining room is large, bright, and pretty, with a pleasing South-of-the-Border flair, and the service is affable if a little slow at times. Mexican beers and wine are available, but you may want to consider one of Gabriela's yummy fruit shakes or tall agua frescas (fresh fruit drinks), which come in a variety of tropical flavors.

Hunan Park. 235 Columbus Ave. (btw. 70th and 71st St.). ☎ **212/724-4411.** Reservations accepted for groups of 5 or more. Main courses $5.25–$10.50 (Peking Duck $24). AE, MC, V. Sun–Thurs noon–11:30pm; Fri–Sat noon–12:30am. Subway: B, C, 1, 2, 3, 9 to 72nd St. HUNAN CHINESE.

This casual place has been earning broad-sweeping kudos for years from Zagat's to *New York* magazine to Alan Alda for its well-prepared, inexpensive Chinese standards. Everything about it—quality, service, decor—is a cut above the standard. Expect all the familiar favorites, plus satisfying specialties like ginger chicken, spicy four-flavor beef, and crispy sea bass in a rich Hunan sauce. Service is quick and efficient, and the convenient location makes this a cheap and easy post–Central Park or pre–Lincoln Center stop.

If you're farther Uptown, there's a second location at 721 Columbus Ave., at 95th St. (☎ **212/222-6511**).

Josie's Restaurant & Juice Bar. 300 Amsterdam Ave. (at 74th St.). ☎ **212/769-1212.** Reservations recommended. Main courses $8–$16. AE, DC, MC, V. Mon 5:30–11pm; Tues–Fri 5:30pm–midnight; Sat 5pm–midnight, Sun 5–11pm. Subway: 1, 2, 3, 9 to 72nd St. HEALTH-CONCIOUS.

You have to admire the sincerity of an organic restaurant that uses chemical-free milk paint on its walls. Chef/owner Louis Lanza doesn't stop there: His adventurous menu shuns dairy, preservatives, and concentrated fats. Free-range and farm-raised meats and poultry augment vegetarian choices like baked sweet potato with tamari brown rice, broccoli, roasted beets, and tahini sauce; eggless Caesar salad; and a great three-grain vegetable burger with homemade ketchup and caramelized onions. The yellowfin tuna wasabi burger with pickled ginger is another signature. Everything is made with organic grains, beans, and flour as well as organic produce when possible. You don't have to be a health nut to enjoy Josie's; Lanza's eclectic cuisine really satisfies. If wheat grass isn't your thing, a full wine and beer list is served in this pleasing modern space, which boasts enough *Jetsons*-style touches to give the room a playful, relaxed feel.

QUICK BITES

For one of the cheapest, most satisfying meal deals in New York, head to the Uptown branch of **Gray's Papaya** (p. 98), 2090 Broadway, at 72nd Street (☎ **212/799-0243**), where first-rate all-beef dogs are just 50¢ each around the clock. Pair your franks with some crispy fries and a tropical juice drink.

WORTH A SPLURGE

Sarabeth's Kitchen. 423 Amsterdam Ave. (btw. 80th and 81st sts.). ☎ **212/496-6280.** Reservations accepted for dinner only. Main courses $5–$11 at lunch and brunch; $10–$22 at dinner. AE, CB, DC, DISC, JCB, MC, V. Mon–Thurs 8am–10:30pm; Fri 8am–11pm; Sat 9am–11pm; Sun 9am–9:30pm. Subway: 1, 9 to 79th St. CONTEMPORARY AMERICAN.

Its 200-year-old family recipe for orange-apricot marmalade first rooted Sarabeth's Kitchen into New York's consciousness, but its fresh-baked goods, award-winning preserves, and creative American cooking with a European touch keep the clientele loyal. This charming country restaurant with a distinct Hamptons feel is best known for its breakfast and weekend brunch, when the menu features such treats as porridge with wheatberries, fresh cream, butter, and brown sugar; pumpkin waffle topped with sour cream, raisins, pumpkin seeds, and honey (a sweet tooth's delight); and a whole host of farm-fresh omelets. But lunch is just as good and a lot less crowded. Offerings might include a generous Caesar salad with aged Parmesan, brioche croutons, and a tangy anchovy dressing accompanied by a hearty from-scratch soup, or some beautifully built country-style sandwiches.

Dinner is more sophisticated—with such specialties as hazelnut-crusted halibut in an aromatic seven-vegetable broth and oven-roasted lamb crusted in black mushrooms, with grilled leeks and Vidalia onion rings on the side—but a splurge, albeit a worthy one. No matter what time you come, leave room for the scrumptious desserts. Or feel free to stop in just for a sweet, as many New Yorkers do.

There are also two East Side locations: 1295 Madison Ave. (☎ **212/410-7335**) and inside the Whitney Museum at 945 Madison Ave. (☎ **212/570-3670**).

12 The Upper East Side

If it's an excellent contemporary meal or a sweet treat you're after, head to **Sarabeth's Kitchen** (p. 116), which has two eastside locations: 1295 Madison Ave., at E. 92nd St. (☎ **212/410-7335**), and at the Whitney Museum, 945 Madison Ave. (☎ **212/570-3670**).

Serendipity 3. 225 E. 60th St. (btw. Second and Third aves.). ☎ **212/838-3531**. Reservations recommended for dinner. Main courses $5.50–$17.95; sweets and sundaes $4.50–$10. AE, DC, DISC, MC, V. Sun–Thurs 11:30am–midnight; Fri 11:30–1am; Sat 11:30–2am. Subway: 4, 5, 6 to 59th St.; N, R to Lexington Ave. AMERICAN.

You'd never guess that this whimsical place was once a top stop on Andy Warhol's agenda. Wonders never cease—and neither does the confection at this delightful restaurant and sweet shop. Tucked into a cozy brownstone a few steps from Bloomingdale's, Serendipity's small front-room curiosity shop overflows with odd objects, from jigsaw puzzles to silly jewelry. But the real action is in back, where the quintessential American soda fountain still reigns supreme. Remember Farrell's? This is the better version (complete with candy to tempt the kids on the way out). Happy people gather at marble-topped ice-cream parlor tables for burgers and foot-long hot dogs, country meat loaf with mashed potatoes and gravy, and salads and sandwiches with cute names like "The Catcher in the Rye" (their own twist on the BLT, with chicken and Russian dressing—on rye, of

Pizza! Pizza!

Leave it to the chi-chi Upper East Side to specialize in designer pizza. **Sofia Fabulous Pizza,** 1022 Madison Ave., at 79th Street (☎ **212/734-2676**), serves pricey but terrific Tuscan-style pizza, and there's even wonderful alfresco rooftop dining. **Pintaile's Pizza,** at 26 E. 91st St., between Fifth and Madison avenues (☎ **212/722-1967**), dresses their crisp organic crusts with layers of plum tomatoes, extra-virgin olive oil, and other fabulously fresh ingredients.

For something more traditional, head to **Totonno's Pizzeria Napolitano,** 1544 Second Ave., between 80th and 81st streets (☎ **212/327-2800**), for killer coal-oven pies. Some naysayers consider this a pale comparison to the Coney Island original, but I think they're just hung up on the fancier digs. A little farther afield, at 408 E. 64th St. between First and York avenues, is a branch of **John's Pizzeria** (☎ **212/935-2895**) that's worth checking out (p. 105).

course). The food isn't great, but the main courses aren't the point—they're just an excuse to get to the desserts. The restaurant's signature is Frozen Hot Chocolate, a slushy version of everybody's cold weather favorite, but other crowd pleasers include dark double devil mousse, celestial carrot cake, lemon ice-box pie, and anything with hot fudge. So cast that willpower aside and come on in—Serendipity is an ironic-free charmer to be appreciated by adults and kids alike.

QUICK BITES

Papaya King, 179 E. 86th St., at Third Avenue (☎ **212/ 369-0648**), is the originator of the two-franks-and-a-fruit-drink combo that **Gray's Papaya** (p. 98) has popularized in other 'hoods. Papaya King isn't quite so cheap as Gray's, but close enough. Open daily from 8:30am to midnight.

13   Harlem

Sylvia's. 328 Lenox Ave. (btw. 126th and 127th sts.). ☎ **212/996-0660.** Reservations accepted for 10 or more. Main courses $8–$16. AE, DISC, MC, V. Mon–Thurs 8am–10:30pm; Fri–Sat 7:30am–10:30pm; Sun 11am–8pm. Subway: 2, 3 to 125th St. SOUL FOOD.

South Carolina–born Sylvia Woods is the last word in New York soul food. The place is so popular with both locals and visitors that the dining room has spilled into the building next door. Since 1962, her Harlem institution has dished up the southern-fried goods: Turkey with down-home stuffing; smothered chicken and pork chops; fried chicken and baked ham; collard greens and candied yams; cavity-inducing sweet tea; and "Sylvia's World Famous, Talked About, Bar-B-Que Ribs Special"—the sauce is sweet, with a potent afterburn. This Harlem landmark is still presided over by 72-year-old Sylvia, who's likely to greet you at the door herself. Some naysayers claim that Sylvia's just isn't what it used to be, but chowing down here is still a one-of-a-kind New York experience. Sunday gospel brunch is a joyous time to go, if you're not put off by the tour buses out front.

5

Exploring New York City

*O*ne of the best—and cheapest—ways to experience New York is to pick a neighborhood and just stroll it. Walk the prime thoroughfares, poke your head into shops, park yourself on a bench or at an outdoor cafe, and just watch the world go by. For tips on where to go, how to get there, and what highlights to be on the lookout for, see the "Manhattan's Neighborhoods in Brief" in chapter 2. If you'd prefer to explore with an expert at the helm, consider taking an organized tour; see "Affordable Sightseeing Tours," later in this chapter.

1 In New York Harbor: Lady Liberty, Ellis Island & the Staten Island Ferry

✪ **Statue of Liberty.** On Liberty Island in New York Harbor. ☎ **212/363-3200** (general info) or 212/269-5755 (ticket/ferry info). www.nps.gov/stli. Ferry ticket/admission to Statue of Liberty and Ellis Island $7 adults, $6 seniors, $3 children under 17. Daily 9am–5pm; extended hours in summer. Subway: 4, 5 to Bowling Green; 1, 9 to South Ferry (the platform at this station is shorter than the train, so ride in the first five cars). From the station, walk south through Battery Park to Castle Clinton, the fort housing the ferry ticket booth.

For the millions who first came by ship to America in the last century—either as privileged tourists or needy, hopeful immigrants—Lady Liberty, standing in the Upper Bay, was their first glimpse of America. Few travel by boat anymore, so it probably won't be your first impression of New York, but you should make it one of the lasting ones. Designed by sculptor Frédéric-Auguste Bartholdi with the engineering help of Alexandre-Gustave Eiffel (responsible for the famed Paris tower) and unveiled on October 28, 1886, no monument so embodies the nation's, and the world's, notion of political freedom and economic potential. Even if you don't make it out to Liberty Island, you can get a spine-tingling glimpse during a free ride on the Staten Island Ferry (see below).

Touring Tips: Ferries leave daily every half hour to 45 minutes from 9:30am to 3:15pm, with more frequent ferries in the morning and extended hours in summer. Try to go early on a weekday to avoid the crowds. Be sure to arrive by noon if your heart's set on experiencing everything; go later, and you may not have time to make it to the crown. A stop at Ellis Island (see below) is included in the fare, but if you catch the last ferry, you can only visit the statue or Ellis Island, not both.

The ferry deposits you, in about 20 minutes, on Liberty Island, a short distance from the statue. Once on the island, you'll start to get an idea of the statue's immensity: She weighs 225 tons and measures 152 feet from foot to flame. Her nose alone is $4^1/_2$ feet long, and her index finger is 8 feet long. You may have to wait as long as 3 hours to walk up into the crown (the torch is not open to visitors). If it's summer, or if you're just not in shape for it, you may want to skip it: It's a grueling 354 steps (22 stories) to the crown, or you can cheat and take the elevator the first 10 stories up (an act I wholeheartedly endorse). But even if you take this shortcut, the interior is stifling once the temperature starts to climb. However, you don't have to go all the way up to the crown; there are a number of **observation decks** at different levels, including one at the top of the pedestal reachable by elevator. Even if you don't go inside, a stroll around the base is an extraordinary experience, and the views of the Manhattan skyline are stellar.

✪ **Ellis Island.** Located in New York Harbor. ☎ **212/363-3200** (general info) or 212/269-5755 (ticket/ferry info). www.ellisisland.org. For subway, hours, and ferry ticket details, see the Statue of Liberty above.

One of New York's most moving sights, the restored Ellis Island opened in 1990. Roughly 40% of Americans can trace their heritage back to an ancestor who came through here (myself included). For the 62 years when it was America's main entry point for immigrants (it closed in 1954), Ellis Island processed some 12 million people. The greeting was often brusque—especially in the early years of the century, when as many as 12,000 came through in a single day. The statistics and their meaning can be overwhelming, but the **Immigration Museum** skillfully relates the story of Ellis Island and immigration in America by putting the emphasis on personal experience.

Today you enter the Main Building's baggage room, just as the immigrants did, and then climb the stairs to the **Registry Room,** where millions waited anxiously for medical and legal processing. A step-by-step account of the immigrants' voyage is detailed in the **"Through America's Gate"** exhibit, with haunting photos and touching oral histories. What might be the most poignant exhibit is **"Treasures from Home,"** 1,000 objects and photos donated by

Downtown Attractions

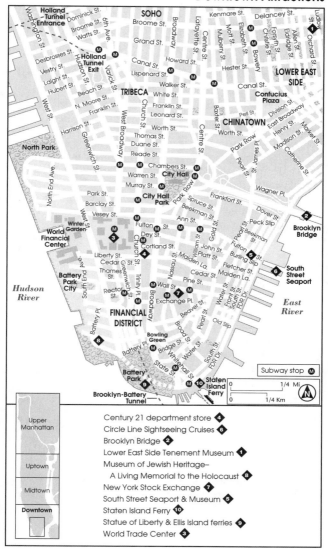

Century 21 department store ◆4
Circle Line Sightseeing Cruises ◆6
Brooklyn Bridge ◆2
Lower East Side Tenement Museum ◆1
Museum of Jewish Heritage–
  A Living Memorial to the Holocaust ◆8
New York Stock Exchange ◆7
South Street Seaport & Museum ◆5
Staten Island Ferry ◆10
Statue of Liberty & Ellis Island ferries ◆9
World Trade Center ◆3

Cheap Thrills: What to See & Do for Free

The Big Apple offers more freebies than you might think:

- **Ride the Staten Island Ferry.** This iconic ride into the world's biggest harbor has many charms, not the least of which is that it's absolutely free. The hour-long excursion offers the same brilliant Lower Manhattan skyline views as private harbor cruises with high price tags.

- **Promenade Across the Brooklyn Bridge.** The easy walk from end to end offers a remarkable, up-close perspective of the marvelous Gothic-inspired stone pylons and intricate steel-cable webs that established the first physical connection between Brooklyn and Manhattan in 1883. Start at the Brooklyn end for the best views, and consider pairing your walk with a stroll through historic Brooklyn Heights for a leafy, lovely, and absolutely free afternoon.

- **Take a Walking Tour.** The best way to get to know New York is to pick one or two of its distinctive neighborhoods and meet them on a human scale. I recommend a number of very good guides that offer affordable walks later in this chapter, but there's no need to spend a dime on one if you don't want to—just take out a map and chart a route for yourself.

- **Ogle the City's Architecture.** New York boasts such a wealth of architectural treasures that this one could easily keep you busy for a full day or more. It doesn't cost a penny to admire such works of art and engineering as the neo-Gothic Woolworth Building; Rockefeller Center, an art-deco delight; and majestic Grand Central Terminal, recently restored to its original glory.

- **Go to the Park.** Lots of travelers don't bother with Central Park—and they're making a huge mistake. An urban miracle, this massive verdant playground forms the backbone of the city, both physically and socially. This is where New Yorkers come year-round to relax, play, commune with nature, and get to know one another. Don't skip the chance to enjoy its many wonders.

descendants of immigrants, including family heirlooms, religious articles, and rare clothing and jewelry. Outside, the **American Immigrant Wall of Honor** commemorates the names of hundreds of thousands of immigrants and their families who have been

- **Attend a TV Show Taping.** With some advance planning—or just the right amount of luck on tape day—you can be an audience member at your favorite morning gabfest, network sitcom, or late-night talk show for absolutely free. See p. 142 for details on getting tickets to shows taped at the NBC studios, or call the NYCVB at ☎ **212/484-1222** for details on how to attend tapings of gabfests like *The View, Live! With Regis & Kathie Lee, Montel,* and *The Late Show with David Letterman,* or sitcoms such as *Cosby* and *Spin City.*
- **Celebrate Sunday Morning in Harlem.** In a mixed blessing for local congregations, Sunday-morning gospel services have become so popular that tour groups sometimes outnumber parishioners. At **Abyssinian Baptist Church,** 132 W. 138th St., between Seventh and Lenox avenues (☎ **212/862-7474**), services are held at 9 and 11am. Another resounding service takes place at the **First Corinthian Baptist Church,** 1912 Adam Clayton Powell Blvd., at West 116th Street (☎ **212/864-5976**), at 11am. Just keep in mind that these are religious services first, not gospel shows.
- **Hear Some Classical Music at Juilliard.** The nation's premier music school sponsors excellent-quality performances, ranging from classical concerts to opera to drama to dance, throughout the year—and most are free. For further details, see chapter 6.
- **Or Head to Brooklyn for Some Livelier Tunes.** The renowned cultural institution known as the **Brooklyn Academy of Music** offers free live music every Friday and Saturday night at **BAMcafé.** Offerings can range from atmospheric electronica to jazz poetics to Harlem-style swing. Performances are in the evening, but come early (between 4 and 6pm) for happy hour, when all drinks are half-price. For more on BAM, see chapter 6.
- **Take Advantage of Summer's Outdoor Events.** New York's parks burst with freebies in the warm months, from **Shakespeare in the Park** (New York's most famous freebie) to the free Monday-night **Bryant Park Film Festival.** See chapter 6.

commemorated by their descendants (all catalogued on a computer registry as well). You can even research your own family's history at the **American Family Immigration History Center.** It's difficult to leave the museum unmoved.

Touring Tips: Ferries run daily to Ellis Island and Liberty Island from Battery Park and Liberty State Park in New Jersey at frequent intervals; see the Statue of Liberty (above) for details.

Staten Island Ferry. Departs from the Staten Island Ferry Terminal at the southern tip of Manhattan. ☎ **718/815-BOAT.** www.SI-Web.com/transportation/dot.htm. Free (fee charged for car transport). 24 hours; every 15–30 min weekdays, less frequently on off-peak and weekend hours. Subway: 1, 9, N, R to South Ferry.

Here's New York's best freebie—especially if you just want to glimpse the Statue of Liberty and not climb her steps. You get an enthralling hour-long excursion (round-trip) into the world's biggest harbor. This is not strictly a sightseeing ride, but commuter transportation to Staten Island. As a result, during business hours, you'll share the boat with working stiffs reading papers and drinking coffee inside, blissfully unaware of the sights outside.

You, however, should go on deck and enjoy the busy harbor traffic. The old orange-and-green boats usually have open decks along the sides or at the bow and stern (try to catch one of these boats if you can; the newer white boats don't have decks). Grab a seat on the right side of the boat for the best view. On the way out of Manhattan, you'll pass the Statue of Liberty, Ellis Island, and (from the left side of the boat) Governor's Island; you'll see the Verranzano Narrows Bridge linking Brooklyn to Staten Island in the distance.

When the boat arrives at St. George, Staten Island, everyone must disembark. Follow the boat loading sign on your right as you get off; you'll circle around to the next loading dock, where there's usually another boat waiting to depart for Manhattan. The skyline views are simply awesome on the return trip. Well worth the time spent—and the fare simply can't be beat.

2 Historic Lower Manhattan's Top Attractions

✪ **Brooklyn Bridge.** Subway: 4, 5, 6 to Brooklyn Bridge–City Hall; A, C to High St.

Its Gothic-inspired stone pylons and intricate steel-cable webs have moved poets like Walt Whitman and Hart Crane to sing the praises of this great span, the first to cross the East River and connect Manhattan to Brooklyn. Begun in 1867 and ultimately completed in 1883, the beautiful Brooklyn Bridge is now the city's best-known symbol of the age of growth that seized the city during the late 19th century. Walk across the bridge, and imagine the awe that New Yorkers of that age felt at seeing two boroughs joined by this monumental span. It's still astounding.

Walking the Bridge: Walking the Brooklyn Bridge is one of my all-time favorite New York activities. A wide wood-plank pedestrian walkway is elevated above the traffic, making it a relatively peaceful, and popular, walk. It provides a great vantage point from which to contemplate skyline.

There's a sidewalk entrance on Park Row, just across from City Hall Park (take the 4, 5, or 6 train to Brooklyn Bridge–City Hall). But why do this walk *away* from Manhattan, toward the far less impressive Brooklyn skyline? For gorgeous Manhattan views, take an A or C train to High Street, one stop into Brooklyn. From there, you'll be on the bridge in no time: Come above ground, then walk through the little park to Cadman Plaza East and head downslope (left) to the stairwell that will take you up to the footpath. (Following Prospect Place under the bridge, turning right onto Cadman Plaza East, will also take you directly to the stairwell.) It's a 20- to 40-minute stroll over the bridge to Manhattan, depending on your pace, the amount of foot traffic, and the number of stops you make to contemplate the spectacular views (there are benches along the way). The footpath will deposit you right at City Hall Park.

New York Stock Exchange. 20 Broad St. (btw. Wall St. and Exchange Place). ☎ **212/656-5165.** www.nyse.com. Free admission. Mon–Fri 9am–4:30pm (ticket booth opens at 8:45am). Subway: 2, 3, 4, 5 to Wall St.; J, M, Z to Broad St.

Wall Street—it's an iconic name, and ground zero for bulls and bears everywhere. This narrow 18th-century lane (you'll be surprised at how little it is) is appropriately monumental, lined with neo-classic towers that reach as far skyward as the dreams and greed of investors who built it into the world's most famous financial market. At the heart of the action is the New York Stock Exchange, the world's largest securities trader, where you can watch the billions change hands and get a fleeting idea of how the money merchants work.

While the NYSE is on Wall Street, the **ticket kiosk** is around the corner at 20 Broad St., where you'll be issued a ticket with a time on it; you must enter during the window of opportunity specified on your ticket. The staff starts handing out tickets at 8:45am, but get in line early if you want to be inside to see all hell break loose at the 9:30am opening bell. The 3,000 tickets issued per day are usually gone by noon; plan on having to return unless you're one of the first in line. Despite the number of visitors, things move pretty quickly.

Don't expect to come out with a full understanding of the market; if you didn't have one going in, you won't leave any more enlightened. Still, it's fun watching the action on the trading floor from the glass-lined, mezzanine-level **observation gallery** (look to the right, and you'll see the Bloomberg people sending their live reports back to the newsroom). You can stay as long as you like, but it doesn't really take more than 20 minutes or so to peruse the other jingoistic exhibits ("NYSE—our hero!"), which include a rather oblique explanation of the floor activities, interactive exhibits, and a short film presentation of the Exchange's history and present-day operations.

South Street Seaport & Museum. At Water and South sts.; museum at 12–14 Fulton St. ☎ **212/748-8600** or 212/732-7678. www.southstseaport.org. Museum admission $6 adults, $5 seniors, $3 children. Museum, Apr–Sept Fri–Wed 10am–6pm, Thurs 10am–8pm; Oct–Mar Wed–Sun 10am–5pm. Subway: 2, 3, 4, 5 to Fulton St. (walk east, or downslope, to Water St.)

This landmark district on the East River encompasses 11 square blocks of historic buildings, a maritime museum, several piers, shops and restaurants (including the authentically old world **North Star Pub;** see chapter 4).

You can explore most of the seaport on your own. It's an odd place. The 18th- and 19th-century buildings lining the cobbled streets and alleyways are beautifully restored but nevertheless have a theme-park air about them, no doubt due to the J. Crews, Brookstones, and Body Shops housed within. The height of the seaport's cheesiness its **Pier 17,** a historic barge converted into a mall, complete with food court and cheap jewelry kiosks.

Despite its rampant commercialism, the seaport is worth a look. There's a good amount of history to be discovered here, most of it around the **South Street Seaport Museum,** a fitting tribute to the sea commerce that once thrived here.

Including the galleries—which house paintings and prints, ship models, scrimshaw, and nautical designs, as well as frequently-changing exhibitions—there are a number of historic ships berthed at the pier to explore. A few of the boats are living museums and restoration works in progress, but you can actually hit the high seas on the 1885 cargo schooner *Pioneer* (☎ 212/748-8786), which offers two-hour public sails daily from early May through September. Tickets are $20 for adults, $15 for seniors and students, and $12 for children. Advance reservations are recommended; always call ahead to confirm sailing times.

At the gateway to the seaport, at Fulton and Water streets, is the *Titanic* **Memorial Lighthouse,** a monument to those who lost their lives when the ocean liner sank on April 15, 1912. It was erected overlooking the East River in 1913, and moved to this spot in 1968, just after the historic district was so designated.

✪ **World Trade Center.** Bounded by Church, Vesey, Liberty, and West sts. ☎ 212/323-2340 for observation deck, 212/435-4170 for general information. www.wtc-top.com. Admission to observation deck $12 adults, $9 seniors, $6 children under 12. Sept–May, daily 9:30am–9:30pm; June–Aug, 9:30am–11:30pm. Subway: C, E to World Trade Center; 1, 9, N, R to Cortlandt St.

Nowhere near as romantic as the Empire State Building, the World Trade Center is nevertheless just as heroic, having withstood a bombing in its basement garage in 1993 without so much as a flinch. Built in 1970, the center is actually an immense complex of seven buildings on 16 acres housing offices, restaurants, a hotel, an underground shopping mall, and an outdoor plaza with fountains, sculpture, and summer concerts and performances. But the parts you'll be interested in are the Twin Towers, which usurped the Empire State to become New York's tallest structures.

The box-like buildings are so nondescript that the local Channel 11 once used them to represent that number in their commercials. Each is 110 stories and 1,350 feet high. The **Top of the World** observation deck is high atop 2 World Trade Center, to the south. On the 107th floor, it's like a mini theme park, offering a 6-minute simulated helicopter tour over Manhattan, high-tech kiosks, a food court, and a nighttime light show. But the reason to come is for those incredible views. The enclosed top floor offers incredible panoramas on all sides, with windows reaching right down to the floor. Go ahead, walk right up to one, and look down—*scaaary.*

Come on a clear day. If you're lucky, you'll be able to go out on the **rooftop promenade,** the world's highest open-air observation deck. (It's only open under perfect conditions; I've only been able to go out once in a lifetime of visits.) You thought inside was incredible? Wait 'til you see this. While you're up here, look straight down and wonder what Frenchman Philippe Petit could've been thinking when in August 1974 he walked across to tower no. 1 on a tightrope, stopping to lie down for a moment in the center.

3 The Top Museums

✪ **American Museum of Natural History.** On Central Park W., btw. 77th and 81st sts. ☎ 212/769-5100. www.amnh.org. Suggested admission $8 adults ($13 with 1 IMAX movie, $16 with 2), $6 seniors and students ($9 with 1 IMAX movie, $12 with 2), $4.50 children 2–12 ($7 with 1 IMAX movie, $9 with 2). Sun–Thurs 10am–5:45pm, Fri–Sat 10am–8:45pm. Subway: B, C to 81st St.; 1, 9 to 79th St.

This 4-block-square museum houses the world's greatest natural-science collection in a group of buildings overflowing with neo-Gothic charm. If you spent the whole day in the museum, you still

Midtown Attractions

Barneys New York
Bloomingdale's
Central Park Wildlife Center/
  Tisch Children's Zoo
Chrysler Building
Circle Line Sightseeing Cruises
Empire State Building
Grand Central Terminal
Henri Bendel
International Center of
  Photography–Midtown
Intrepid Sea-Air-Space
  Museum
Macy's
Morgan Library
Museum of Modern Art
NYCVB Visitor Information
  Center
Rockefeller Center
Saks Fifth Avenue
Times Square Visitors Center
United Nations

Uptown Attractions

American Museum of
  Natural History 5
Barneys New York 10
Bloomingdale's 11
Central Park 6
Central Park Wildlife Center/
  Tisch Children's Zoo 9
Cooper-Hewitt National
  Design Museum 2
The Frick Collection 8
International Center of
  Photography 1
Metropolitan Museum of Art 4
Solomon R. Guggenheim
  Museum 3
Whitney Museum of
  American Art 7

wouldn't get to everything. If you don't have a lot of time, you can see the best of the best on free **highlights tours** offered daily every hour at 15 minutes after the hour from 10:15am to 3:15pm. Free daily **spotlights tours,** thematic tours that change monthly, are also offered; stop by an information desk for the day's schedule. **Audio Expeditions,** high-tech audio tours that allow you to access narration in the order you choose, are also available to help you make sense of it all.

If you only see one exhibit, see the ✪ **dinosaurs**, which take up the entire fourth floor. Start in the **Orientation Room,** where a

short video gives an overview of the 500 million years of evolutionary history that led to you. Continue to the **Vertebrate Origins Room,** where huge models of ancient fish and turtles hang overhead, with plenty of interactive exhibits and kid-level displays on hand to keep young minds fascinated. Next come the great **dinosaur halls,** with mammoth, spectacularly reconstructed skeletons and more interactive displays. **Mammals and Their Extinct Relatives** shows how yesterday's prehistoric monsters have evolved into today's modern animals. Simply marvelous—you could spend hours in these halls alone.

Many other areas of the museum pale in comparison. The **animal habitat dioramas** and **halls of peoples** seem a bit dated but still have something to teach, especially the Native-American halls. Other than peeking in to see the giant whale (viewable from the cafe below) skip the **Ocean Life** room altogether; let's hope this is next on the restoration agenda. The new **Hall of Biodiversity** is an impressive multimedia exhibit, but the doom-and-gloom story it tells about the future of rain forests and other natural habitats may be too much for the little ones. Kids 5 years and older should head to the **Discovery Room,** with lots of hands-on exhibits and experiments.

The museum excels at **special exhibitions,** so I recommend checking to see what will be on while you're in town. In addition, an **IMAX Theater** shows neat films like *Cosmic Voyage* and *Africa's Elephant Kingdom* on a four-story screen. The **Hayden Planetarium** closed in 1997 for demolition and reconstruction that should be completed in 2000, but Beavis and Buttheads (and I say that fondly) can still see **laser light shows**—including U2 and Laser Zeppelin in 3D—Friday and Saturday at 9 and 10pm. Tickets are $9; call ☎ 212/769-5200 to reserve.

☼ Metropolitan Museum of Art. Fifth Ave. at 82nd St. ☎ **212/535-7710.** www.metmuseum.org. Suggested admission (includes same-day entrance to the Cloisters) $10 adults, $5 students and seniors, free for children under 12 when accompanied by an adult. Tues–Thurs and Sun 9:30am–5:15pm, Fri–Sat 9:30am–8:45pm. No strollers allowed Sun (back carriers available at 81st St. entrance coat-check area). Subway: 4, 5, 6 to 86th St.

Home to blockbuster after blockbuster exhibition, the Metropolitan Museum of Art attracts some 5 million people a year, more than any other spot in New York City. And it's no wonder—this place is magnificent. At 1.6 million square feet, this is the largest museum in the Western Hemisphere. Nearly all the world's cultures are on display through the ages—from Egyptian mummies to Islamic carvings to Renaissance paintings to Native-American masks to 20th-century decorative arts—and masterpieces are the rule. You could go once a week for a lifetime and still find something new on each visit.

So unless you plan on spending your entire vacation in the museum (some people do), you cannot see the entire collection. My recommendation is to give it a good day—or better yet, 2^1/2 days so you don't burn out. One good way to get an overview is to take advantage of the little-known **Highlights Tour.** Call ☎ **212/570-3711** (Mon–Fri 9am–5pm) or visit the museum's Web site for a schedule of this and subject-specific tours.

The least overwhelming way to see the Met on your own is to pick up a map in the entry hall and concentrate on what you like. Highlights include the American Wing's **Garden Court,** with its 19th-century sculpture, the lower-level **Costume Hall,** and the **Frank Lloyd Wright Room.** The **Roman and Greek galleries** are overwhelming, but in a marvelous way, as is the collection of later **Chinese art.** The setting of the **Temple of Dendur** is dramatic, in a specially built glass-walled gallery with Central Park views. But it all depends on what your interests are. Don't forget the marvelous **special exhibitions.** If you'd like to plan your visit ahead of time, the museum's Web site is a useful tool; there's also a list of current exhibitions in the Friday and Sunday editions of *The New York Times.*

Special programs abound. To purchase tickets for concerts and lectures, call ☎ **212/570-3949** (Mon–Sat 9:30am–5pm). On Friday and Saturday evenings, the Met stays open late not only for art viewing but also for cocktails in the Great Hall Balcony Bar (4–8:30pm) and classical music.

If you're interested in the medieval age, head to the **Cloisters,** a branch of the Met in uptown Manhattan, at the north end of Fort Tryon Park (☎ **212/923-3700;** www.metmuseum.org/htmlfile/gallery/cloister/cloister.html).

✪ **Museum of Modern Art.** 11 W. 53rd St. (btw. Fifth and Sixth aves.). ☎ **212/708-9400.** www.moma.org. Admission $9.50 adults ($13.50 with audio tour), $6.50 seniors and students ($10.50 with audio tour), free for children under 16 accompanied by an adult; pay as you wish Fri 4:30–8:15pm. Sat–Tues and Thurs 10:30am–5:45pm, Fri 10:30am–8:15pm. Subway: E, F to Fifth Ave.; B, D, F, Q to 47–50th sts./Rockefeller Center.

MoMA boasts the world's greatest collection of painting and sculpture ranging from the late 19th century to the present, including everything from van Gogh's *Starry Night,* Picasso's early *Les Demoiselles d'Avignon,* Monet's *Water Lilies,* and Klimt's *The Kiss* to later masterworks by Frida Kahlo, Andy Warhol, Robert Rauschenberg, and many others. Top that off with an extensive collection of photography, architectural models and furniture (including the Mies van der Rohe Collection), iconic design objects ranging from tableware to sports cars, and film and video, and you have quite a museum. If you're into modernism, this is the place.

While not quite Met-sized, MoMA is probably still more than you can see in a day. In true modern style, the museum is efficient and well organized, so it's easy to focus on your primary interests. For an overview, take the **self-guided tour** that stops at the collection's highlights. Be sure to check out the sculpture garden—an island of trees and fountains containing works by Calder, Moore, and Rodin. In addition, there's usually at least one beautifully mounted special exhibition in house that's worth a trip. MoMA boasts a host of special programs, from hour-long family-oriented gallery on Saturdays at 10am to live jazz three evenings a week in **Sette MoMA,** the museum's notable Italian restaurant; call ☎ 212/708-9781 or visit the museum's Web site to see what's on while you're in town. Additionally, there's always a multifaceted film and video program on the schedule; call the main number to see what's on. Films are included in the price of admission, but arrive early to make sure you get a seat.

Solomon R. Guggenheim Museum. 1071 Fifth Ave. (at 88th St.). ☎ **212/423-3500.** www.guggenheim.org. Admission $12 adults, $7 seniors, children under 12 free; Fri 6–8pm pay what you wish. Two-museum pass, which includes one admission to the SoHo branch valid for 1 week, $16 adults, $10 seniors. Sun–Wed 10am–6pm, Fri–Sat 10am–8pm. Subway: 4, 5, 6 to 86th St.

It has been called a bun, a snail, a concrete tornado, and even a giant wedding cake. Whatever descriptive you choose to apply, Frank Lloyd Wright's only New York building, completed in 1959, is undeniably a brilliant work of architecture—so impressive that it competes with the art for your attention. If you're looking for the city's best modern art, head to MoMA or the Whitney first; come to the Guggenheim to see the house.

It's easy to see the bulk of what's on display in 2 to 4 hours. Inside, a spiraling rotunda circles over a slowly inclined ramp that leads you past changing exhibits, which can range from modern masterworks from the Centre Pompidou to the Art of the Motorcycle. Usually the progression is counterintuitive: from the first floor up, rather than from the sixth floor down. If you're not sure, ask a guard before you begin. Permanent exhibits of 19th- and 20th-century art, including strong holdings of Kandinsky, Klee, Picasso, and French impressionists, occupy a stark annex called the **Tower Galleries,** an addition accessible at every level.

The Guggenheim runs some interesting special programs, including free docent tours (there's a one-hour highlights tour daily at noon), film screenings, and the World Beat Jazz Series on Friday and Saturday evenings from 5 to 8pm.

✪ **Whitney Museum of American Art.** 945 Madison Ave. (at 75th St.). ☎ **212/570-3600** or 212/570-3676. www.echonyc.com/~whitney. Admission $9 adults, $7 seniors and students, free for children under 12; pay as you wish Thurs 6–8pm. Wed and Fri–Sun 11am–6pm, Thurs 11am–8pm. Subway: 6 to 77th St.

What is arguably the finest collection of 20th-century American art in the world belongs to the Whitney thanks to the efforts of Gertrude Vanderbilt Whitney. A sculptor herself, she organized exhibitions by American artists shunned by traditional academies, assembled a sizable personal collection, and founded the museum in 1930 in Greenwich Village.

Today's museum is an imposing presence on Madison Avenue—an inverted three-tiered pyramid of concrete and gray granite with seven seemingly random windows designed by Marcel Breuer, a leader of the Bauhaus movement. The rotating permanent collection consists of an intelligent selection of major works by Edward Hopper, Georgia O'Keeffe, Roy Lichtenstein, Jasper Johns, and other significant artists. A pleasing new fifth-floor exhibit space, the museum's first devoted exclusively to works from its permanent collection from 1900 to 1950, opened in 1998.

There are usually several simultaneous shows, typically all well curated and more edgy than what you'd see at MoMA or the Guggenheim. Topics range from topical surveys, such as "American Art in the Age of Technology" to in-depth retrospectives of famous or lesser-known movements (such as Fluxus, the movement that spawned Yoko Ono, among others) and artists (Mark Rothko, Keith Haring, Duane Hanson, Bob Thompson).

The next **Whitney Biennial** is scheduled for spring 2000. A major event on the national museum calendar, the Biennials serve as the premier launching pad for new American artists working in the vanguard of every media. The millennial edition promises to be an exciting and much-talked-about event.

Free **gallery tours** are offered daily; call ☎ **212/570-3676** for the current schedule, or check at the Information desk when you arrive.

MORE MUSEUMS

✪ **Cooper-Hewitt National Design Museum.** 2 E. 91st St. (at Fifth Ave.). ☎ **212/849-8300.** www.si.edu/ndm. Admission $5 adults, $3 seniors and students, free for children under 12; free to all Tues 5–9pm. Tues 10am–9pm, Wed–Sat 10am–5pm, Sun noon–5pm. Subway: 4, 5, 6 to 86th St.

Part of the Smithsonian Institution, the Cooper-Hewitt is housed in the Carnegie Mansion, built by steel magnate Andrew Carnegie in 1901. Some 11,000 square feet of gallery space is devoted to changing exhibits that are invariably well conceived, engaging, and educational. Exhibitions scheduled for late 1999–2000 include a retrospective on the work of Charles and Ray Eames and the National Design Triennial, featuring the work of both well-known and emerging talents as they address the pressing design issues of today.

✪ **The Frick Collection.** 1 E. 70th St. (at Fifth Ave.). ☎ **212/288-0700.** www.frick.org. Admission $7 adults, $5 seniors and students. Children under 10 not admitted; children 10–16 must be accompanied by an adult. Tues–Sat 10am–6pm, Sun and minor holidays 1–6pm (closed all major holidays). Subway: 6 to 68th St./Hunter College.

To house his treasures and himself, steel magnate Henry Clay Frick hired architects Carrère & Hastings to build this 18th-century-French–style mansion (1914), one of the most beautiful remaining on Fifth Avenue. This is a living testament to New York's vanished Gilded Age: The interior still feels like a private home (albeit a really, really rich guy's home) graced with beautiful paintings, rather than a museum. Come here to see the classics, by some of the world's most famous painters: Titian, Rembrandt, Turner, Vermeer, El Greco, and Goya, to name only a few. A highlight is the **Fragonard Room,** graced with the sensual rococo series *The Progress of Love.* The portrait of Montesquiou by Whistler is also stunning. Sculpture, furniture, Chinese vases, and French enamels complement the paintings and round out the collection. Included in the price of admission, the AcousticGuide audio tour is particularly useful, because it allows you to follow your own path rather than a proscribed route.

In addition to the permanent collection, the Frick regularly mounts small, well-focused temporary exhibitions, such as "Victorian Fairy Painting" and "Constable, A Master Draughtsman."

International Center of Photography & ICP–Midtown. Uptown branch: 1130 Fifth Ave. (at 94th St.) ☎ **212/860-1777.** Midtown branch: 1133 Sixth Ave. (at 43rd St.). ☎ **212/768-4682.** www.icp.org. Admission (includes both Uptown and Midtown locations) $6 adults, $4 seniors, $1 children under 13; Tues 5–8pm pay what you wish. Tues–Thurs 10am–5pm, Fri 10am–8pm, Sat and Sun 10am–6pm. Subway: 6 to 96th St. to ICP Uptown; B, D, F, Q to 42nd St. to ICP Midtown.

The ICP is one of the world's premier collectors and exhibitors of photographic art, mounting some of the most interesting changing art exhibits in the city. The original ICP is also worth a look, but the Midtown branch is twice the size of the original and usually has two mounted exhibitions rather than just one. The emphasis is on contemporary photographic works, but historically important photographers aren't ignored. Topics can range from "Man Ray: Photography and its Double" to "Soul of the Game: Images and Voices of Street Basketball." A must on any photography buff's list.

***Intrepid* Sea-Air-Space Museum.** Pier 86 (W. 46th St. at Twelfth Ave.).
☎ **212/245-0072.** www.intrepid-museum.com. Admission $10 adults; $7.50
veterans, seniors, and students; $5 children 6–11; first child under 6 free, each
extra child $1. May–Sept, Mon–Sat 10am–5pm (last admission 4pm),
Sun 10am–6pm (last admission 5pm); Oct–Apr, Wed–Sun 10am–5pm (last
admission 4pm). Subway: A, C, E to 42nd St. Bus: M42 crosstown.

The most astonishing thing about the aircraft carrier USS *Intrepid*
is how it can be simultaneously so big and so small. It's a few
football fields long, holds 40 aircraft, and sometimes doubles as a
ballroom for society functions. But stand there and think about
landing an A-12 jet on the deck and suddenly, it's minuscule. Now
a National Historic Landmark, the exhibit also includes the
destroyer USS *Edison,* the submarine USS *Growler,* and the lightship
Nantucket, as well as a collection of vintage and modern aircraft.
Kids just love this place. But think twice about going in winter—
it's almost impossible to heat an aircraft carrier.

⊙ **Lower East Side Tenement Museum.** Visitors' Center at 90 Orchard St.
(at Broome St.). ☎ **212/431-0233.** www.wnet.org/tenement. $8 adults, $6
seniors and students for 1 tenement tour; $14 adults, $10 seniors and students
for any 2 tours; $20 adults, $14 seniors and students for all 3 tours. Tenement
tours depart Tues–Fri every half hour 1–4pm; Thurs hourly 6pm–9pm; Sat–Sun
every half hour 11am–4:30pm. Subway: F to Delancey St.; B, D, Q to Grand St.

This decade-old museum is the first-ever National Trust for Historic
Preservation site that was not the home of someone rich or famous.
It's something quite different: A five-story tenement that 10,000
people from 25 countries called home between 1863 and 1935—
people who had come to the United States looking for the American dream, and made 97 Orchard St. their first stop. This living history museum tells the story of the great immigration boom of the
late 19th and early 20th centuries, when the Lower East Side was
considered the "Gateway to America." A visit here makes a good
follow-up to an Ellis Island trip—what happened to all the people
who passed through that famous waystation?

The only way to see the museum is by guided tour. The primary
tenement tour, offered on all open days, is a satisfying way to explore
the museum. A knowledgeable guide leads you into the dingy urban
time capsule, where several apartments have been faithfully restored
to their exact lived-in condition, and recounts the real-life stories of
the families who occupied them in fascinating detail. Tours are limited in number, so it pays to reserve ahead.

❖ **Morgan Library.** 29 E. 36th St. (at Madison Ave.). ☎ **212/685-0008.**
www.shop.morganlibrary.org. Admission $7 adults, $5 seniors, children under
12 free. Tues–Thurs 10:30am–5pm, Fri 10:30am–8pm, Sat 10:30am–6pm, Sun
noon–6pm. Subway: 6 to 33rd St.

Here's an undiscovered New York treasure, boasting one of the
world's most important collections of original manuscripts, rare
books and bindings, master drawings, and personal writings. Among
the remarkable artifacts on display are stunning illuminated manuscripts (including Guttenberg bibles); a working draft of the U.S.
Constitution bearing copious handwritten notes; and handwritten
scores by the likes of Beethoven, Mozart, and Puccini. The collection of mostly 19th-century drawings—featuring works by Seurat,
Degas, Rubens, and other great masters—have an excitement of
immediacy about them that the artists' more well-known paintings
often lack. This rich repository originated as the private collection
of turn-of-the-century financier J. Pierpont Morgan and is housed
in a landmark Renaissance-style palazzo building (1906) he commis-
sioned from McKim, Mead & White. Morgan's library and study
are preserved virtually intact, and worth a look. The special exhibitions are particularly well chosen and curated, and a reading room
is available by appointment.

Museum of Jewish Heritage—A Living Memorial to the Holocaust.
18 First Place (at Battery Place), Battery Park City. ☎ **212/968-1800.**
www.mjhnyc.org. Admission $7 adults, $5 seniors and students, children under 5 free. Sun–Wed 9am–5pm, Thurs 9am–8pm, Fri and evenings of Jewish
holidays 9am–2pm. Subway: 1, 9 to South Ferry; 4, 5 to Bowling Green.

Located in the south end of Battery Park City, the Museum of
Jewish Heritage occupies a strikingly spare six-sided building designed
by award-winning architect Kevin Roche, with a six-tier roof evoking
the Star of David and the 6 million murdered in the Holocaust. The
permanent exhibits—"Jewish Life a Century Ago," "The War Against
the Jews," and "Jewish Renewal"—recount the daily pre-war lives, the
unforgettable horror that destroyed them, and the tenacious renewal
experienced by European and immigrant Jews. Their stories are
powerfully told through the objects, photographs, documents, and,
most poignantly, through the videotaped testimonies of Holocaust vic-
tims, survivors, and their families, all chronicled by Steven Spielberg's
Survivors of the Shoah Visual History Foundation.

   Advance tickets are highly recommended to guarantee admission,
and can be purchased by calling ☎ **212/786-0820, ext. 111** or
Ticketmaster (☎ **800/307-4007** or 212/307-4007; www.
ticketmaster.com).

4 The Top Skyscrapers & Architectural Marvels

For details on the **World Trade Center,** see p. 127. For the **Brooklyn Bridge,** see p. 124.

Chrysler Building. 405 Lexington Ave. (at 42nd St.). Subway: 4, 5, 6, 7, S to 42nd St.–Grand Central.

Built as Chrysler Corporation headquarters in 1930 (they moved out decades ago), this is perhaps the 20th century's most romantic architectural achievement, especially at night, when the lights in its triangular openings play off its steely crown. A recent cleaning added new sparkle. As you admire its facade, be sure to note the gargoyles reaching out from the upper floors, looking for all the world like streamline-Gothic hood ornaments.

The observation deck closed long ago, but you can visit the lavish ground-floor interior, which is art deco to the max. The ceiling mural depicting airplanes and other early marvels of the first decades of the 20th century evince the bright promise of technology. The elevators are works of art, masterfully covered in exotic woods.

✪ Empire State Building. 350 Fifth Ave. (at 34th St.). ☎ **212/736-3100.** www.esbnyc.com. Observatory admission $6 adults, $3 seniors and children under 12, free for children under 5. Daily 9:30am–midnight (tickets sold until 11:30pm). Subway: B, D, F, Q, N, R to 34th St.; 6 to 33rd St.

King Kong climbed it in 1933. A plane slammed into it in 1945. The World Trade Center superseded it in 1970 as the island's tallest building. And in 1997, a gunman ascended it to stage a deadly shooting. But through it all, the Empire State Building has remained one of the city's favorite landmarks, and its signature high-rise. Completed in 1931, it climbs 102 stories (1,454 feet) and now harbors the offices of fashion firms and, in its upper reaches, a jumble of high-tech broadcast equipment.

Always a conversation piece, the Empire State Building glows every night, bathed in colored floodlights to commemorate events of significance (red, white, and blue for Independence Day; green for St. Patrick's Day; even lavender and white for Gay Pride Day). The familiar silver spire can be seen from all over the city. My favorite view of the building is from 23rd Street, where Fifth Avenue and Broadway converge: On a lovely day, stand at the base of the Flatiron Building and gaze up Fifth; the crisp, gleaming deco tower jumps out, soaring above the sooty office buildings that surround it.

But the views that keep nearly 3 million visitors coming every year are the ones from the 86th- and 102nd-floor **observatories.** The

Empire State Ticket-Buying Tip

Lines can be frightfully long at the concourse-level ticket booth, so be prepared to wait. Or, if time is more precious than money to you, consider purchasing **advance tickets** online using a credit card at **www.esbnyc.org.** You'll pay a $2 service charge for the service, but it's well worth it, especially if you're visiting during a busy season. You're not required to choose a time or date for your tickets in advance; they can be used on any regular open day. However, order them well before you leave home, because they'll take 7 to 10 days to reach you (longer if you live out of the country). With tickets in hand, you're allowed to proceed directly to the second floor—past everyone who didn't plan as well as you did!

lower one is best—you can walk out on a windy deck and look through coin-operated viewers (bring quarters!) over what, on a clear day, can be as much as an 80-mile visible radius. The citywide panorama is magnificent. The higher observation deck is glass-enclosed and cramped.

Light fog can create an admirably moody effect, but it goes without saying that a clear day is best. Dusk brings the most remarkable views, and the biggest crowds. Consider going in the morning, when the light is still low on the horizon, keeping glare to a minimum. Starry nights are pure magic.

✪ **Grand Central Terminal.** 42nd St. at Park Ave. www.grand centralterminal.com. Subway: 4, 5, 6, 7, S to 42nd St.–Grand Central.

After more than two years and $175 million, Grand Central Terminal has come out from under the tarps and scaffolding. Rededicated with all the appropriate pomp and circumstance on October 1, 1998, the 1913 landmark has been reborn as one of the most magnificent public spaces in the country.

By all means, come and visit, even if you're not catching one of the subway lines or Metro North commuter trains that rumble through the bowels of this great place. And even if you arrive and leave by subway, be sure to exit the station, walking a couple of blocks south, to about 40th Street, before you turn around to admire Jules-Alexis Coutan's neoclassical sculpture *Transportation* hovering over the south entrance, with a majestically buff Mercury, the Roman god of commerce and travel, as its central figure.

The greatest visual impact hits when you enter the vast **main concourse.** Cleansed of decades of grime and cheezy advertisements, it boasts renewed majesty. The masterful **sky ceiling,** again a brilliant greenish blue, depicts the constellations of the winter sky above New York. The stars are surrounded by dazzling 24-karat gold and emit light fed through fiber-optic cables, their intensities roughly replicating the magnitude of the actual stars as seen from Earth. Look carefully, and you'll see a patch near one corner left unrestored as a reminder of the neglect once visited on this splendid overhead masterpiece. On the east end of the main concourse, a grand **marble staircase** has been built, as the original plans had always intended.

This dramatic beaux-arts splendor serves as a hub of social activity as well. New retail shops and restaurants have taken over the mezzanine and lower levels. The highlight of the mezzanine is **Michael Jordan's—The Steak House,** a gorgeous art-deco space; stop into the welcoming, comfortable bar, where you can enjoy the marvelous views for the price of a drink. Off the main concourse at street level there's a nice mix of specialty shops and national retailers, including **Banana Republic** and **Kenneth Cole.** The **lower concourse** houses newsstands, a food court, and the famous **Oyster Bar,** also restored to its original Old World glory (see chapter 4).

✪ **Rockefeller Center.** Between 47th and 50th sts., from Fifth to Sixth aves. ☎ **212/632-3975.** Subway: B, D, F, Q to 47th–50th sts./Rockefeller Center.

A streamline moderne masterpiece, Rockefeller Center is one of New York's central gathering spots for visitors and New Yorkers alike. A prime example of the city's skyscraper spirit and historic sense of optimism, it was erected mainly in the 1930s, when the city was deep in a depression as well as its most passionate art deco phase. Designated a National Historic Landmark in 1988, it's now the world's largest privately owned business-and-entertainment center, with 18 buildings on 21 acres.

For a dramatic approach to the entire complex, start at Fifth Avenue between 49th and 50th streets. The builders purposely created the gentle slope of the Promenade, known here as the **Channel Gardens** because it's flanked to the south by La Maison Française and to the north by the British Building (the Channel, get it?). You'll also find a number of attractive shops along here, including a big branch of the **Metropolitan Museum of Art Store,** a good stop for elegant gifts (many of them quite affordable. The Promenade leads to the **Lower Plaza,** home to the famous ice-skating rink in winter (see below) and alfresco dining in summer in the shadow of Paul Manship's gilded bronze statue *Prometheus*, more notable for its setting than its magnificence as an artwork. All around the flags of the United Nations' member countries flap in the breeze. Just behind *Prometheus*, in December and early January, towers the city's official and majestic Christmas tree.

The **Rink at Rockefeller Plaza** (☎ 212/332-7654), is tiny but positively romantic, especially during the holidays, when the giant Christmas tree's multicolored lights twinkle from above. It's open from mid-October to mid-March, and you'll skate under the magnificent tree for the month of December.

The focal point of this "city within a city" is the **GE Building,** at 30 Rockefeller Plaza, a 70-story showpiece towering over the plaza. You can pick up a walking tour brochure highlighting the center's art and architecture at the main information desk in this building.

NBC television maintains studios throughout the complex. *Saturday Night Live,* the *Rosie O'Donnell Show,* and *Late Night with Conan O'Brien* originate in the GE Building; call ☎ 212/664-4000 for tips on getting tickets. If you're a fan of NBC's *Today Show,* the glass-enclosed studio from which the show is broadcast live weekdays from 7 to 9am is on the southwest corner of 49th Street and Rockefeller Plaza; come early if you want a visible spot, and bring your HI MOM! sign. Who knows? You may even get to chat with Katie, Matt, or Al in a segment. One-hour **NBC Studio Tours** (☎ 212/664-7174) are $10 per person (children under 6 are not admitted).

United Nations. At First Ave. and 46th St. ☎ **212/963-8687.** www.un.org. Guided tours $7.50 adults, $5.50 seniors, $4.50 students, $3.50 children (those under 5 not permitted). Daily tours every half hour 9:15am–4:45pm; closed weekends Jan–Feb. Subway: 4, 5, 6, 7, S to 42nd St.–Grand Central.

In the midst of what some consider the world's most cynical city is this working monument to world peace. The U.N. headquarters occupies 18 acres of international territory—neither New York City nor the United States has jurisdiction here—along the East River from 42nd to 48th streets. Designed by an international team of architects (led by American Wallace K. Harrison and including Le Corbusier) and finished in 1952, the complex weds the 39-story glass slab Secretariat with the free-form General Assembly on beautifully landscaped grounds donated by John D. Rockefeller, Jr., along the East River. One hundred eighty nations use the facilities to arbitrate worldwide disputes.

Guided one-hour tours take you to the General Assembly Hall and the Security Council Chamber and introduce the history and activities of the United Nations and its related organizations. Along the tour you'll see donated objects and artwork, including charred artifacts that survived the atomic bombs at Hiroshima and Nagasaki, stained-glass windows by Chagall, a replica of the first *Sputnik*, and a colorful mosaic called *The Golden Rule,* based on a Norman Rockwell drawing, which was a gift from the United States in 1985.

The **Delegates' Dining Room** (☎ 212/963-7625), which affords great views of the East River, is open to the public on weekdays for lunch 11:30am to 2:30pm (reserve in advance). The **post office** sells unique United Nations stamps that can be purchased and posted only here.

5 Affordable Sightseeing Tours

DOUBLE-DECKER BUS TOURS

Taking a narrated sightseeing tour is one of the best ways to see and learn quickly about New York's major sights and neighborhoods. However, keep in mind that the commentary is only as good as the guide, who is seldom an expert. Enjoy the ride—and take the "facts" you hear along the way with a grain of salt.

Gray Line New York Tours. In the Port Authority Bus Terminal, Eighth Ave. and 42nd St. ☎ **212/397-2600.** www.graylinenewyork.com. Hop-on, hop-off bus tours from $22 adults, $13 children 5–11; basic full-city tour $33 adults, $21 children. Check Web site for online booking discounts (10% at press time). Operates daily. Subway: A, C, E to 42nd St.

Gray Line offers just about every sightseeing tour option and combination you could want. There are double-decker bus tours by day and by night that run uptown, downtown, and all around the town, as well as bus combos with Circle Line cruises, helicopter flights, museum entrances, and guided visits of sights. Two-day options are available, as are some out-of-town day trips (even a full day at Woodbury Commons, if you can't resist an opportunity for outlet shopping).

There's no real point to purchasing some combination tours—you don't need a guide to take you to the top of the World Trade Center or to the Statue of Liberty, and you don't save any money on admission by buying the combo ticket—but others, such as the Sunday Harlem Gospel tour, which features a tour of Harlem's top sights and a gospel service, is well worth the $33 price tag ($24 for kids 5 to 11). I've found Gray Line to put a higher premium on accuracy than the other big tour-bus operators, so this is your best bet among the biggies. There's also a sales office in the **Times Square Visitors Center,** 1560 Broadway, between 46th and 47th streets.

HARBOR CRUISES

If you'd like to sail the New York Harbor aboard the 1885 cargo schooner *Pioneer*, see the listing for **South Street Seaport & Museum** on p. 126.

✪ **Circle Line Sightseeing Cruises.** Departing from Pier 83, at W. 42nd St. and Twelfth Ave and Pier 16 at South Street Seaport. ☎ **212/563-3200.** Also departing from Pier 16 at South Street Seaport, 207 Front St. ☎ **212/630-8888.** www.circleline.com. Cruises from $12 adults, $6 children under 12; 3-hour Full Island cruise $22 adults, $12 children. Operates daily. Subway to Pier 83: A, C, E to 42nd St. Subway to Pier 16: J, M, Z, 2, 3, 4, 5 to Fulton Street.

Circle Line is the only tour company that circumnavigates the entire 35 miles around Manhattan, and I love this ride. It takes three hours and passes by the World Trade Center, the Statue of Liberty, Ellis Island, the Brooklyn Bridge, the United Nations, Yankee Stadium, the George Washington Bridge, and more, including Manhattan's wild northern tip. The panorama is riveting, and the commentary is surprisingly good. The big boats are basic but fine, with lots of deck room for everybody to enjoy the view. Snacks and drinks are available on-board for purchase.

If three hours is more than you or the kids can handle, go for either the 1¹/₂-hour **Semi-Circle** or **Sunset** cruise ($18 adults, $10 kids), both of which show you the highlights of the skyline. There's also a one-hour **Seaport Liberty** version ($12 adults, $6 kids) that sticks close to the south end of the island. But of all the tours, the kids might like *The Beast* best, a thrill-a-minute speedboat ride offered in summer only ($15 adults, $10 kids).

SPECIALTY TOURS
MUSEUMS & CULTURAL ORGANIZATIONS

The **92nd Street Y** (☎ 212/415-5628 or 212/415-5420; www.92ndsty.org) offers a wonderful variety of **walking tours,** many featuring funky themes or behind-the-scenes visits. Subjects can range from "Diplomat for a Day at the U.N" to "Artists of the Meatpacking District" to "Jewish Harlem." Prices range from $18 to $60, but many include ferry rides, afternoon tea, dinner, or whatever suits the program. Advance registration is required for all tours. Schedules are planned out a few months in advance, so check the Web site for tours that might interest you.

One of the most highly praised sightseeing organizations in New York is ✪ **Big Onion Walking Tours** (☎ 212/439-1090; www.bigonion.com). Enthusiastic Big Onion guides (all hold an advanced degree in American history from Columbia or New York

Show Me, Show Me, Show Me: Free Walking Tours

A number of neighborhood organizations and business improvement districts (BIDs) offer free guided walks to highlight the new developments and hidden joys of their neighborhoods. For travelers on a budget, these introductory freebies are well worth taking advantage of:

The **34th Street Tour,** sponsored by the 34th Street Partnership (☎ **212/868-0521**), reveals the stories behind the buildings under the guidance of an architectural historian and an architect. Tours are offered Thursdays at 12:30pm; meet at the Fifth Avenue entrance to the Empire State Building.

The **Times Square Tour,** sponsored by the Times Square Visitors Center, 1560 Broadway, between 46th and 47th streets (☎ **212/768-1560;** www.timessquarebid.org), offers a behind-the-scenes look at the Theater District's architecture, history, and current trends. Led by an actor, the tours are animated and enlightening. Be at the center Friday at noon.

The **Orchard Street Bargain District Tour,** sponsored by the Lower East Side Business Improvement District (☎ **888/VALUES-4-U** or 212/226-9010), explores the general history and long-standing retail culture of this historic neighborhood. This is a particularly good bet for bargain-hunters, who will learn all about the famous Old World shops and newer outlet stores in this discount-shopping destination. The free tours are offered Sundays at 11am from April to December, rain or shine, and no reservation is required. Meet up with the guide in front of Katz's Delicatessen, 205 E. Houston St., at Ludlow Street.

Although none of the above tours require reservations, it's a good idea to call ahead to confirm meeting times and places, since life is always subject to change.

On Wednesdays at 12:30pm, the Municipal Art Society sponsors a free tour of **Grand Central Terminal** (although donations are accepted); call ☎ **212/935-3960** to confirm the schedule and meeting spot.

If you're looking to tour another neighborhood with an expert guide, call **Big Apple Greeter** (☎ **212/669-8159;** www.bigapplegreeter.org). This non-profit organization is comprised of specially trained New Yorkers who volunteer to take visitors around town for a free 2- to 4-hour tour of a particular neighborhood. Reservations must be made in advance, preferably at least 1 week ahead of your arrival.

universities) peel back the layers of history to reveal the city's inner secrets on two-hour walking tours that range from "Presidential New York" to a multi-ethnic eating tour of the Lower East Side. Prices range from $10 to $16 for adults, $8 to $14 for students and seniors. No reservations are necessary, but Big Onion strongly recommends that you call to verify schedules.

All tours offered by ✪ **Joyce Gold History Tours of New York** (☎ 212/242-5762; www.nyctours.com) are led by Joyce Gold herself, an instructor of Manhattan history at New York University and the New School for Social Research. Joyce is full of fascinating stories about Manhattan and its people. Tours are arranged around themes like "The Colonial Settlers of Wall Street," "The Genius and Elegance of Gramercy Park," and "TriBeCa: The Creative Explosion." Tours are offered most weekends March to December and last from 2 to 4 hours. The price is $12 per person; no reservations are required.

Behind the scenes is the focus of **Adventure on a Shoestring** (☎ **212/265-2663**), a membership organization that offers 1¼-hour public walking tours on weekends year-round for just $5. Howard Goldberg has provided unique views of New York since 1963, exploring Manhattan's neighborhoods with a breezy, man-of-the-people style. Call for reservations.

For 18 years Larcelia Kebe, owner of **Harlem Your Way! Tours Unlimited** (☎ 212/690-1687; www.harlemyourway.com), has been leading visitors around Harlem on bus and walking tours that take you beyond the snapshot stops at major sights (though they're all included). She shares Harlem's distinct culture on spirited tours of brownstones, churches, jazz clubs, and soul-food restaurants. Walking tours are $25 to $48 per person, and bus tours are $35 to $55.

6 Central Park

Without this miracle of civic planning, Manhattan would be a virtual unbroken block of buildings. Instead, smack in the middle of Gotham, an 843-acre natural retreat provides a daily escape valve and tranquilizer for millions of New Yorkers.

While you're in the city, be sure to take advantage of the park's many charms—not the least of which is its sublime layout. Frederick Law Olmstead and Calvert Vaux won a competition with a plan that marries flowing paths with sinewy bridges, integrating them into the natural rolling landscape with its rocky outcroppings, man-made lakes and wooded pockets. The designers predicted the hustle and bustle to come, and tactfully hid traffic from the eyes and ears of parkgoers by building roads that are largely hidden from the bucolic view.

Central Park

American Museum of
    Natural History **6**
Alice in Wonderland Statue **12**
Arsenal **25**
The Bandshell **17**
Belvedere Castle **8**
Bethesda Terrace
    & Bethesda Fountain **15**
Bow Bridge **14**
Carousel **20**
Central Park Wildlife Center **26**
Charles A. Dana
    Discovery Center **1**
Chess and Checkers House **21**
Conservatory Garden **1**
Conservatory Water **11**
The Dairy Information Center **22**
Delacorte Clock **24**
Delacorte Theater **7**
Diana Ross Playground **6**
Hans Christian Anderson
    Statue **10**
Harlem Meer **1**
Hecksher Playground **28**
Henry Luce
    Nature Observatory **8**
Imagine Mosaic **16**
Loeb Boathouse **13**
The Mall **18**
Metropolitan Museum of Art **3**
The Obelisk
    (Cleopatra's Needle) **5**
Park View at the Boathouse **11**
Pat Hoffman Friedman
    Playground **9**
Shakespeare Garden **8**
Spector Playground **2**
Swedish Cottage
    Marionette Theatre **8**
Tavern on the Green **19**
Tisch Children's Zoo **23**
Wollman Rink **27**

Subway stop **M**

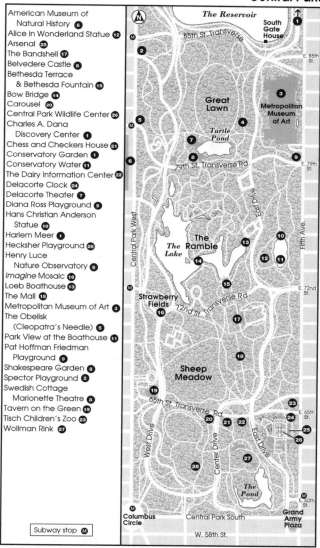

On just about any day, Central Park is crowded with New Yorkers and visitors alike. On nice days, especially weekends, it's the city's party central. Families come to play in the snow or the sun, depending on the season; in-line skaters come to fly through the crisp air and twirl in front of the bandshell; couples come to stroll or paddle the lake; and just about everybody comes to sunbathe at the first sign of summer. On beautiful days, the crowds are part of the appeal—everybody's come here to peel off their urban armor and relax, and the common goal puts a general feeling of camaraderie in the air. On these days, the people-watching is more compelling than anywhere else in the city. But one of Central Park's great appeals is that even on the most crowded days, there's always somewhere to get away from it all, if you just want a little peace and quiet, and a moment to commune with nature.

ORIENTATION & GETTING THERE   Look at your map—that great green swath in the center of Manhattan is Central Park. It runs from 59th Street (also known as Central Park South) at the south end to 110th Street at the north end, and from Fifth Avenue on the east side to Central Park West (the equivalent of Eighth Avenue) on the west side. A 6-mile rolling road, **Central Park Drive,** circles the park, and has a lane set aside for bikers, joggers, and in-line skaters. A number of **transverse** (crosstown) **roads** cross the park at major points—at 65th, 79th, 86th, and 97th streets—but they're built down a level, largely out of view, to minimize intrusion on the bucolic nature of the park.

A number of subway stops and lines serve the park, and which one you take depends on where you want to go. To reach the southernmost entrance on the west side, take an A, B, C, D, 1, or 9 to 59th Street/Columbus Circle. To reach the southeast corner entrance, take the N, R to Fifth Avenue; from this stop, it's an easy walk into the park to the **Information Center** in the **Dairy** (☎ 212/794-6564; open daily 11am to 5pm, to 4pm in winter), midpark at about 65th Street. Here you can ask questions, pick up park information, and purchase a good park map. If your time for exploring is limited, I suggest entering the park at 72nd or 79th streets for maximum exposure (subway: B, C to 72nd St. or 81st St./Museum of Natural History). From here, you can pick up park information at the visitor center at **Belvedere Castle** (☎ 212/772-0210; open Wed–Sun 11am–4pm), mid-park at 79th Street.

Food carts and vendors are set up at all of the park's main gathering points, selling hot dogs, pretzels, and ice cream, so finding a bite to eat is never a problem. You'll also find a fixed food counter at the **Conservatory,** on the east side of the park north of the 72nd Street entrance, and both casual snacks and more sophisticated drinks and dining at **Park View at the Boathouse.**

GUIDED TOURS   **Trolley tours** of the park are offered weekdays from May through November; call ☎ **212/397-3809** for details. The **Charles A. Dana Discovery Center,** at the northeast corner of the park at Harlem Meer, hosts ranger-guided tours on occasion (☎ **212/860-1370**).

FOR FURTHER INFORMATION   Call the main number at ☎ **212/360-3444** for recorded information, or 212/794-6564 to talk to a real person at the Dairy Information Center. The park also has a comprehensive Web site at **www.centralpark.org**.

SAFETY TIP   Even though the park has the lowest crime rate of any of the city's precincts, be wary, especially in the more remote northern end. It's a good idea to avoid the park entirely after dark, unless you're heading to one of the restaurants for dinner or to a Summerstage or Shakespeare in the Park event (see chapter 6), when you should stick with the crowds.

EXPLORING THE PARK

The best way to see Central Park is to wander along its 58 miles of winding paths, keeping in mind the following highlights.

Before starting your stroll, stop by the Information Center in the Dairy, midpark in a 19th-century–style building overlooking Wollman Rink at about 65th Street, to get a good park map and other information on sights and events, and to peruse the kid-friendly exhibit on the park's history and design.

The southern part of Central Park is more formally designed and heavily visited than the relatively rugged and remote northern end. Not far from the Dairy is the **carousel** with 58 hand-carved horses (open daily 10:30am to 6pm, to 5pm in winter; rides are 90¢); the **zoo** (see below), and the **Wollman Rink** for roller- or ice-skating (see "Activities," below).

Where's Balto?

The people at Central Park say that the question they're asked almost more than any other these days is "Where is the statue of Balto?" The heroic dog is just northwest of the zoo, mid-park at about 66th Street.

The Mall, a long formal walkway lined with elms shading benches and sculptures of sometimes forgotten writers, leads to the focal point of Central Park, **Bethesda Fountain** (along the 72nd Street transverse road). **Bethesda Terrace** and its grandly sculpted entryway border a large lake where dogs fetch sticks, rowboaters glide by, and dedicated early-morning anglers try their luck at catching carp, perch, catfish, and bass. You can rent a rowboat at or take a gondola ride from **Loeb Boathouse,** on the eastern end of the lake (see "Activities," below). Boats of another kind are at **Conservatory Water** (on the east side at 73rd Street), a stone-walled pond flanked by statues of both Hans Christian Andersen and Alice in Wonderland. On Saturdays at 10am, die-hard yachtsmen race remote-controlled sailboats in fierce competitions following Olympic regulations. (Sorry, model boats aren't for rent.)

If the action there is too intense, **Sheep Meadow** on the southwestern side of the park is a designated quiet zone, where Frisbee throwing and kite flying are as energetic as things get. Another respite is ✪ **Strawberry Fields,** at 72nd Street on the West Side. This memorial to John Lennon, who was murdered across the street at the Dakota apartment building (72nd Street and Central Park West, northwest corner), is a gorgeous garden centered around an Italian mosaic bearing the title of the lead Beatle's most famous solo song, and his lifelong message: IMAGINE. In keeping with its goal of promoting world peace, the garden has 161 varieties of plants, donated by each of the 161 nations in existence when it was designed in 1985. This is a wonderful place for peaceful contemplation.

Bow Bridge, a graceful lacework of cast-iron designed by Calvert Vaux, crosses over the lake and leads to the most bucolic area of Central Park, **the Ramble.** This dense 38-acre woodland with spiraling paths, rocky outcroppings, and a stream is the best spot for bird-watching and feeling as if you've discovered an unimaginably leafy forest right in the middle of the city.

North of the Ramble, **Belvedere Castle** is home to **the Henry Luce Nature Observatory** (☎ **212/772-0210**), worth a visit if you're with children. From the castle, set on Vista Rock (the park's highest point at 135 feet), you can look down on the **Great Lawn,** which has emerged lush and green from renovations, and the **Delacorte Theater,** home to **Shakespeare in the Park** (☎ **212/ 861-7277** or 212/539-8500; www.publictheater.org).

At the northeast end, **Conservatory Garden** (at 105th Street and Fifth Avenue), Central Park's only formal garden, is a magnificent display of flowers and trees reflected in calm pools of water. **Harlem**

Meer and its boathouse were recently renovated, and look beautiful. The boathouse now berths the **Dana Discovery Center** (☎ 212/860-1370; open daily 11am–5pm, to 4pm in winter), where children can learn about the environment and borrow fishing poles at no charge.

GOING TO THE ZOO

Central Park Wildlife Center/Tisch Children's Zoo. At Fifth Ave. and E. 64th St. ☎ **212/861-6030.** www.wcs.org/zoos. Admission $3.50 adults, $1.25 seniors, 50¢ children 3–12, under 3 free. Apr–Oct, Mon–Fri 10am–5pm, Sat–Sun 10:30am–5:30pm; Nov–Mar, daily 10am–4:30pm. Subway: N, R to Fifth Ave.

It has been nearly a decade since the zoo in Central Park was renovated, making it in the process both more human and more humane. Lithe sea lions frolic in the central pool area with beguiling style. The gigantic but graceful polar bears glide back and forth across a watery pool that has glass walls through which you can observe very large paws doing very smooth strokes. The monkeys seem to regard those on the other side of the fence with knowing disdain.

Because of its small size, the zoo is at its best with its displays of smaller animals. The indoor, multi-level Tropic Zone is a real highlight, its steamy rainforest home to everything from black-and-white Colobus monkeys to Emerald tree boa constrictors to a leaf-cutter ant farm. So is the large penguin enclosure in the Polar Circle, which is better than the one at San Diego's Sea World. In the Temperate Territory, look for the Asian red pandas (cousins to the big black-and-white ones), which look like the world's most beautiful raccoons. Despite their pool and piles of ice, however, the polar bears still look sad.

The entire zoo is good for short attention spans; you can cover the whole thing in 1¹/₂ to 3 hours, depending on the size of the crowds and how long you like to linger. It's also very kid-friendly, with lots of well-written and -illustrated placards that older kids can understand. For the littlest ones, there's the **Tisch Children's Zoo.** With pigs, llamas, potbellied pigs, and more, this petting zoo and playground is a real blast for the five-and-under set.

ACTIVITIES

The 6-mile road circling the park, **Central Park Drive,** has a lane set aside for bikers, joggers, and in-line skaters. The best time to use it is when the park is closed to traffic: Monday to Friday 10am to 3pm (except Thanksgiving to New Year's) and 7 to 10pm. It's also closed from 7pm Friday to 6am Monday, but when the weather is nice, the crowds can be hellish. For a shorter jogging loop, try the midpark 1.58-mile track around the **Reservoir,** recently renamed for Jacqueline Kennedy Onassis, who often enjoyed a jog here (keep your eyes ready for spotting Madonna and other famous bodies). It's safest to jog only during daylight hours and where everybody else does.

BIKING   Off-road biking isn't permitted; stay on Central Park Drive or your bike may be confiscated by park police. You can rent 3- and 10-speed bikes as well as tandems in Central Park at the **Loeb Boathouse,** midpark near 74th Street and East Drive (☎ 212/861-4137 or 517-3623).

BOATING   From spring to fall, gondola rides and canoe rentals are available at the **Loeb Boathouse,** midpark near 74th Street and East Drive (☎ 212/517-3623). Rentals are $10 for the first hour, $2.50 every 15 minutes thereafter, and a $30 deposit is required.

HORSE-DRAWN CARRIAGE RIDES   At the entrance to the park at 59th Street and Central Park South, you'll see a line of **horse-drawn carriages** waiting to take passengers on a ride through the park or along certain of the city's streets. You won't need me to tell you how forlorn most of these horses look; if you insist, a ride is about $50 for two for a half-hour, but I suggest skipping it.

ICE SKATING   Central Park's **Wollman Rink,** at 59th Street and Sixth Avenue (☎ 212/396-1010), is the city's best outdoor skating spot. It's open for skating generally from mid-October to mid-April, depending on the weather. Rates are $7 for adults, $3.50 for seniors and kids under 12, and skate rental is $3.50; lockers are available.

IN-LINE SKATING   Central Park is the city's most popular place for blading. See the top of this section for details on **Central Park Drive,** main drag for skaters. On weekends, head to **West Drive** at 67th Street, behind Tavern on the Green, where you'll find trick skaters weaving through an NYRSA slalom course at full speed, or the **Mall** in front of the bandshell (above Bethesda Fountain) for twirling to tunes. In summer, **Wollman Rink** converts to a hot-shot roller rink, with half-pipes and lessons available (see "Ice Skating," above).

You can rent skates for $15 a day weekdays and $25 a day weekends from **Blades East,** 160 E. 86th St. (☎ 212/996-1644), and **Blades West,** 120 W. 72nd St. (☎ 212/787-3911). April to October. Wollman also rents in-line skates for park use at similar rates.

Especially for Kids

Probably the best place of all to entertain the kids is in **Central Park,** which has kid-friendly diversions galore; see p. 146.

Kids of all ages can't help but turn dizzy with delight at the incredible views from atop the **Empire State Building** (p. 139) and the **World Trade Center** (p. 127). The Empire State Building also offers the **New York Skyride** (☎ **888/SKYRIDE** or 212/279-9777; www.skyride.com), which offers a stomach-churning virtual tour of New York—just in case the real one isn't enough for them.

Designed for kids 2 to 12, the **Children's Museum of Manhattan,** 212 W. 83rd St., between Broadway and Amsterdam Avenue on the Upper West Side (☎ **212/721-1234;** www. cmom.org), is a great place to take the kids when they're tired of being told not to touch. Interactive exhibits and activity centers encourage self-discovery, and a recent expansion means that there's now more than ever before to keep the kids busy and learning. The Time Warner Media Center takes children through the world of animation and helps them produce their own videos. New in 1999 was the Body Odyssey, a zany, scientific journey through the human body (just like Will Robinson on *Lost in Space* or *Sabrina the Teenage Witch,* depending on which TV generation you belong to). Admission is $5 for kids and adults, $2.50 for seniors. Open Wednesday through Sunday from 10am to 5pm.

The **Sony Wonder Technology Lab,** at Sony Plaza, 550 Madison Ave., at 56th Street (☎ **212/833-8100**), is not as much of an infomercial as you'd expect. Both kids and adults love this high-tech science and tech center, which explores communications and information technology. You can experiment with robotics, explore the human body through medical imaging, mix a hit song, design a video game, and save the day at an environmental command center. Open Tuesday through Saturday from 10am to 6pm (until 8pm on Thursday), Sunday from noon to 6pm. Admission is free.

Also consider the following museums, discussed elsewhere in this chapter: The **American Museum of Natural History** (p. 127), whose dinosaur displays are guaranteed to wow both you and the kids; the *Intrepid* **Sea-Air-Space Museum** (p. 137), on a real battle-ship with an amazing collection of vintage and high-tech airplanes; the **Lower East Side Tenement Museum** (p. 137), whose living-history approach really intrigues school-age kids; and the **South Street Seaport & Museum** (p. 126), which little ones will love for its theme park–like atmosphere and old boats bobbing the harbor.

PLAYGROUNDS Nineteen Adventure Playgrounds are scattered throughout the park, perfect for jumping, sliding, tottering, swinging, and digging. At Central Park West and 81st Street is the **Diana Ross Playground,** voted the city's best by *New York* magazine. Also on the west side is the **Spector Playground,** at 85th Street and Central Park West, and, a little farther north, the **Wild West Playground** at 93rd Street. On the east side is the **Rustic Playground,** at 67th Street and Fifth Avenue, a delightfully landscaped space rife with islands, bridges, and big slides; and the **Pat Hoffman Friedman Playground,** right behind the Metropolitan Museum of Art at East 79th Street, is geared towards older toddlers.

7 Shopping Highlights for Bargain Hunters

THE TOP SHOPPING STREETS & NEIGHBORHOODS

CHINATOWN

Don't expect to find the purchase of a lifetime on Chinatown's streets, but there's some fun browsing to be had. The fish markets along Canal, Mott, Mulberry, and Elizabeth streets are fun to explore for their bustle and exotica. Especially along Canal, you'll find an astounding collection of super-cheap knock-offs—mostly sunglasses, designer bags, and watches. **Mott Street** between Pell Street and Chatham Square boasts the most interesting of Chinatown's off-Canal shopping, with an antique shop or two dispersed among the tiny storefronts selling blue-and-white dinnerware. But the definite highlight is the three-story **Pearl River Mart** (see "The Big Department Stores," below).

THE LOWER EAST SIDE

The bargains aren't quite what they used to be in the **Historic Orchard Street Shopping District**—which basically runs from Houston to Canal along Allen, Orchard, and Ludlow streets, spreading outward along both sides of Delancey Street—but prices on leather bags, shoes, luggage, fabrics on the bolt, and men's and women's clothes are still quite good. Be aware, though, that the hard-sell on Orchard Street can be pretty hard to take. Still, the district is a nice place to discover a part of New York that's disappearing. Come during the week, since most stores are Jewish-owned, and therefore close Friday afternoon and all day Saturday. Sundays tend to be a madhouse. Stop in first at the **Lower East Side Visitor Center,** 261 Broome St., between Orchard and Allen streets (☎ **888/825-8374** or 212/226-9010; open Sun–Fri 10am–4pm) for a shopping guide.

A little farther west, the stretch of the Bowery from Canal to Houston streets is considered the "light-fixture district" for its huge selections and great bargains on light fixtures, lamps, and ceiling fans. The best of the bunch is **Lighting by Gregory,** 158 Bowery (☎ **212/226-1276**).

SoHo

People love to complain about super-fashionable SoHo—it's become too trendy, too tony, too Mall of America. True, J. Crew is only one of many big names to have supplanted the galleries that used to inhabit the historic cast-iron buildings, but SoHo is still one of the best shopping neighborhoods in the city—and few are more fun to browse. You'll find few bargains here, as rents are too high for merchants to sell at anything but a premium. This is the epicenter of cutting-edge haute couture. Most of these designer shops are likely to be *way* out of your price range (they're way outta mine, that's for sure), but the streets are chock-full of unique boutiques, some hawking more affordable wares, and the eye candy is tops. End-of-season sales, when racks are cleared for incoming merchandise, are the best bet for those who actually want to buy.

SoHo's prime shopping grid is from Broadway east to Sullivan Street, and from Houston down to Broome, although Grand Street, one block south of Broome, has been sprouting shops of late. If you're less interested in designer fashions and more interested in unique mid-priced wearables, consider **Anthropologie,** 375 W. Broadway (☎ **212/343-7070**), whose funky-chic, affordable clothes mix with fun gifts and home decorating items—much like Urban Outfitters for grown-ups. High-end home stores are another huge part of the SoHo scene, but **Global Table,** 107 Sullivan St. (☎ **212/431-5839**), is a great source for beautiful, affordable tableware from around the world.

SoHo is also popular for its high-end street peddlers, hawking hand-crafted silver jewelry, coffee-table books, and their own art, mainly along **Prince Street** on weekends.

NoLiTa

Just east of SoHo, **Elizabeth Street** is now the grooviest shopping strip in town, star of the neighborhood known as NoLita. Elizabeth and neighboring Mott and Mulberry streets are dotted with an increasing number of shops between Houston and Spring streets, with a few pushing one more block south to Kenmare. It's an easy walk from the Broadway–Lafayette stop on the B, D, F, Q line.

Don't expect cheap—NoLiTa is clearly a stepchild of SoHo. Its boutiques are largely the province of sophisticated shopkeepers specializing in high-quality, fashion-forward products and design.

Prince Street is probably the best stretch for affordable treasures. There's **Dö Kham** at no. 51 (☎ 212/966-2404), for Tibetan bags, rugs, and other Himalayan imports; **Cocoon & Co.** at no. 25 (☎ 212/966-8680) for a charmingly quirky mix of well-priced vintage housewares and contemporary gifts; and **Gates of Morocco,** at no. 8 (☎ 212/925-2650), for traditional Moroccan goodies. At 235 Elizabeth St. is **Daily 235** (☎ 212/334-9728), a cool candy and card store for artsy grown-ups that's terrific for under-$10 tchotchkes.

THE EAST VILLAGE

The East Village remains the international standard of bohemian hip. The easiest subway access is the 6 train to Astor Place, which lets you right out at **Kmart;** from here, it's just a couple blocks east to the prime hunting grounds. Note that some East Village shops don't open until 2pm, so your best bet is to come in the afternoon; most stay open until 8pm, some later.

East 9th Street between Second Avenue and Avenue A has become one of my favorite shopping strips in the entire city. Lined with an increasingly smart collection of boutiques, it proves that the East Village isn't just for kids anymore. Up-and-coming designers selling good-quality and affordably priced original fashions for women have set up shop along here, the best of which is the utterly fabulous ✪ **Jill Anderson,** at 331 E. 9th St. (☎ 212/253-1747), one of New York's few designers creating clothes for real women to wear for real life—not just for 22-year-old size-2s to match with a pair of Pradas and wear out clubhopping. For stylish gifts and little luxuries, there's **H,** at no. 335 (☎ 212/477-2631). There's also the factory store for super-hip **Manhattan Portage,** at no. 333 (☎ 212/995-1949), if you're looking for something to stash your booty in.

If it's strange, illegal, or funky, it's probably available on **St. Marks Place,** which takes over for 8th Street running east from Third Avenue to Avenue A. This skanky strip is a permanent street market, with countless T-shirt and boho jewelry stands. The height of the action is between Second and Third avenues, which is prime hunting grounds for used-record collectors.

GREENWICH VILLAGE

The West Village is great for browsing and gift shopping. Specialty book- and record stores, antiques and craft shops, and gourmet food

Where the Fleas Are

For those in search of vintage treasures, the Big Apple is also a flea market bonanza. City fleas operate on weekends throughout the year, so even winter visitors can enjoy the prowl.

Usually called the 26th Street flea market, the famous **Annex Antiques Fair and Flea Market** (☎ 212/243-5343) is an outdoor emporium of nostalgia, filling a few parking lots along Sixth Avenue between 24th and 27th streets on weekends year-round. The assemblage is hit or miss—some days you'll find treasures galore, and others it seems like there's nothing but junk. A few quality vendors are almost always on hand, though, and prices are usually negotiable. The truly dedicated arrive at 6:30am, but the browsing is still good as late as 4pm. Sunday is always best, since there's double the booty on hand. One lot charges $1 admission both days, but the rest are free. Die-hards can continue the hunt at the **Garage,** an indoor two-story parking garage at 112 W. 25th St., between Sixth and Seventh avenues (☎ 212/647-0707), then proceed to 26th Street and Seventh Avenue, where another lot fills up with dealers on Sunday.

Another popular weekend market is the **SoHo Antiques and Collectibles Market,** at Broadway and Grand Street, on Saturdays and Sundays starting at 9am. Knowledgeable fleabees don't consider this the prime hunting ground it once was, but prices are reasonable and real finds surface every so often. The collections tend toward mid-century kitsch, vintage clothes, old records, old-fashioned kitchen appliances, and the like.

Uptown, the **Greenflea Market** (☎ 212/721-0900) operates at two different venues: on the east side on East 67th Street, between First and York avenues, on Saturday from 6am to 6pm; and on the west side on Columbus Avenue at West 77th Street, Sundays from 10am to 6pm. Both markets operate as both green and flea markets (hence the name). I'm not a big fan, but some people just love the west side Sunday event, where goods run from used records to Turkish kilims to discount pet supplies. Costume jewelry hunters, in particular, should enjoy the east side Saturday event.

markets dominate. The best **Tower Records** in the country is at West 4th Street and Broadway (☎ 212/505-1500). NYU territory is good for cheap fashions: **8th Street** between Broadway and Sixth Avenue for trendy footwear and affordable fashions, and **Broadway** from 8th Street south to Houston, anchored by **Urban Outfitters** (☎ 212/475-0009) and dotted with skate and sneaker shops.

The prime drag for strolling is bustling **Bleecker Street,** where you'll find lots of leather shops and record stores interspersed with a good number of interesting and artsy boutiques. Narrow **Christopher Street** is another fun street to browse, because it's loaded with genuine Village character.

THE FLATIRON DISTRICT & UNION SQUARE

When 23rd Street was the epitome of New York Uptown fashion more than a hundred years ago, the major department stores stretched along **Sixth Avenue** for about a mile from 14th Street up. In the last few years, the area has turned into the city's discount shopping center, with superstores and off-pricers filling up the renovated cast-iron buildings: **Filene's Basement, TJ Maxx,** and **Bed Bath & Beyond,** are all at 620 Sixth Ave., while witty **Old Navy,** the cheaper version of the Gap, is next door.

The city's best **Barnes & Noble** towers over Union Square at 22 E. 17th St. (☎ 212/253-0810). On the other side of the square is the city's second **Virgin Megastore** (☎ 212/598-4666). Just a few blocks north is ☎ **ABC Carpet & Home,** 888 Broadway at 19th St. (☎ 212/473-3000), a magnet for aspiring Martha Stewarts. Even if you can't afford anything, ABC is well worth a peek, and the first-floor gallery often boasts a gorgeous array of reasonably priced goodies.

THE GARMENT DISTRICT

On Seventh Avenue between 34th and 42nd street is the grimy, heavily industrial Garment District. This is, however, where you'll find that quintessential New York experience, the sample sale. You won't know where to find them if you just walk the streets, so point your web browser for **www.samplesale.com** for the latest on sales in New York City.

TIMES SQUARE & THE THEATER DISTRICT

This neighborhood has become increasingly family oriented: hence, **Disney** and **Warner Bros.** outposts at the crossroads of Times Square, and Richard Branson's rollicking **Virgin Megastore,** Broadway at 45th St. (☎ 212/921-1020).

West 47th Street between Fifth and Sixth avenues is the city's famous **Diamond District.** More than 90% of the diamonds sold in the United States come through this neighborhood first, so there are some great deals to be had if you're in the market for a nice rock

---

Theater District Shopper's Alert

You'll also notice a wealth of electronics stores throughout the neighborhood, many trumpeting GOING OUT OF BUSINESS sales. These guys have been going out of business since the Stone Age. That's the bait and switch; pretty soon you've spent too much money for not enough stereo. If you want to check out what they have to offer, go in knowing what going prices are on that PDA or digital camera you're interested in. You can negotiate a good deal if you know exactly what the market is—I've seen prices tumble precipitously the closer I got to the door—but these guys will be happy to suck you dry given half a chance. Trust me on this: The only way you'll do well is if you know your stuff.

---

or another piece of fine jewelry. Be ready to wheel and deal with the largely Hasidic dealers. For a complete introduction to the district, including smart buying tips, visit **www.47th-street.com**. For semiprecious stones, head one block over to the **New York Jewelry Mart,** 26 W. 46th St. (☎ **212/575-9701**). Virtually all of these dealers are open Monday through Friday only.

FIFTH AVENUE & 57TH STREET

The heart of Manhattan retail is the corner of Fifth and 57th. Home to high-ticket names like Gucci, Chanel, and Cartier, this tony shopping neighborhood has long been the province of the über-rich. In recent years, however, it has become more accessible as wallet-friendlier retailers like **Niketown,** 6 E. 57th St. (☎ **212/891-6453**), and the dazzling new **NBA Store,** at Fifth Avenue and 52nd Street (☎ **212/515-NBA1**), have joined the fold.

Still, the window shopping is classic. And if you, like Holly Golightly, always dreamed of shopping at **Tiffany & Co.,** Fifth Avenue at 57th Street (☎ **212/755-8000**), the most famous jewelry store in New York is well worth a stop. The multilevel showroom is so full of tourists at all times that it's easy to browse without having any intention of buying. If you do want to indulge, your best bet is to head upstairs to the gift level, where you'll find a number of gifts to suit a $50 budget.

THE BIG DEPARTMENT STORES

✪ **Bloomingdale's.** 1000 Third Ave. (Lexington Ave. at 59th St.). ☎ **212/705-2000.** Subway: 4, 5, 6 to 59th St.

This is my favorite of New York's big department stores. It's more accessible than Barneys or Bergdorf's and more affordable than Saks, but still has the New York pizzazz that Macy's and Lord & Taylor now largely lack. Taking up the space of a city block, Bloomie's has just about anything you could want, from clothing (both designer and everyday basics) and fragrances to a full range of housewares. Service is a step above increasingly lackluster Macy's. The frequent sales can yield unbeatable bargains; look for full-page ads in the daily *New York Times*.

✪ Century 21. 22 Cortlandt St. (btw. Broadway and Church St.). ☎ **212/227-9092.** Subway: 1, 9, N, R to Cortlandt St.; 4, 5 to Fulton St.; C, E to World Trade Center.

Just across from the World Trade Center, Century 21 long ago achieved legend status as *the* designer discount store. If you don't mind wrestling with the aggressive, ever-present throngs, this is where you'll find those $20 Todd Oldham pants or the $50 Bally loafers you've been dreaming of—not to mention underwear, hosiery, and ties so cheap that they're almost free. The shoe department is an outlet-style madhouse, but the bargains can be incredible. The whole store's an utter hassle, but always worth it. To avoid the bulk of the crowds, avoid lunch hour, the after-work hours, and weekends; weekday mornings are best.

Kmart. 770 Broadway (at Astor Place, btw. 8th and 9th sts.). ☎ **212/673-1540.** Subway: 6 to Astor Place.

Kmart is so out of place in the East Village that it has turned the mundane into marvelous camp: Japanese kids stare and marvel at gargantuan boxes of laundry detergent as if they were Warhol designed, while multi-pierced and mohawked locals navigate the name-brand maze alongside stroller-pushing housewives. U2 even held a press conference/performance here to announce their consumption-minded *Popmart* tour back in 1998. Kitsch value aside, this multilevel megastore is a great bet for discount prices on practicals, from socks to shampoo. You'll also find a pharmacy, a sizable food department where you can stock up on Cocoa Puffs and other kitchenette supplies (sale prices on snack foods are rock-bottom), and even a photography studio.

There's a second Kmart in midtown at 1 Penn Plaza, on 34th Street between Seventh and Eighth avenues (☎ **212/760-1188**).

Lord & Taylor. 424 Fifth Ave. (at 39th St.). ☎ **212/391-3344.** Subway: B, D, F, Q to 42nd St.

Okay, so maybe Lord & Taylor isn't the first place you'd go for a vinyl miniskirt. But I like Lord & Taylor's understated, elegant mien. Their house-brand clothes are well-made and a great bargain.

Sales can be stellar, especially around holidays. The Christmas window displays are an annual delight.

Macy's. At Herald Square, W. 34th St. and Broadway. ☎ **212/695-4400.** Subway: 1, 2, 3, 9, B, D, F, Q, N, R to 34th St.

A four-story sign on the side of the building trumpets, MACY'S, THE WORLD'S LARGEST STORE—a hard fact to dispute, since the 10-story behemoth covers an entire city block, even dwarfing Bloomie's on the other side of town. Macy's is a hard place to shop: The size is unmanageable, the service is dreadful, and the incessant din from the crowds on the ground floor alone will kick your migraine into action. But they do sell *everything*. The store's one-of-a-kind flair that I remember so well from my childhood is just a memory now. Still, sales run constantly, so bargains are guaranteed. And because so many feel adrift in this retail sea, the store provides personal shoppers to serve as guides at absolutely no charge.

Tips for Sale Seekers: One-day sales usually occur on Wednesdays, and sometimes on Saturdays. Extended hours are common on sale days. Call the store when you arrive to find out if your visit overlaps with one. It's also a terrific idea to check the A (front) section of *The New York Times* any day of the week for full-page advertisements, which sometimes include clip-out coupons for additional 10 to 15% discounts.

✪ **Pearl River Mart.** 277 Canal St., at Broadway. ☎ **212/431-4770.** Subway: N, R to Canal St.

It doesn't look like much more than your average storefront from the street, but this three-floor Chinatown emporium overflows with affordable Asian exotica. Cool goods run the gamut from colorful paper lanterns to Chinese snack foods to Mandarin-collared silk pajamas to mah jongg sets to Hong Kong action videos. This fascinating place can keep you occupied for hours, and it's a great source for cheap, creative souvenirs.

Saks Fifth Avenue. 611 Fifth Ave. (btw. 49th and 50th sts.). ☎ **212/753-4000.** Subway: B, D, F, Q to 47–50th sts.–Rockefeller Center; E, F to Fifth Ave.

There are branches of Saks all over the country now, but this is it: Saks *Fifth Avenue*. This legendary flagship is well worth an hour or two for real department-store aficionados, and the smaller-than-most size makes it manageable in that amount of time. As department stores go, there's something for everyone, and every budget, here. And the store's location, right across from Rockefeller Center, makes it a convenient stop for those on the sightseeing circuit. Don't miss the holiday windows.

6

New York City After Dark

*F*or the latest, most comprehensive arts and entertainment listings, pick up a copy of *Time Out New York,* or the free weekly *Village Voice,* the city's legendary alterna-paper. Another great weekly is *New York* magazine. *The New York Times* features terrific nightlife coverage, particularly in the two-part Friday "Weekend" section.

Some of your best, most comprehensive and up-to-date information sources for what's going on about town are in cyberspace, of course. Excellent sources worth scanning are **www.newyork.citysearch.com**, and **www.nytoday.com** plus **www.papermag.com** for opinionated coverage of the downtown club and bar scenes.

1 All the City's a Stage: The Theater Scene

Nobody does theater better than New York. No other city—not even London—has a theater scene with so much breadth and depth, with so many wide-open alternatives. Broadway, of course, gets the most ink and the most airplay, and deservedly so: Broadway is where you'll find the big stage productions and the moneymakers, from crowd-pleasing warhorses like *Cats* to phenomenal newer successes like *The Lion King.* But today's scene is thriving beyond the bounds of just Broadway: With bankable stars on stage, crowds lining up for hot tickets, and hits popular enough to generate major-label cast albums, off-Broadway isn't just for culture vultures anymore.

Despite this vitality, plays and musicals close all the time, often with little warning, so I can't tell you precisely what will be on while you're in town. Your best bet is to check the publications and Web sites listed at the start of this chapter to get an idea of what you might like to see. A particularly useful source is the **Broadway Line** (☎ 888/BROADWAY or 212/302-4111; www.broadway.org), where you can obtain details and descriptions on current Broadway shows, hear about special offers and discounts, and choose to be transferred to Tele-charge to buy tickets. **NYC/Onstage** (☎ 212/ 768-1818; www.tdf.org) offers similar service for both Broadway and off-Broadway productions.

ADVANCE TICKET-BUYING TIPS

Phone ahead or go online for tickets to the most popular shows as far in advance as you can—in the case of shows like *The Lion King* and, thus far, *Cabaret,* it's never too early.

Buying tickets can be simple, if the show you want to see isn't sold out and you don't mind paying full price. You need only call such general numbers as **Tele-Charge** (☎ **212/239-6200;** www. telecharge.com), which handles most Broadway and off-Broadway shows and some concerts; or **Ticketmaster** (☎ **212/307-4100;** www.ticketmaster.com), which also handles Broadway and off-Broadway shows and most concerts.

If you're an American Express gold card holder, see if tickets are being sold through **American Express Gold Card Events** (☎ **800/ 448-TIKS;** www.americanexpress.com/gce). You'll pay full price, but AmEx has access to blocks of preferred seating specifically set aside for gold-card holders, so you may be able to get tickets to a show that's otherwise sold out, or better seats than you would be able to buy through other outlets.

Theatre Direct International (TDI) is a ticket broker that sells tickets to select Broadway and off-Broadway shows direct to individuals and travel agents. Check to see if they have seats to the shows you're interested in by calling ☎ **800/334-8457** or pointing your web browser to **www.theatredirect.com**. (Disregard the discounted prices, unless you're buying for a group of 20 or more; tickets are full price for smaller quantities.) With a service charge of $12.50 per ticket, you'll do better by trying TicketMaster or Tele-charge first; but because they act as a consolidator, TDI may have tickets left for a specific show even if the major outlets don't. Other reputable ticket brokers include **Keith Prowse & Co.** (☎ **800/669-8687;** www.keithprowse.com) and **Edwards & Edwards Global Tickets** (☎ **800/223-6108**).

If you don't want to pay a service charge, try calling the **box office** directly. Broadway theaters don't sell tickets over the telephone, but a good number of off-Broadway theaters do.

GETTING TICKETS WHILE YOU'RE HERE

Once you arrive in the city, getting your hands on tickets can take some street smarts—and failing those, good hard cash. Even if it seems unlikely that seats are available, always **call or visit the box office** before attempting any other route. Single seats are often easiest to obtain, so people willing to sit apart may find themselves in luck.

Bargain Alert—How to Save on Theater Tickets

If you employ a little patience, flexibility, and know-how, there are ways to pay less than full price for your theater tickets—sometimes a lot less.

Joining the **Playbill Online Theater Club** (**www. playbillclub.com**) can yield substantial savings on advance-purchase theater tickets for select Broadway and off-Broadway shows. Becoming a member is free; all you have to do is register, and you'll have access to discounts that can range from a few dollars to as much as 45% off regular ticket prices.

If you're visiting the city early in the year, be sure to look into the **Passport to Off Broadway.** The Alliance of Resident Theaters/New York sponsors this campaign, which offers 10 to 50% discounts on tickets to more than 200 off- and off-off-Broadway shows from February through April. You can download the discount coupon as many times as you want by visiting **www. newyork.sidewalk.com/passport**. Note, however, that restrictions may apply: For instance, some theaters don't accept the coupons for Friday or Saturday night performances, and some will accept them only for cash purchases. Still, the inconveniences are minimal, and it's a great deal.

Even blockbusters can have a limited number of cheaper tickets for **students and seniors,** and they may even be available at the last minute. Your best bet is to call the box office direct to inquire.

You should also try the **Broadway Ticket Center** at the Times Square Visitors Center, 1560 Broadway, between 46th and 47th streets (open daily 8am–8pm). They often have tickets available for otherwise sold-out shows, and only charge $4 extra per ticket.

If you want to deal with a licensed broker direct, **Global Tickets Edwards & Edwards** has a local office that accommodates drop-ins at 1270 Sixth Ave., on the 24th floor (☎ **212/332-2435;** open Monday to Saturday 9am to 9pm, Sunday noon to 7pm).

If you buy from one of the **scalpers** selling tickets in front of the theater doors, you're taking a risk. They may be perfectly legitimate—a couple from the 'burbs whose companions couldn't make it for the evening, say—but they could be swindlers passing off fakes for big money. It's a risk not worth taking.

The best deal in town on **same-day tickets** for both Broadway and off-Broadway shows is at the ✪ **Times Square Theatre Centre,** better known as the **TKTS booth,** run by the nonprofit Theatre Development Fund in the heart of the Theater District at Duffy Square, 47th Street and Broadway (open 3–8pm for evening performances, 10am–2pm for Wednesday and Saturday matinees, from 11am on Sunday for all performances). Tickets for that day's performances are usually offered at half price, with a few reduced only 25%, plus a $2.50 per ticket service charge. Boards outside the ticket windows list available shows; you're unlikely to find certain perennial or outsize smashes, but most other shows turn up. Cash and traveler's checks only are accepted. There's often a huge line, so show up early for the best availability and be prepared to wait—but frankly, the crowd is all part of the fun. If you don't care much what you see and you'd just like to go to a show, you can walk right up to the window later in the day and something's always available.

Run by the same group and offering the same discounts is the **TKTS Lower Manhattan Theatre Centre,** on the mezzanine of 2 World Trade Center (open Mon–Fri 11am–5:30pm and Sat 11am–3:30pm). All the same policies apply. The advantages to coming down here is that the lines are generally shorter; your wait is sheltered indoors; and matinee tickets are available a day in advance, so you can plan ahead.

2 The Performing Arts: Concert Halls & Companies

✪ **Bargemusic.** At the Fulton Ferry Landing (just south of the Brooklyn Bridge), Brooklyn. ☎ **718/624-2083** or 718/624-4061. www.bargemusic.org. Subway: 2, 3 to Clark St.

Many thought Olga Bloom peculiar, if not deranged, when she transformed a 40-year-old barge into a chamber-music concert hall. More than 20 years later, Bargemusic is an internationally reputed recital room boasting more than 100 first-rate chamber music performances a year. There are two shows per week, on Thursday evening and Sunday afternoon; from June through August, there's also a Friday-evening performance.

The musicians perform on a small stage in a cherry-paneled, fireplace-lit room accommodating 130. The barge may creek a bit and an occasional boat may speed by, but the music rivals what you'll find in almost any other New York concert hall—and the panoramic view through the glass wall behind the stage can't be beat. Neither can the price: Tickets are just $23 ($20 seniors, $15 students). Reserve well in advance.

Brooklyn Academy of Music. 30 Lafayette Ave., Brooklyn. ☎ **718/ 636-4100.** www.bam.org. Subway: 2, 3, 4, 5, D, Q to Atlantic Ave.; B, M, N, R to Pacific Ave.

BAM, as it's known, is the city's most renowned contemporary arts institution. Offerings have included historically informed presentations of baroque opera by William Christie and Les Arts Florissants; Marianne Faithfull singing the music of Kurt Weill; dance by Mark Morris, Merce Cunningham, and Mikhail Baryshnikov; the Royal Dramatic Theater of Sweden directed by Ingmar Bergman; and many more experimental works by both renowned and lesser-known international artists as well as visiting companies from all over the world. Of particular note is the **Next Wave Festival,** from September through December, this country's foremost showcase for new experimental works.

Carnegie Hall. 881 Seventh Ave. (at 57th St.). ☎ **212/247-7800.** www. carnegiehall.org. Subway: N, R or B, Q to 57th St.

Perhaps the world's most famous performance space, the 2,804-seat main hall welcomes visiting orchestras from across the country and the world. Many of the world's premier soloists and ensembles give recitals. The legendary hall is both visually and acoustically brilliant; don't miss an opportunity to experience it if there's something on that interests you. There's also the intimate 284-seat **Weill Recital Hall,** usually used to showcase chamber music and vocal and instrumental recitals.

City Center. 131 W. 55th St. (btw. Sixth and Seventh aves.). ☎ **212/ 581-7907.** Subway: N, R or B, Q to 57th St.; B, D, E to Seventh Ave.

Modern dance usually takes center stage in this Moorish dome-topped performing arts palace. Regular performances by the companies of Merce Cunningham, Paul Taylor, Trisha Brown, Alvin Ailey, Twyla Tharp, and the American Ballet Theatre are often on the calendar. Don't expect cutting edge—but do expect excellence. Sightlines are terrific from all corners.

Joyce Theater. 175 Eighth Ave. (at 19th St.). ☎ **212/242-0800.** www. joyce.org. Subway: C, E to 23rd St.; 1, 9 to 18th St.

Housed in an old art deco movie house, the Joyce has grown into one of the world's greatest modern dance institutions. You can see everything from Native American ceremonial dance to Maria Benites Teatro Flamenco to the innovative works of Pilobolus to the Martha Graham Dance Company. In residence annually is Ballet Tech, which WQXR radio's Francis Mason called "better than a whole month of namby-pamby classical ballets."

✪ **Lincoln Center for the Performing Arts.** 70 Lincoln Center Plaza (at Broadway and 64th St.). ☎ **212/546-2656.** www.lincolncenter.org. Subway: 1, 9 to 66th St.

New York is the world's premier performing arts city, and Lincoln Center is its premier institution. Lincoln Center's many buildings serve as permanent homes to their own companies as well major stops for world-class performance troupes from around the globe.

Resident companies include the **Metropolitan Opera** (☎ 212/ **362-6000;** www.metopera.org), whose full productions of the classics, regularly starring world-class grand sopranos and tenors, makes the Met the world's premier opera house. The opera house also hosts the **American Ballet Theatre** (www.abt.org) each spring, as well as such visiting companies as the Kirov, Royal, and Paris Opéra ballets.

The **New York State Theater** (☎ 212/870-5570 or 212/ 307-4100) is home to the ✪ **New York City Opera** (www. nycopera.com), a superb company that attempts to reach a wider audience than the Metropolitan with its more "human" scale and significantly lower prices. It's also committed to adventurous premieres, newly composed operas, and American operettas, plus the occasional avant-garde work. Also based here is the world-renowned **New York City Ballet** (www.nycballet.com), highly regarded for its unsurpassed technique. The cornerstone of the annual season is the Christmastime production of *The Nutcracker.*

Symphony-wise, you'd be hard-pressed to do better than the phenomenal ✪ **New York Philharmonic** (☎ 212/875-5030 or 212/ 721-6500 for tickets; www.newyorkphilharmonic.org), performing at Avery Fisher Hall. The country's oldest philharmonic orchestra is under the strict but ebullient guidance of music director Kurt Masur. He's retiring in 2002, so don't miss this chance to see the master conductor leading his orchestra. ✪ **Jazz at Lincoln Center** (☎ 212/875-5299; www.jazzatlincolncenter.org), is led by the incomparable Wynton Marsalis, with the orchestra usually performing at Alice Tully Hall. The **Chamber Music Society of Lincoln Center** (☎ 212/875-5788; www.chamberlinc.org)

Last-Minute Discount Ticket-Buying Tips

The majority of seats at **New York Philharmonic** performances are sold to subscribers, with just a few left for the rest of us. But there are still ways to get tickets. When subscribers can't attend, they may turn their tickets back to the theater, which then resells them at the last moment. The hopeful form "cancellation lines" 2 hours or more before curtain time for a crack at returned tickets on a first-come, first-serve basis. And periodically, a number of **same-day orchestra tickets** are set aside at the philharmonic, and sold first thing in the morning for $25 a pop (maximum 2). **Senior/student/disabled rush tickets** may be available for $10 (maximum 2) on concert day, but never at Friday matinees or Saturday evening performances. To check availability for all **New York Philharmonic** performances, call the Audience Services Department at ☎ **212/875-5656.**

Note that Lincoln Center's **Alice Tully Hall** (where the Chamber Music Society performs and other concerts are held), the **Metropolitan Opera,** and **Carnegie Hall** offer similar last-minute and discount programs. It makes sense to call the box office first to check on same-day availability before heading to the theater— or, if you're willing to take the risk of coming away empty-handed, be there at opening time for first crack.

If all else fails and your heart is set on seeing a sold-out perfor-mance, you can call or go to the box office to see if **standing room** is available (usually around $20). The best standing room is at the Met, where you get to lean against plush red bars. (Don't tell them I told you, but if subscribers fail to show, I've seen standees with eagle eyes fill the empty seats at intermission.)

performs at Alice Tully Hall or the Rose Rehearsal Studio, often in the company of such high-caliber guests as Anne Sofie Von Otter and Midori.

The **Film Society of Lincoln Center** (☎ **212/875-5600;** www.filmlinc.com), screens a daily schedule of movies at the Walter Reade Theater, and hosts a number of important annual film and video festivals.

Most of the companies' **major seasons** run from about October to May or June. **Special series** like Great Performers help round out the calendar. Indoor and outdoor events are held in warmer months;

check the "New York City Calendar of Events" in chapter 1 or Lincoln Center's Web site to see what events will be on while you're in town.

Tickets for all performances at Avery Fisher and Alice Tully halls can be purchased through **CenterCharge** (☎ 212/721-6500) or online at www.lincolncenter.org. Tickets for all Lincoln Center Theater performances can be purchased thorough **Tele-Charge** (☎ 212/239-6200; www.telecharge.com). Tickets for New York State Theater productions are available through **Ticketmaster** (☎ 212/307-4100; www.ticketmaster.com), while film tickets can be bought via **Movie Phone** (☎ 212/777-FILM; www.777film. com; the theater code is 954).

✪ **92nd Street Y.** 1395 Lexington Ave. (at 92nd St.). ☎ **212/996-1100.** www.92ndsty.org. Subway: 4, 5, 6 to 86th St.; 6 to 96th St.

This community center offers a phenomenal slate of top-rated cultural happenings. Just because you see "Y", don't think this place is small potatoes: The greatest classical performers—Isaac Stern, Janos Starker, Nadja Salerno-Sonnenberg—give recitals here. In addition, the full concert calendar often includes musical programs from luminaries such as Max Roach and John Williams; Jazz at the Y from Dick Hyman and guests; plus regular chamber music and cabaret programs. The lectures and literary readings calendar is unparalleled, with featured speakers ranging from Lorne Michaels to Ann Richards to Charles Frazier. Readings and lectures are usually priced between $10 and $15 for non-members (although select lectures can be priced as high as $30), and concert tickets generally go for $25 to $35—half or a third of what you'd pay at comparable venues.

The Classical Learning Curve

The **Juilliard School,** Lincoln Center at Broadway and 65th Street (☎ 212/769-7406; www.juilliard.edu), the nation's premier music education institution, sponsors about 550 performances of the highest quality—at the lowest prices. With most concerts free and $15 as a maximum ticket price, Juilliard is one of New York's greatest cultural bargains. In addition to classical concerts, Juilliard offers other music as well as drama, dance, opera, and interdisciplinary works. The best way to find out about the wide array of productions is to call, visit the school's Web site, or consult the bulletin board in the building's lobby. Watch for master classes and discussions open to the public featuring celebrity guest teachers.

Park It! Shakespeare & Other Free Fun

As the weather warms, New York culture comes outdoors to play.

Shakespeare in the Park, held at Central Park's Delacorte Theater, is by far the city's most famous alfresco arts event. Organized by the Joseph Papp Public Theater, the schedule consists of summertime productions of usually two of the Bard's plays (although the 1997 season also saw a restaging of the 1944 musical *On the Town*). Productions often feature big names, and range from traditional interpretations (Patrick Stewart as Prospero, Andre Braugher as an armor-clad *Henry V*) to avant-garde presentations (Morgan Freeman, Tracey Ullman, and David Alan Grier in *Taming of the Shrew* as Wild-West showdown). The theater itself, next to Belvedere Castle near 79th Street and West Drive, is a dream—on a beautiful starry night, there's no better stage in town. Tickets are given out free on a first-come, first-serve basis (two per person), at 1pm on the day of the performance at the theater. Each of the 1,881 seats is a hot commodity, so people generally line up on the baseball field next to the theater about 2 to 3 hours in advance. You can also pick up tickets between 1 and 3pm at the Joseph Papp Public Theater, at 425 Lafayette St., where the Shakespeare Festival continues throughout the year. For more information, call the Public Theater at ☎ **212/539-8500** or the Delacorte at **212/861-7277,** or go online at **www.publictheater.org**.

With summer comes the sound of music to Central Park, where the **New York Philharmonic** and the **Metropolitan Opera** regularly entertain beneath the stars; for the current

Radio City Music Hall. 1260 Sixth Ave. (at 50th St.). ☎ **212/247-4777,** or 212/307-1000 for tickets. www.radiocity.com. Subway: B, D, F, Q to 49th St./Rockefeller Center.

This stunning 6,200-seat art deco theater opened in 1932 and continues to be a choice venue, where the theater alone adds a dash of panache to any performance. Star of the Christmas season is the **Radio City Music Hall Christmas Spectacular,** starring the legendary Rockettes. Visiting chart-toppers, from Stevie Nicks to Radiohead, also perform here. Thanks to perfect acoustics and uninterrupted sightlines, there's hardly a bad seat in the house. The theater also hosts a number of annual awards shows—such as the ESPYs and anything MTV is holding in town—so this is a good place to celeb-spot on show nights.

schedule, call ☎ **212/360-3444** or 212/875-5709. But the most active music stage in the park is **SummerStage,** at Rumsey Playfield, mid-park around 72nd Street. Recent offerings have included concerts by Yoko Ono, Rocket from the Crypt, and Peter, Paul, and Mary; readings by authors Grace Paley, Paul Auster, and Tom Robbins; and "Viva, Verdi!" festival performances by the **New York Grand Opera.** The season usually lasts from mid-June to early August. Tickets aren't usually required, but donations are warmly accepted. For the latest, call ☎ **212/360-2777** or visit **www.summerstage.org**.

The **Bryant Park Film Festival** takes place every Monday night throughout July and August, starting at sunset. This charming block-square park is blanket-to-blanket as crowds come to watch classic and family-friendly films such as *Breakfast at Tiffany's* under the stars. The crowds can get thick, especially for popular ones, so stake out your spot early. Rain dates are Tuesday. Call ☎ **212/512-5700** for this season's schedule.

And keep in mind that Lower Manhattan is rife with free arts and entertainment during the daytime, too. Trinity Church, on Broadway at Wall Street, hosts a chamber music and orchestral **Noonday Concert series** each Thursday at 1pm, and each Monday at noon at nearby St. Paul's, on Broadway at Fulton Street. This excellent program isn't quite free, but almost: The suggested donation is just $2. Call the concert hot line at ☎ **212/602-0747** or visit **www.trinitywallstreet.org**.

3 Live Rock, Jazz, Blues & More

Below, you'll find only a handful of special venues; there are far more than these around town, and there's always something going on. Checking the listings in the *Village Voice* or *Time Out New York* to see what's on around town while you're here.

If you're looking for a rock or pop show by a national act, see what's happening at **The Bottom Line,** 15 W. 4th St. (☎ **212/228-7880** or 212/228-6300), one of the city's most comfortable and well-respected venues, especially for acoustic acts; the ✪ **Bowery Ballroom,** 6 Delancey St., at Bowery (☎ **212/533-2111**), a marvelous space accommodating a crowd of 500 or so; **Irving Plaza,** 17 Irving Place, at 15th Street (☎ **212/777-6800**), another pleasing mid-sized hall; **Roseland,** 239 W. 52nd St. (☎ **212/247-0200**), an old warhorse of a general-admission venue that has hosted everybody from Big Bad Voodoo Daddy to Busta Rhymes to Jeff Beck; and the **Hammerstein Ballroom,** at the Manhattan Center, 311 W. 34th St. (☎ **212/564-4882**), a general-admission hall with very good sound and sightlines.

Be aware that a night at a top-flight jazz club can be expensive. For serious fans, it's worth splurging on a night at one of New York's world-class showcases for the top talents in the jazz world: the **Blue Note,** 131 W. 3rd St., at Sixth Avenue (☎ **212/475-8592;** www.bluenote.net); the **Village Vanguard,** 178 Seventh Ave. South, just below 11th Street (☎ **212/255-4037**); or **Iridium,** 44 W. 63rd St., at Columbus Avenue (☎ **212/582-2121;** www.iridiumjazz. com), Monday-night home of the Les Paul Trio. However, cover charges can vary dramatically—from as little as $10 to as high as $65, depending on who's taking the stage—and there's likely to be an additional drink minimum, or maybe even a dinner requirement. Call ahead so you know what you're getting into; reservations are an excellent idea.

Arlene Grocery. 95 Stanton St. (btw. Ludlow and Orchard sts.). ☎ **212/ 358-1633.** www.arlene-grocery.com. Subway: F to Second Ave.

Live music is always free at this Lower East Side club, which boasts a friendly bar and a good sound system. Arlene Grocery primarily serves as a showcase for unknown bands looking for a deal or promoting their self-pressed record. Still, there's little risk involved thanks to the no-cover policy, and bookers who know what they're doing. The crowd is an easygoing mix of club hoppers, rock fans looking for a new fix, and industry scouts looking for new blood.

Cafe Wha? 115 MacDougal St. (btw. Bleecker and W. 3rd sts.). ☎ **212/ 254-3706.** Subway: A, B, C, D, E, F, Q to W. 4th St.

You'll find a carefree crowd dancing in the aisles of this casual basement club just about any night of the week. From Wednesday through Sunday, the stage features the house's own Wha Band, which does an excellent job cranking out crowd-pleasing covers of familiar rock-and-roll hits from the '70s, '80s, and '90s. Monday night is the hugely popular Brazilian Dance Party, while Tuesday night is Funk Night. Expect to be surrounded by lots of Jersey kids and out-of-towners on the weekends, but so what? You'll be having as much fun as they are.

CBGB's. 315 Bowery (at Bleecker St.). ☎ **212/982-4052,** or 212/677-0455 for CB's 313 Gallery. www.cbgb.com. Subway: 6 to Bleecker St.; F to Second Ave.

The original downtown rock club has seen much better days, but no other spot is so rich with rock-and-roll history—this was the launching pad for New York punk and New Wave. The occasional names still show up (at press time, Tom Tom Club was doing a special 25th Anniversary show) but most acts performing here these days you've never heard of. Never mind—CB's still rocks. Expect loud and cynical, and you're unlikely to come away disappointed. Come early if you have hopes of actually seeing the stage, and avoid the bathrooms at all costs.

More today than yesterday is ✪ **CB's 313 Gallery,** a welcome spin-off that showcases alternative art on the walls and mostly acoustic singer/songwriters on stage. Within striking distance of the history, but much more pleasant all the way around.

Chicago B.L.U.E.S. 73 Eighth Ave. (btw. 13th and 14th sts.). ☎ **212/ 924-9755.** Subway: A, C, E, L to 14th St.

Here's the best blues joint in the city, with a genuine Windy City flair. The contrived decor makes the place feel more theme-park than roadhouse, but the music is the real thing. Kick back on the comfortable couches for some of the best unadulterated blues around, which can include big names like Buddy Miles and Lonnie Brooks.

The Knitting Factory. 74 Leonard St. (btw. Broadway and Church St.). ☎ **212/219-3006.** www.knittingfactory.com. Subway: 1, 9 to Franklin St.

New York's premier avant-garde music venue has four separate spaces, each showcasing performances ranging from experimental jazz and acoustic folk to spoken-word and poetry readings to out-there multimedia works. Regulars who use the Knitting Factory as their lab of choice include former Lounge Lizard John Lurie; around-the-bend experimentalist John Zorn; and guitar gods Vernon Reid, Eliot Sharp, and David Torn. (If these names mean nothing to you, chances are good that the Knitting Factory is not for you.) The schedule is peppered with edgy star turns from the likes of Taj Mahal, Faith No More's Mike Patton, and folky charmer Jill Sobule ("I Kissed a Girl"). There are often two shows a night in the remarkably pleasing main performance space.

✪ **Mercury Lounge.** 217 E. Houston St. (at Essex St./Ave. A). ☎ **212/ 260-4700.** Subway: F to Second Ave.

The Merc is everything a top-notch live music venue should be: unpretentious, extremely civilized, and outfitted with a killer sound system. The rooms themselves are nothing special: a front bar and an intimate back-room performance space with a low stage and a few

Free Music

Arlene Grocery and **Rodeo Bar** (see below) are the city's top no-cover clubs, but they're far from the only free shows in town.

East Village stalwart **Sidewalk Cafe,** 94 Ave. A, at 6th Street (☎ 212/473-7373), hosts live bands in the back room most nights. Pretty good cheap eats and two-for-one drinks before 8pm serve as additional attractions for the monetarily challenged.

On the Lower East Side is comfy **Luna Lounge,** 171 Ludlow St., between Houston and Stanton streets (☎ 212/260-2323), which usually hosts two bands per night, and is a popular venue for local record-release parties. Monday's comedy night, however, has become so popular that a $5 cover is now charged.

One of my favorite coffeehouses, **Eureka Joe,** 168 Fifth Ave., at 22nd Street (☎ 212/741-7500, or 212/741-7504 for recorded schedule information), hosts a mix of eclectic acoustic acts and readings in its cozy, velvet-curtained environs. The cappuccino, sandwiches, and pastries are great, and there's also a beer and wine bar.

Jazz fans will want to try **Arthur's Tavern,** 57 Grove St., at Seventh Avenue South (☎ 212/675-6879), a comfortable club and piano bar attracting a mixed gay-and-straight crowd. Beware of the drinks, however, which can be pricey.

Louisiana Community Bar & Grill, 622 Broadway, at Houston Street (☎ 212/460-9633), is a great place to do the swing thing for free. There's live music 7 nights a week, and acts like the Flipped Fedoras, the Harlem Jazz Legends, and George Gee and the Jump, Jive and Wailers have been dominating the bill of late.

Also keep in mind that a number of clubs offer free music one or more nights a week, such as **Cafe Wha?** and **Chicago B.L.U.E.S.;** the **Knitting Factory** offers free music in its Tap Bar. The easiest way to check for free events while you're in town is to peruse the music calendar in the weekly *Time Out New York,* which announces no-cover shows with an easy-to-spot FREE! Sunday night, in particular, is a big night for freebies.

Remember that schedules and no-cover policies can change at any time, so it's a good idea to confirm in advance.

tables along the wall. The calendar is filled with a mix of accomplished local rockers and up-and-coming national acts. The crowd is grown-up and easygoing. The only downside is that it's consistently packed thanks to the high quality of the entertainment and all-around pleasing nature of the experience.

Rodeo Bar. 375 Third Ave. (at 27th St.). ☎ **212/683-6500.** www.rodeobar. com. Subway: 6 to 28th St.

Here's New York's oldest—and finest—honky-tonk. Hike up your Wranglers and head those Fryes inside, where you'll find longhorns on the walls, peanut shells underfoot, and Tex-Mex on the menu. But this place is really about the music: urban-tinged country, foot-stompin' bluegrass, swinging rockabilly, Southern-flavored rock. While bigger names like Rosie Flores and up-and-comers on the tour circuit occasionally grace the stage, regular acts like Dixieland swingers the Flying Neutrinos and Simon and the Bar Sinisters usually supply the free music, keeping the urban cowboys plenty happy.

✪ **S.O.B's.** 204 Varick St. (at W. Houston St.). ☎ **212/243-4940.** Subway: 1, 9 to Houston St.

This is the city's top world-music venue, specializing in Brazilian, Caribbean, and Latin sounds. The packed house dances and sings along nightly to calypso, samba, mambo, African drums, reggae, or other global grooves, united in the high-energy, feel-good vibe. Bookings include top-flight performers from around the globe; luminaries who have graced the stage include Marc Anthony, Astrud Gilberto, King Sunny Ade, and the unsurpassed Celia Cruz. The room's Tropicana Club style has island pizzazz that carries through to the Caribbean-influenced cooking and tropical drinks menu. This place is so popular that it's an excellent idea to book in advance, especially if you'd like table seating.

4 Stand-Up Comedy

Cover charges are generally in the $8 to $15 range, with all-star **Caroline's,** 1626 Broadway, between 49th and 50th streets (☎ **212/757-4100**), going as high as $25 on occasion. Unless you're enamored with seeing a big name that's scheduled there, I suggest that those of you watching your wallets opt for a less-expensive club, where you're likely to enjoy just as many yuks.

Keep in mind that many clubs have a two-drink minimum, and may raise their covers if a famous name is in the house; be sure to ask about the night's cover and requirements when you reserve. And ask about open-mike shows if you want to try to tickle some funny bones yourself.

✪ **Comedy Cellar.** 117 MacDougal St. (btw. Bleecker and W. 3rd sts.). ☎ **212/254-3480.** Subway: A, B, C, D, E, F, Q to W. 4th St. (use 3rd St. exit).

This intimate subterranean spot is the club of choice for stand-up fans in the know, thanks to the best, most consistently impressive lineups in the business. I'll always love the Comedy Cellar for introducing me to an uproariously funny unknown comic named Ray Romano a few years back. Just $5 weekdays, $12 weekends.

Gotham Comedy Club. 34 W. 22nd St. (btw. Fifth and Sixth aves.). ☎ **212/367-9000.** www.citysearch.com/nyc/gothamcomedy. Subway: N, R or F to 23rd St.

Here's the city's trendiest and most sophisticated comedy club. The young talent—Tom Rhodes, Jeff Ross, Paul Mercurio, Lynn Harris—is red-hot. Look for theme nights like the lovelorn laugh riot "Breakup Girl Live!" and "A Very Jewish Thursday." The cover is $8 cover weekdays, $12 weekends.

New York Comedy Club. 241 E. 24th St. (btw. Second and Third aves.). ☎ **212/696-5233.** Subway: 6 to 23rd St.

With a $5 cover charge on weekdays ($10 Friday and Saturday), this club offers the best laugh value for your money. Despite what the owners call their "Wal-Mart approach" to comedy, the club has presented Damon Wayans, Chris Rock, and Brett Butler, among others, in its two showrooms. Fridays feature African-American comics, while Saturdays save time for Hispanic comics.

5 Bars & Cocktail Lounges

DOWNTOWN

Barmacy. 538 E. 14th St. (btw. aves. A and B). ☎ **212/228-2240.** Subway: L to First Ave.

Barmacy is just what you'd guess—a bar housed in a vintage pharmacy, complete with shelves of classic toiletries and a drugstore counter that would make Lana Turner smile. On an otherwise desolate stretch of East 14th, it's really a fun place to spend an evening, complete with a youngish party-hearty crowd and DJs spinning tunes in the back room that range from earnest Britpop to modern funk to makeout music, depending on the evening.

Chumley's. 86 Bedford St. (btw. Grove and Barrow sts.). ☎ **212/675-4449.** Subway: 1, 9 to Christopher St.–Sheridan Square.

A classic. Many bars in New York date their beginnings to Prohibition, but Chumley's still has the vibe. The circa college-age crowd doesn't date back nearly as far, however. Come to warm yourself by the fire and indulge in a once-forbidden pleasure: beer. The door is unmarked, with a metal grille on the small window; another entrance is at 58 Barrow St., which takes you in through a back courtyard.

✪ **dba.** 41 First Ave. (btw. 2nd and 3rd sts.). ☎ **212/475-5097.** Subway: F to Second Ave.

dba has completely bucked the loungey trend that has taken over the city, instead remaining firmly and resolutely an unpretentious neighborhood bar, where everyone is welcome and at home. Most importantly, dba is a beer- and scotch-lover's paradise. Owner Ray Deter specializes in British-style cask-conditioned ales (the kind that you pump by hand) and stocks a phenomenal collection of 90 single-malt scotches. The relaxed crowd is a pleasing mix of connoisseurs and casual drinkers who like the unlimited choices and egalitarian vibe. Excellent jukebox, too.

Double Happiness. 173 Mott St. (at Broome St.). ☎ **212/941-1282.** Subway: 6 to Spring St.; B, D, Q to Grand St.

This new kid on a new block has already shown itself to be quite a star. The only indicator to the subterranean entrance is a vertical WATCH YOUR STEP sign. Once through the door, you'll find a beautifully designed lounge with artistic nods to the neighborhood throughout. The space is large, but a low ceiling and intimate nooks enhance its romantic vibe (although the loud funkified music mix may deter true wooing). Don't miss the green-tea martini, an inspired house creation.

✪ **The Greatest Bar on Earth.** 1 World Trade Center, 107th floor (on West St., btw. Liberty and Vesey sts.) ☎ **212/524-7000.** www. windowsontheworld.com. Subway: 1, 9, C, E to Church St.; N, R to Cortlandt St.

High atop the World Trade Center sits the Greatest Bar on Earth, whose name is only a slight exaggeration. This is a magical spot for cocktails and dancing (mostly swing); the music is loud, and the joint really jumps as the night goes on. No matter how many times I come up here, I'm wowed by the incredible views. The place is huge, but intimate nooks and a separate back room bring the scale down to comfortable proportions. The crowd is a lively mix of

in-the-know locals and stylish out-of-towners. Quintessentially—
and spectacularly—New York.

Idlewild. 145 E. Houston St. (btw. First and Second aves., on the south side
of Houston). ☎ **212/477-5005.** Subway: F to Second Ave.

It may look unapproachable from the street, with nothing but an
unmarked stainless-steel facade, but inside you'll find a fun, easy-
going bar that's perfect for lovers of retro-kitsch. The interior is a
larger-scale repro of a jet airplane, complete with reclining seats, tray
tables, an Austin Powers–style bar to gather around at center stage,
and too-small bathrooms that will transport you back to your favorite mid-air moments in no time. The DJ spins a listener-friendly mix
of light techno, groovy disco in the Funkadelic vein, and '80s tunes
from the likes of the Smiths and the Cure.

The Sporting Club. 99 Hudson St. (btw. Franklin and Leonard sts.). ☎ **212/
219-0900.** www.thesportingclub.net. Subway: 1, 9 to Franklin St.

The city's best sports bar is a guy's joint if there ever was one. The
space is as big as a linebacker, with giant TV screens at every turn
tuned to just about every game on the planet. (Wall Streeters bring
their international cohorts here to catch everything from English
football to Japanese sumo.) There's no better place for sports fans
to get crazy at Super Bowl time and during March Madness. When
the big games are over, this turns into a surprisingly popular singles
place.

Wall St. Kitchen & Bar. 70 Broad St. (btw. Beaver and S. William sts., about
1¹/₂ blocks south of New York Stock Exchange). ☎ **212/797-7070.** www.
citysearch.com/nyc/wallstkitchen. Subway: 4, 5 to Bowling Green; J, M, Z to
Broad St.

Want to rub elbows with some genuine bulls and bears after a hard
day of downtown sightseeing? Head to this surprisingly appealing
and affordable bar, housed (appropriately enough) in a spectacular
former bank in the heart of the financial district. Wall St. Kitchen
specializes in on-tap beers and "flight" menus of wines and
microbrews for tasting. The familiar bar food is well prepared and
reasonably priced.

MIDTOWN

Divine Bar. 244 E. 51st St. (btw. Second and Third aves.). ☎ **212/319-9463.**
Subway: 6 to 51st St.; E, F to Lexington Ave.

This glowing hacienda-style wine bar is a big hit with a cute and
sophisticated under-40 crowd (think up-and-coming media types
and you'll get the picture), with a few older patrons in the mix who

come for the excellent selection of wines and microbrews rather than the pick-up scene. I prefer the more relaxed, fireplace-lit upstairs over the first floor bar. The DJ plays a radio-friendly mix, and there's live acoustic music on Sundays. Good tapas and an extensive humidor round out the appeal.

The Ginger Man. 11 E. 36th St. (btw. Fifth and Madison aves.). ☎ **212/532-3740.** Subway: 6 to 33rd St.

The big bait at this appealing and cigar-friendly beer bar is the 66 gleaming tap handles lining the wood-and-brass bar, dispensing everything from Sierra Nevada and Hoegaarden to cask-conditioned ales. The cavernous space has a clubby feel, as Cohiba-toking Wall Streeters lounge on sofas and chairs. The limited menu is well prepared, and prices are better than you'd expect from an upmarket place like this.

Heartland Brewery. 35 Union Sq. W. (16th St.). ☎ **212/645-3400.** Subway: 4, 5, 6, N, R, L to 14th St.–Union Sq.

The food leaves a bit to be desired, but the house-brewed beers are first-rate. Brewmaster Jim Migliorini's two-time award-winner, Farmer Jon's Oatmeal Stout, is always on hand, as are four other hand-crafted brews. The wood-paneled, two-level bar is big and appealing, but expect a loud, boisterous after-work crowd. There's now a Midtown location, too: 1285 Sixth Ave., at 51st Street (☎ **212/582-8244**).

Joe Allen. 326 W. 46th St. (btw. Eighth and Ninth aves.). ☎ **212/581-6464.** Subway: A, C, E to 42nd St.

An upscale pub peopled with Broadway types gives this atmospheric place the edge on Restaurant Row. More than 30 bottled beers are on the shelves. The bar is always hopping, but the American food is reliable and well-priced if you'd rather sit down at a table for a bite. You'll thoroughly enjoy perusing the walls, which are covered with posters and other memorabilia from legendary Broadway flops.

✪ **King Cole Room.** At the St. Regis hotel, 2 E. 55th St. (at Fifth Ave.). ☎ **212/339-6721.** Subway: E, F to 53rd St.

The birthplace of the Bloody Mary, this theatrical spot may just be New York's best hotel bar. The Maxfield Parrish mural alone is worth the price of a classic cocktail. The sophisticated setting demands proper attire, so be sure to dress for the occasion. *The New York Times* calls the bar nuts "the best in town," but there's an elegant bar food menu if you'd like something more substantial. A worthy splurge.

Mickey Mantle's. 42 Central Park S. (btw. Fifth and Sixth aves). ☎ **212/688-7777.** Subway: B, Q to 57th St.

If you're a fan, it's definitely worth a visit to the Mick's sports bar and restaurant, which chronicles his life and career in photos. A great place to watch the game, too. Don Imus, a self-styled sports expert, has been known to wander in on occasion.

Pete's Tavern. 129 E. 18th St. (at Irving Place). ☎ **212/473-7676.** Subway: 4, 5, 6, N, R, L to 14th St./Union Square.

This old-timer features sidewalk space for summer imbibing, Guinness on tap, and a St. Patrick's Day party that makes the neighbors crazy. But the best thing in Pete's (opened in 1864—while Lincoln was still president!) is the happy hour, where drinks are cheap and the crowd is a mix of locals from ritzy Gramercy Park and more down-to-earth types.

The View Lounge. On the 48th floor of the New York Marriott Marquis, 1535 Broadway (btw. 45th and 46th sts.). ☎ **212/398-1900.** Subway: 1, 2, 3, 9, N, R to Times Sq.; N, R to 49th St.

If it's a clear night, head up to this aptly named three-story revolving rooftop bar for great views and decent cocktails. Grab a window seat if you can; it takes about an hour to see the 360-degree view of Times Square go by.

UPTOWN

Brandy's Piano Bar. 235 E. 84th St. (btw. Second and Third aves.). ☎ **212/650-1944.** Subway: 4, 5, 6 to 86th St.

A mixed crowd—Upper East Side locals, waiters off work, gays, straights, all ages—comes to this intimate, old-school piano bar for the friendly atmosphere and nightly entertainment. The talented waitstaff does most of the singing while waiting for their big break, but enthusiastic patrons join in on occasion.

Hi-Life Bar & Grill. 477 Amsterdam Ave. (at 83rd St.). ☎ **212/787-7199.** Subway: 1, 9 to 86th St.

During the week, expect a few quiet drinks with a slightly older crowd in this casual retro-style bar and restaurant. Come the weekend, youth reigns, the volume cranks up, and the dating game zooms into full gear. The classic martinis couldn't be better.

O'Neal's. 49 W. 64th St. (btw. Broadway and Central Park West). ☎ **212/787-4663.** Subway: 1, 9 to 66th St.

O'Neal's easygoing, old-time atmosphere makes it a favorite among a grown-up neighborhood crowd as well as students from nearby

Juilliard. Lincoln Center is a stone's throw away, making this a great place for a pre-theater cocktail or a reasonably priced, if unremarkable, bite to eat.

Shark Bar. 307 Amsterdam Ave. (btw. 74th and 75th sts.). ☎ **212/874-8500.** Subway: 1, 2, 3, 9 to 72nd St.

This perennially popular upscale spot is well known for its good soul food and even better singles' scene. It's also a favorite hangout for sports celebs, so don't be surprised if you spot a New York Knick or two.

6 Dance Clubs & Party Scenes

First things first: Finding and going to the latest hotspot is not worth agonizing over. Clubbers spend their lives obsessing over the scene. My rule of thumb is that if I know about a place, it must not be hip anymore. Even if I could tell you where the hippest club kids hang out today, they'll have moved on by the time you arrive in town.

You can find listings for the most current hotspots and moveable parties in the publications and online sources listed at the start of this chapter. *Time Out New York* is a great source to check, because it lists cover charges for the week's big events and clearly indicates which are free. Another good bet is to cruise hip boutiques in SoHo, the East Village, and the Lower East Side, where party planners usually leave flyers advertising the latest goings-on. No matter what, **always call ahead,** because schedules change constantly, and can do so at the last minute.

New York nightlife starts late: With the exception of places that have scheduled performances, it's almost useless to show up anywhere before about 11pm. Bring cash, and plan on dropping a wad at most places. Cover charges start out high—anywhere from $10 to $25—and often get more expensive as the night wears on.

Life. 158 Bleecker St. (Sullivan and Thompson sts.). ☎ **212/420-1999.** Subway: A, B, C, D, E, F, Q to W. 4th St.

This velvet-drenched, faux-deco nightclub was *the* clubbers' hotspot a few years back, and it just keeps on going. The formula changes every night, from Lifestyle Fridays, drawing a fabulous fashion crowd, to Boy's Life Sundays, when beautiful Chelsea boys come looking for the same. The cover ranges from $10 to $20.

✪ **Mother.** 432 W. 14th St. (at Washington St.). ☎ **212/366-5680.** Subway: A, C, E to 14th St.

Fabulous hipsters, both gay and straight, crowd this joint for a variety of hugely popular events. On Tuesday it's Jackie 60 (☎ 212/929-6060; www.echonyc.com/~interjackie), which *Paper* magazine calls "the mother of all freak fests." Almost as popular is Saturday's Click + Drag, a futuristic techno-fetish party from the same team. Performance art, poetry readings, and other multimedia fun round out the goings-on. The cover ranges from $5 to $15; call to check if a strict dress code is being enforced the night you go.

✪ **Nell's.** 246 W. 14th St. (btw. Seventh and Eighth aves.). ☎ **212/675-1567.** Subway: 1, 2, 3, 9, A, C, E to 14th St.

Nell's was the first to establish a lounge-like atmosphere years ago, and still attracts a huge crowd comprised of everyone from homies to Wall Streeters. Most of the parties have a soulful edge. Look for the hugely popular laid-back Voices, sort of a sophisticated weekly *Star Search* that's a showcase for a surprising number of new talents. The cover runs $10 to $15.

Polly Esther's. 1487 First Ave. (btw. 77th and 78th sts.). ☎ **212/628-4477.** Subway: 6 to 77th St. Also at 186 W. 4th St. (btw. Sixth and Seventh aves.). ☎ **212/924-5707.** Subway: 1, 9 to Christopher St.–Sheridan Sq.

Here's the ultimate 1970s theme club, where you can groove to the sounds of the Bee Gees, Gloria Gaynor, Abba, and every other band you loved when you still listened to AM radio and turned the dial on the TV set. This cheesy place is geared to tourists, but who cares? Arrive before 10pm to avoid the $8 cover (no cover on Wednesday and Thursday).

If you're more Karma Chameleon than Dancing Queen, then head to the similarly silly **Culture Club,** 179 Varick St., between King and Charlton streets (☎ **212/243-1999**), where the big '80s come to life.

Roxy. 515 W. 18th St. (at Tenth Ave.). ☎ **212/645-5156.** Subway: 1, 9 to 18th St.

This club scene stalwart could be the single best place to see the Manhattan night mix, worth the (usually) $20 cover. You'll find fashion models, city club kids, wide-eyed kids from the 'burbs, straights and gays of every color, lights, sound, and action. At press time, the schedule featured in-line roller disco on Tuesday (predominantly gay) and Wednesday (mixed). Friday nights draw a big hetero Hispanic crowd with salsa and merengue, while Saturdays bring in a committed, mostly gay crowd in love with the tribal house mix. There's also a martini lounge, a cigar bar, and two VIP rooms.

13. 35 E. 13th St. (btw. Broadway and University Place), 2nd floor. ☎ **212/979-6677.** Subway: 4, 5, 6, N, R, L to Union Sq.

This little lounge is a great place to dance the night away. It's stylish but unpretentious, with a steady roster of fun weekly parties. If there's a cover, it's usually just $5. Arrive extra-early, between 4 and 8pm, for two-for-one happy hour.

Webster Hall. 125 E. 11th St. (btw. Third and Fourth aves.). ☎ **212/353-1600.** www.webster-hall.com. Subway: 6 to Astor Place.

Five floors and a seemingly endless warren of rooms mean that there's something for everyone at this old war horse of a nightclub. Even though it's dominated by a bridge-and-tunnel crowd, Webster Hall is still a plenty interesting place to hang on the weekends, especially if you're looking for a straightforward crowd and music mix. Expect to wait in line to get in. The standard cover is $22, but add your name to the guest list via the Web, and you can enter for as little as $5 before midnight. Ladies free on Thursdays.

XIT. 511 Lexington Ave. (btw. 47th and 48th sts.). ☎ **212/371-1600.** Subway: 4, 5, 6, 7 to Grand Central.

At this popular baby-boomer hangout, thirty-, forty-, and fiftysomethings boogie to a mainstream mix of tunes from the 1960s to the top hits of today. The owners have issued a "no attitude" promise to the press, so everyone should feel comfortable here. Admission is $10.

7   The Lesbian & Gay Scene

For an up-to-date take on what's happening in gay and lesbian nightlife, pick up a free copy of *Homo Xtra (HX)* or *HX for Her,* available for free in bars and clubs or at the Lesbian and Gay Community Services Center (see "Tips for Travelers with Special Needs" in chapter 1), or go online at **www.hx.com**. *Time Out New York* also boasts a terrific gay and lesbian section.

These days, many bars, clubs and cocktail lounges are neither gay nor straight but a bit of both. Most of the clubs listed under "Dance Clubs & Party Scenes," above, cater to a gay crowd, some predominately so.

Barracuda. 275 W. 22nd St. (btw. Seventh and Eighth aves.). ☎ **212/645-8613.** Subway: 1, 9 or C, E to 23rd St.

Chelsea is now central to gay life—and gay bars. This trendy, loungy place was voted "Best Bar" by *HX* and *New York Press* magazines, while *Paper* singles out the hunky bartenders. Look for the regular drag shows.

Henrietta Hudson. 438 Hudson St. (at Morton St.). ☎ **212/924-3347.** Subway: 1, 9 to Houston St.

This friendly and extremely popular women's bar is known for drawing in an attractive crowd that comes for the great jukebox and videos as well as the pleasingly low-key atmosphere.

✪ **Meow Mix.** 269 E. Houston St. (btw. avenues A and B) ☎ **212/254-0688.** Subway: F to Second Ave.

This funky two-level East Villager is the city's best, and probably its most popular, lesbian hangout. It draws in a young, attractive, arty crowd with nightly diversions like groovy DJs and the hugely popular Xena Night. Meow Mix is also booking an increasing number of good local bands, with most nights dedicated to the girls but one night set aside for all-boy bands.

Stonewall. 53 Christopher St. (just east of Seventh Ave. South). ☎ **212/463-0950.** Subway: 1, 9 to Christopher St.–Sheridan Square.

A new bar at the spot where it all started. A mixed male crowd—old and young, beautiful and great personalities—makes this an easy place to begin.

✪ **Wonder Bar.** 505 E. 6th St. (btw. avenues A and B). ☎ **212/777-9105.** Subway: 6 to Astor Place.

The "sofa look" has lent a loungier, more stylish tone to this packed-on-weekends East Village hangout. There's some male cruising, but fun and friendly Wonder Bar gets points for making straights feel welcome, too. DJs now spin a listener-friendly mix from the revamped back room.

Index

See also separate Accommodations and Restaurant indexes, below.

GENERAL INDEX

ABC Carpet & Home, 158
Abyssinian Baptist Church, 123
Accommodations, 47–77. *See also* Accommodations index
 chains, 64–65
 money-saving tips, 5–8, 48, 73
 package deals, 21, 54–55
 reservation services, 6
Activities, 151–52
Adventure on a Shoestring, 146
Airfares, 3–4
Airlines, 2–3, 19–21, 24
Airports, 2, 19–20
 safety warning, 25
 transportation to/from, 21–26
Airport shuttles, 21–22, 23–24
Air-Ride, 21
Alice Tully Hall, 168
American Art, Whitney Museum of, 134–35
American Ballet Theatre, 166, 167
American Express, 9, 28, 45, 163
American Family Immigration History Center (Ellis Island), 123
American Immigrant Wall of Honor (Ellis Island), 122–23

American Museum of Natural History, 127, 130–32, 153
Amtrak, 4, 26
Annex Antiques Fair and Flea Market, 157
Anthropologie, 155
Area codes, 45
Arlene Grocery, 172, 174
Arthur's Tavern, 174
Art museums
 the Cloisters, 133
 Cooper-Hewitt National Design Museum, 135
 Frick Collection, 136
 Guggenheim Museum, 134
 International Center of Photography, 136
 Metropolitan Museum of Art, 132–33, 141
 Morgan Library, 138
 Museum of Modern Art, 133–34
 Whitney Museum of American Art, 134–35
ATM networks, 5

Baby-sitters, 17
Ballet, 166, 167
Balto statue, in Central Park, 149
BAM. *See* Brooklyn Academy of Music

Bargemusic (Brooklyn), 165–66

Barmacy, 176

Barnes & Noble, 158

Bars, 176–81
    gay and lesbian, 183–84

Battery Park City, 32, 138

Bed-and-breakfasts, 7–8

Bed, Bath & Beyond, 158

Belvedere Castle (Central Park), 148, 150

Bethesda Fountain (Central Park), 150

Bethesda Terrace (Central Park), 150

Bicycling, 152

Big Apple Circus, 17

Big Apple Greeter, 145

Big Apple Visitors Kit, 11

Big Onion Walking Tours, 144, 146

Bleecker Street, 158

Bloomingdale's, 159–60

Blue Note, 172

Blues, 171–75

Boating, 150, 152

Boat travel and cruises, 126, 144. *See also* Ferries

Bookstores, 158

Bottom Line, 171

Bow Bridge (Central Park), 150

Bowery, 32, 155

Bowery Ballroom, 171

Brandy's Piano Bar, 180

Bridge, Brooklyn, 122, 124–25, 139

Broadway, 31, 32
    shopping, 157–58
    theater. *See* Theater

Broadway on Broadway, 15

Brooklyn Academy of Music (BAM), 123, 166
    Next Wave Festival, 16, 123, 166

Brooklyn Bridge, 122, 124–25, 139

Bryant Park Film Festival, 123, 171

Bucket shops, 3

Buses, 41–42
    to/from airports, 22–24
    for disabled travelers, 18
    to New York City, 4, 26
    tours, 143

Cabs, 31, 42–44
    to/from airports, 24–25
    for disabled travelers, 18

Cafe Wha?, 172, 174

Canal Street, 34

Carnegie Hall, 166, 168

Caroline's, 175

Carousel, in Central Park, 149

Car services, 25–26

Car travel, 26
    parking, 8, 39, 46

CBGB's, 172–73

Central Park, 122, 146–52
    activities, 16, 151–52
    for children, 153
    free events in, 170–71
        Shakespeare in the Park, 14, 123, 150, 170
    guided tours, 149
    Information Center, 148
    playgrounds, 154
    safety tip, 149
    sightseeing, 149–51
    traveling to, 148

Central Park Drive, 148, 151–52

Central Park Wildlife Center, 151
Century 21, 160
Channel Gardens (Rockefeller Center), 141
Charles A. Dana Discovery Center (Central Park), 149, 151
Chelsea, 36
    accommodations, 56–57
    flea market, 157
    gay and lesbian nightlife, 183–84
    restaurants, 103–4
Chelsea Piers, 36
Chicago B. L. U. E. S., 173, 174
Children
    sights and activities, 153–54
    travel tips, 17
Children's Museum of Manhattan, 153
Children's Zoo (Central Park), 151
Chinatown, 12, 32, 34
    restaurants, 84–85
    shopping, 154
Chinese New Year, 12
Christmas Spectacular, Radio City Music Hall, 16, 170
Christopher Street, 158, 184
Chrysler Building, 139
Chumley's, 177
Circle Line Sightseeing Cruises, 144
Circuses, 13, 17
City Center, 166
City layout, 30–39
CityPass, 9–10
Citysearch, 11, 162

Classical music, 123, 165, 167–71
Climate, 12
Cloisters, the, 133
Clothing. See Fashion
Cocktail lounges, 176–81
Comedy Cellar, 176
Comedy clubs, 175–76
Concert halls, 165–71
Concerts, 14, 123, 165–66, 167–75. See also Music
Conservatory Garden (Central Park), 150
Conservatory Water (Central Park), 150
Consolidators, 3
Cooper-Hewitt National Design Museum, 135
Courier flights, 3–4
Crime, 44–45
Cruises, 126, 144
Currency and exchange, 28
Cybercafes, 46

Dana Discovery Center (Central Park), 149, 151
Dance clubs, 181–83
    gay and lesbian, 183–84
Dance troupes, 166–67
dba, 177
Delacorte Theater (Central Park), 14, 123, 150, 170
Delis, 92–93
Department stores, 159–61
    Christmas windows, 17
Design Museum, Cooper-Hewitt National, 135
Diamond District, 158–59
Diana Ross Playground, 154
Dining. See Restaurants
Dinosaurs, 127, 130–32, 153

Disabled travelers, 17–18
Discounts, 9. *See also* Money-
 saving tips
  CityPass, 9–10
  MetroCard, 4, 29, 40, 41, 42
  New York for Less, 2
  Playbill Online Theater
   Club, 6, 9, 10, 164
  on tickets, 10, 164–65
Disney Store, 158
Divine Bar, 178–79
Dog Show, Westminster
 Kennel Club, 12–13
Dö Kham, 156
Double-decker bus tours, 143
Double Happiness, 177
Downtown, 32–36. *See also*
 specific neighborhoods
  bars, 176–78
Drugstores, 46

Easter Parade, 13
East Side, 31. *See also* East
 Village; Gramercy Park; Lower
 East Side; Midtown East;
 Upper East Side
East Village, 35
  bars, 176–78
  gay and lesbian nightlife,
   183–84
  restaurants, 89–94
  shopping, 156
Electronics stores, 159
Elizabeth Street, 155–56
Ellis Island, 120, 122–24
Emergencies, 45–46
Empire State Building,
 139–40, 153
Entry requirements, 26–27
Eureka Joe, 174

Families. *See* Children
FAO Schwarz, 17

Farmers' markets, 37
Fashion, 154, 156
  department stores, 159–61
  Garment District, 158
Feast of San Gennaro, 15
Ferries
  to Ellis Island, 124
  Staten Island Ferry, 122,
   124
Festivals, 10–11, 12–17,
 170–71
Fifth Avenue, 30, 31
  shopping, 159
Filene's Basement, 158
Film festivals
  Bryant Park Film Festival,
   123, 171
  New York Film Festival, 15
Financial District, 32, 125–26
  restaurants, 79–80, 82
First Corinthian Baptist
 Church, 123
Flatiron District, 36, 37
  accommodations, 50–56
  restaurants, 98–103
  shopping, 158
Flea markets, 157
Fleet Week, 13
Flushing Meadows Park
 (Queens), 15
Foreign visitors, 26–28
Fourth of July Fireworks
 Spectacular, 14
Free activities, 10, 122–23
Free music, 174
Frick Collection, 136
Fringe Festival, 14–15

Garment District, 158
Gay and lesbian travelers, 19
  accommodations, 56–57
  Lesbian and Gay Pride
   Week and March, 14

nightlife, 182–84
  Wigstock, 15
GE Building, 142
Ginger Man, 179
Global Table, 155
Gotham Comedy Club, 176
Gramercy Park, 36, 37
  accommodations, 50–56
  restaurants, 98–103
Grand Central Terminal, 23,
  24, 140–41
  guided tours, 145
  restaurants, 113–14
Gray Line Air Shuttle, 23
Gray Line New York Tours,
  143
Greatest Bar on Earth, 177–78
Great Lawn (Central Park),
  150
Greenflea Market, 157
Greenmarket, 37
Greenwich Village, 35–36
  accommodations, 50
  Halloween Parade, 16
  restaurants, 94–98
  shopping, 156–58
Greyhound, 4, 26
Guggenheim Museum, 134
Guided tours. See Tours

Hammerstein Ballroom, 172
Harbor. See New York Harbor
Harlem, 39, 123
  accommodations, 76–77
  guided tours, 146
  restaurants, 118
Harlem Meer (Central Park),
  150–51
Harlem Week, 15
Hayden Planetarium, 132
Heartland Brewery, 179
Henry Luce Nature Observatory
  (Central Park), 150

Hi-Life Bar & Grill, 180
HIV-positive travelers, 28
Holocaust memorial, 138
Homestays, 7–8
Horse-drawn carriages, in
  Central Park, 152
Hospitals, 45–46
Hostels, 8, 75–76
Hotels. See Accommodations;
  Accommodations index

Ice skating, 16, 142, 149, 152
Idlewild, 178
IMAX Theater, 127, 132
Immigration Museum (Ellis
  Island), 120
Independence Day Harbor
  Festival, 14
Information sources, 11, 29–30
In-line skating, 152
International Center of
  Photography, 136
Internet access, 46
Intrepid Sea-Air-Space
  Museum, 13, 137, 153
Iridium, 172
Irving Plaza, 171
Islip Airport, 24

Jazz, 167, 171–75
Jewish Heritage, Museum of,
  138
Jill Anderson, 156
Joe Allen, 179
John F. Kennedy International
  Airport, 19, 21–26
Joyce Gold History Tours, 146
Joyce Theater, 166–67
Juilliard School, 123, 169

Kennedy International Airport,
  19, 21–26
King Cole Room, 179

Kmart, 156, 160
Knitting Factory, 173, 174

La Guardia Airport, 19, 21–26
Late Night with Conan O'Brien
(TV show), 142
Layout, 30–39
Lennon, John, memorial, 150
Lesbian and Gay Pride Week
and March, 14
Liberty Island, 119–20
Life, 181
Lighting by Gregory, 155
Limousine services, 25–26
Lincoln Center for the
Performing Arts, 38, 167–69
Out-of-Doors, 14
Liquor laws, 46
Little India, restaurants, 91
Little Italy, 34
San Gennaro Feast, 15
Live music. *See* Concerts;
Music
Loeb Boathouse (Central Park),
150, 152
Lord & Taylor, 17, 160–61
Louisiana Community Bar &
Grill, 174
Lower East Side, 34
accommodations, 49
guided tours, 145
shopping, 154–55
Visitor Center, 154
Lower East Side Tenement
Museum, 137, 153
Lower Manhattan, 32, 119–27.
See also Financial District;
South Street Seaport
Luna Lounge, 174

Macy's, 161
Fourth of July Fireworks
Spectacular, 14
Thanksgiving Day Parade,
16–17
Mad About You (TV show), 99
Madison Square Garden,
12–13
Magazines, 30, 162
Manhattan neighborhoods,
32–39. *See also specific
neighborhoods*
Manhattan Portage, 156
Marathon, New York City, 16
Markets
farmers', 37
flea, 157
Medical requirements, 27–28
Mercury Lounge, 173, 175
MetroCard, 4, 29, 40, 41, 42
Metropolitan Museum of Art,
132–33, 141
Metropolitan Opera, 167, 168,
170–71
Mickey Mantle's, 180
Midtown. *See also* Midtown
East; Midtown West
bars, 178–80
neighborhoods, 36–38
Midtown East, 38
accommodations, 66–69
restaurants, 109–14
Midtown West, 37. *See also*
Times Square
accommodations, 57–63
restaurants, 104–9
shopping, 158–59
MOMA (Museum of Modern
Art), 133–34
Money, 28
Money-saving tips, 2–11. *See
also* Discounts
Morgan Library, 138
Mother, 181–82
Mulberry Street, 15, 34,
86–87, 155

Murray Hill, 38
    accommodations, 66–69
    restaurants, 109–14
Museum of Jewish Heritage–A
  Living Memorial to the
  Holocaust, 138
Museum of Modern Art,
  133–34
Museum of Natural History,
  127, 130–32, 153
Music, 171–75
    classical, 123, 165, 167–71
    free, 174
    jazz, 167, 171–75
    opera, 167, 168, 170–71,
      171
    rock, 171–75
    shopping for, 157, 158
    tickets, 168

Natural History, American
  Museum of, 127, 130–32,
  153
NBA Store, 159
NBC, 123, 142
Neighborhoods, 32–39. *See also*
  specific neighborhoods
Nell's, 182
Newark International Airport,
  19, 21–26
Newspapers, 30, 162
New Year's Eve, 17
New York (magazine), 11, 30,
  162
New York Airport Service, 23
New York City Ballet, 167
New York City Marathon, 16
New York City Opera, 167
New York Comedy Club, 176
New York Convention &
  Visitors Bureau, 11, 29–30
New York Film Festival, 15
New York for Less, 2

New York Fringe Festival,
  14–15
New York Grand Opera, 171
New York Harbor, 119–24
    cruises, 126, 144
New York Philharmonic, 167,
  168, 170–71
New York Public Library, 17
New York Skyride, 153
New York Stock Exchange,
  125–26
New York Times, 11, 30, 162
Next Wave Festival (Brooklyn),
  16, 166
Nightlife, 162–84. *See also*
  Bars; Comedy clubs; Dance
  clubs; Music; Performing arts;
  Theater
    current schedule, 11, 30,
      162
    money-saving tips, 10–11
Niketown, 159
9th Street, East, shopping, 156
92nd Street Y, 76, 144, 169
Ninth Avenue International
  Food Festival, 13
NoLiTa (*North of Little Italy*),
  35
    restaurants, 85–89
    shopping, 155–56

Old Navy, 158
Olympia Trails, 24
O'Neal's, 180–81
Opera, 167, 168, 170–71, 171
Orchard Street, 34, 137, 145,
  154
Organized tours. *See* Tours

Package tours, 2, 20–21
Parking, 8, 39, 46
Passport to Off Broadway, 10,
  164

Pat Hoffman Friedman Playground, 154
Pearl River Mart, 154, 161
Penn Station, 26
Performing arts, 162–71. *See also* Dance troupes; Music; Theater
    current schedule, 11, 30, 162
    money-saving tips, 10–11
    tickets, 10, 163–65
Pete's Tavern, 180
Pharmacies, 46
Photography, International Center of, 136
Pier 17, 126
Pier 83, 144
Pioneer, 126, 144
Pizza, 98, 102, 105, 117
Planetarium, 132
Playbill Online Theater Club, 6, 9, 10, 164
Playgrounds, 154
Police, 46
Polly Esther's, 182
Port Authority Terminal, 26
Post office, 46
Prince Street, 155

Radio City Music Hall, 170
    Christmas Spectacular, 16, 170
Ramble, the (Central Park), 150
Recreational activities, 151–52
Reservations
    accommodations, 6
    restaurants, 78
Reservoir (Central Park), 152
Restaurants, 78–118. *See also* Restaurant index
    money-saving tips, 9

    reservations, 78
    theme, 110–11
Restaurant Week, 14
Ringling Bros. and Barnum & Bailey Circus, 13
Rockefeller Center, 141–42
    ice skating, 16, 142
    Lighting of the Christmas Tree, 17
Rockettes, the, 16, 170
Rock music, 171–75
Rodeo Bar, 174, 175
Roller blading, 152
Roseland, 172
Rosie O'Donnell Show (TV show), 142
Roxy, 182–83
Rustic Playground, 154

Safety, 44–45
St. Marks Place, 156
St. Patrick's Day Parade, 13
Saks Fifth Avenue, 17, 161
Sample sales, 158
San Gennaro Feast, 15
Saturday Night Live (TV show), 142
Seasons, 2, 12
Seinfeld (TV show), 109
Senior citizen travelers, 18
Shakespeare in the Park, 14, 123, 150, 170
Shark Bar, 181
Sheep Meadow (Central Park), 150
Shopping, 154–61
Sidewalk Cafe, 174
Sightseeing, 119–51
    money-saving tips, 9–10
Sightseeing tours. *See* Tours
Sixth Avenue, 31
    shopping, 158

Skating
   ice, 16, 142, 149, 152
   in-line, 152
Skyscrapers, 139–43
Smoking, 46, 78–79
S. O. B.'s, 175
SoHo (South of Houston
   Street), 34–35
   restaurants, 85–89
   shopping, 155, 157
SoHo Antiques and
   Collectibles Market, 157
Solomon R. Guggenheim
   Museum, 134
Sony Wonder Technology Lab,
   153
South Street Seaport, 32, 126,
   144, 153
   accommodations, 64–65
   restaurants, 79–80, 80, 82
South Street Seaport Museum,
   126, 153
Spector Playground, 154
Sporting Club, 178
Staten Island Ferry, 122, 124
Statue of Liberty, 119–20
Stock Exchange, New York,
   125–26
Strawberry Fields (Central
   Park), 150
Student travelers, 19
Subway, 39–41
   to/from airports, 22
   for disabled travelers, 18
   safety, 44
SummerStage, 171
Super Shuttle, 23
Symphony orchestras, 167–71

Taxes, 46
Taxis, 31, 42–44
   to/from airports, 24–25
   for disabled travelers, 18

Tele-Charge, 163
Telephones, 5–6
Television tapings, 123, 142
Tenement Museum, Lower
   East Side, 137, 153
Tennis Championships, U. S.
   Open, 15
Theater, 162–65
   BAM Next Wave Festival,
      16, 166
   Broadway on Broadway, 15
   current schedule, 11, 30,
      162
   New York Fringe Festival,
      14–15
   Shakespeare in the Park, 14,
      123, 150, 170
   tickets, 10, 163–65
Theme restaurants, 110–11
34th Street Tour, 145
Ticketmaster, 163
Tickets, 163–65, 168, 169
   discounted, 10, 164–65
Tiffany & Company, 17, 159
Time Out New York, 11, 19,
   30, 162, 174, 181, 183
Times Square, 37
   accommodations, 57–63
   bars, 178–80
   guided tours, 145
   New Year's Eve, 17
   restaurants, 104–9
   shopping, 158–59
   Visitors Center, 29, 46
Tipping, 79
Tisch Children's Zoo (Central
   Park), 151
Titanic Memorial Lighthouse,
   126
TJ Maxx, 158
TKTS booths, 10, 165
Today Show (TV show), 142
Top of the World, 127

Tourist information, 11, 29–30
Tours, 143–46
    package, 2, 20–21
Tower Records, 157
Train travel, 4, 26
Transportation, 39–44
    to/from airports, 21–26
    for disabled travelers, 18
    MetroCard, 4, 29, 40, 41,
        42
    money-saving tips, 4–5, 42
    transit info, 41
Traveling to New York City,
    19–26
    money-saving tips, 2–4
Travel Web sites, 3, 6, 21
TriBeCa (*Tri*angle *Be*low
    *Ca*nal Street), 32
    accommodations, 48–49
    restaurants, 82–84
Trinity Church, 171
26th Street flea market, 157

Union Square, 36, 37
    restaurants, 98–103
    shopping, 158
United Nations, 142–43
Upper East Side, 38
    accommodations, 76
    restaurants, 117–18
Upper West Side, 38
    accommodations, 69–76
    restaurants, 114–16
Uptown. *See also* Harlem;
    Upper East Side; Upper West
    Side
    bars, 180–81
    neighborhoods, 38–39
Urban Outfitters, 158
U. S. Open Tennis
    Championships, 15

View Lounge, 180
Village, the. *See* Greenwich
    Village
Village Vanguard, 172
Village Voice, 30, 162
Virgin Megastore, 158
Visas, 27
Visitor information, 11, 29–30

Walking, 4–5, 39, 122
Walking tours, guided, 144–46
Wall Street, 125
Weather, 12
    updates, 46
Web sites, 11
Webster Hall, 183
West Chelsea, art galleries, 36
Westminster Kennel Club Dog
    Show, 12–13
West Side, 31. *See also* Battery
    Park City; Chelsea; Midtown
    West; Upper West Side; West
    Village
West Village, 35–36. *See also*
    Greenwich Village
    shopping, 156–58
Whitney Museum of American
    Art, 134–35
Wigstock, 15
Wild West Playground, 154
Wollman Rink (Central Park),
    16, 149, 152
World Trade Center, 127, 139,
    153, 177–78
    food court, 80, 82
Wright, Frank Lloyd, 133,
    134

YMCA, 8, 69, 74–75, 76

Zoo, in Central Park, 151

ACCOMMODATIONS

Americana Inn, 57
Amsterdam Inn, 69, 72
Apple Core Hotels, 65
Belvedere Hotel, 57, 63
Best Western Manhattan, 65
Best Western President, 65
Best Western Seaport Inn,
  64–65
Best Western Woodward, 65
Broadway Inn, 57–58
Carlton Arms, 66
Chelsea Savoy Hotel, 56
Colonial House Inn, 56–57
Comfort Inn Manhattan, 65
Comfort Inn Midtown, 58, 65
Cosmopolitan Hotel-Tribeca,
  48–49
Crowne Plaza at the United
  Nations, 55
De Hirsch Residence at the
  92nd Street YM-YWCA, 76
Gershwin Hotel, 8, 50–51
Gramercy Park Hotel, 54–56
Habitat Hotel, 66–67
Hostelling International-
  New York, 75–76
Hotel 17, 51
Hotel 31, 67–68
Hotel Edison, 59
Hotel Grand Union, 67
Hotel Newton, 72
Hotel Riverside, 72–73
Hotel Wolcott, 59–60
Larchmont Hotel, 50
Loews New York, 65
Malibu Hotel, 73–74
Marriott Financial Center, 54
Marriott World Trade Center,
  54–55
Milburn, The, 74

Millenium Hilton, 54
Millennium Broadway, 55
Off SoHo Suites, 49
Park Savoy Hotel, 60
Pickwick Arms Hotel, 68
Portland Square Hotel, 60–61
Quality Hotel Eastside, 65,
  68–69
Quality Hotel & Suites
  Midtown, 61, 65
Travel Inn, 61–62
Urban Jem Guest House,
  76–77
Vanderbilt YMCA, 69
Washington Jefferson Hotel,
  62
West Side YMCA, 74–75
Wyndham, The, 62–63
YMCA of Greater New York,
  8, 69, 74–75, 76

RESTAURANTS

Acme Bar & Grill, 89
Aggie's, 94
Amy's Bread, 109
Angelica Kitchen, 90
Bar Pitti, 96
Big Nick's Burger Joint, 114
Boca Chica, 90
Bombay Dining, 91
British Open, 109–10
Cafe de Bruxelles, 96
Cafe Gitane, 85–86
Cafe Habana, 86
Cafeteria, 103–4
California Pizza Oven, 102
Canova Market, 108
Carnegie Deli, 92
Chat 'n' Chew, 98–99
Coffee Shop, 99
Corner Bistro, 96–97

Cucina di Pesce, 90–92
Delegates' Dining Room, 143
Empire Diner, 104
ESPN Zone, 110
Ess-A-Bagel, 110–12
Eureka Joe, 103
Franklin Station Cafe, 82–83
Gabriela's, 114–15
Gandhi, 91
Gray's Papaya, 98, 115, 118
Hard Rock Cafe, 110
Harley-Davidson Cafe, 110
Haveli, 91
Housing Works Used Books
  Cafe, 89
Hunan Park, 115
Island Burgers & Shakes,
  104–5
Jekyll & Hyde Club, 111
Joe's Shanghai, 84
John's Pizzeria, 98, 105, 114,
  117
Josie's Restaurant & Juice Bar,
  115–16
Katz's Delicatessen, 93
Kitchenette, 83
La Bonne Soupe, 105
Lombardi's, 86, 88
Los Dos Rancheros Mexicanos,
  106
Mangia, 79–80, 109, 113
Mars 2112, 111
Michael Jordan's–The Steak
  House, 141
Mitali East, 91
Moustache, 89, 97
New York Noodletown, 84–85
Nha Trang, 85
North Star Pub, 80
Official All-Star Cafe, 111
Old Town Bar & Restaurant,
  99, 102

Oyster Bar, 113–14, 141
Papaya King, 118
Paradise & Lunch, 109
Passage to India, 91
Pietrasanta, 106
Pintaile's Pizza, 102, 117
Pisces, 92–93
Planet Hollywood, 111
Pó, 97–98
Pongal, 112
Prime Burger, 112
Pump, The, 113
Rainforest Cafe, 110
Raw Restaurant, 110
Republic, 102
Rice 'n' Beans, 107
Riverrun Cafe, 83–84
Salaam Bombay, 83
Sapporo, 89, 107
Sarabeth's Kitchen, 116,
  117
Second Avenue Deli, 93
Serendipity 3, 117–18
Siam Inn Too, 107–8
Sofia Fabulous Pizza, 117
SoHo Kitchen & Bar, 79, 88
Soup Kitchen International,
  109
Spring Street Natural
  Restaurant, 88–89
Stage Deli, 92
Sylvia's, 118
Taco & Tortilla King, 112–13
Tavern Room at Gramercy
  Tavern, 103
Totonno's Pizzeria Napolitano,
  117
Veselka, 93–94
Village Yokocho, 94
Virgil's Real BBQ, 108
Wall Street Kitchen & Bar, 79,
  88, 178

FROMMER'S® COMPLETE TRAVEL GUIDES

Alaska
Amsterdam
Arizona
Atlanta
Australia
Austria
Bahamas
Barcelona, Madrid & Seville
Beijing
Belgium, Holland & Luxembourg
Bermuda
Boston
Budapest & the Best of Hungary
California
Canada
Cancún, Cozumel & the Yucatán
Cape Cod, Nantucket & Martha's Vineyard
Caribbean
Caribbean Cruises & Ports of Call
Caribbean Ports of Call
Carolinas & Georgia
Chicago
China
Colorado
Costa Rica
Denmark
Denver, Boulder & Colorado Springs
England
Europe
Florida
France
Germany
Greece
Greek Islands
Hawaii
Hong Kong
Honolulu, Waikiki & Oahu
Ireland
Israel
Italy
Jamaica & Barbados
Japan
Las Vegas
London
Los Angeles
Maryland & Delaware
Maui
Mexico

Miami & the Keys
Montana & Wyoming
Montréal & Québec City
Munich & the Bavarian Alps
Nashville & Memphis
Nepal
New England
New Mexico
New Orleans
New York City
Nova Scotia, New Brunswick & Prince Edward Island
Oregon
Paris
Philadelphia & the Amish Country
Portugal
Prague & the Best of the Czech Republic
Provence & the Riviera
Puerto Rico
Rome
San Antonio & Austin
San Diego
San Francisco
Santa Fe, Taos & Albuquerque
Scandinavia
Scotland
Seattle & Portland
Singapore & Malaysia
South Africa
Southeast Asia
South Pacific
Spain
Sweden
Switzerland
Thailand
Tokyo
Toronto
Tuscany & Umbria
USA
Utah
Vancouver & Victoria
Vermont, New Hampshire & Maine
Vienna & the Danube Valley
Virgin Islands
Virginia
Walt Disney World & Orlando
Washington, D.C.
Washington State

FROMMER'S® DOLLAR-A-DAY GUIDES

Australia from $50 a Day
California from $60 a Day
Caribbean from $70 a Day
England from $70 a Day
Europe from $60 a Day
Florida from $60 a Day

Hawaii from $70 a Day
Ireland from $50 a Day
Israel from $45 a Day
Italy from $70 a Day
London from $85 a Day
New York from $80 a Day

New Zealand from $50 a Day
Paris from $85 a Day
San Francisco from $60 a Day
Washington, D.C., from $60 a Day

FROMMER'S® PORTABLE GUIDES

Acapulco, Ixtapa & Zihuatanejo
Alaska Cruises & Ports of Call
Bahamas
Baja & Los Cabos
Berlin
California Wine Country
Charleston & Savannah

Chicago
Dublin
Hawaii: The Big Island
Las Vegas
London
Maine Coast
Maui
New Orleans
New York City

Paris
Puerto Vallarta, Manzanillo & Guadalajara
San Diego
San Francisco
Sydney
Tampa & St. Petersburg
Venice
Washington, D.C.

FROMMER'S® NATIONAL PARK GUIDES

Family Vacations in the National Parks
Grand Canyon
National Parks of the American West
Rocky Mountain

Yellowstone & Grand Teton
Yosemite & Sequoia/Kings Canyon
Zion & Bryce Canyon

FROMMER'S® GREAT OUTDOOR GUIDES

New England
Northern California

Southern California & Baja
Washington & Oregon

FROMMER'S® MEMORABLE WALKS

Chicago
London

New York
Paris

San Francisco
Washington D.C.

FROMMER'S® IRREVERENT GUIDES

Amsterdam
Boston
Chicago
Las Vegas

London
Los Angeles
Manhattan

New Orleans
Paris
San Francisco

Seattle & Portland
Vancouver
Walt Disney World
Washington, D.C.

FROMMER'S® BEST-LOVED DRIVING TOURS

America
Britain
California

Florida
France
Germany

Ireland
Italy
New England

Scotland
Spain
Western Europe

THE UNOFFICIAL GUIDES®

Bed & Breakfast in New England
Bed & Breakfast in the Northwest
Beyond Disney
Branson, Missouri
California with Kids
Chicago
Cruises
Disneyland
Florida with Kids
The Great Smoky & Blue
   Ridge Mountains
Inside Disney
Las Vegas

London
Miami & the Keys
Mini Las Vegas
Mini-Mickey
New Orleans
New York City
Paris
San Francisco
Skiing in the West
Walt Disney World
Walt Disney World for Grown-ups
Walt Disney World for Kids
Washington, D.C.

SPECIAL-INTEREST TITLES

Born to Shop: France
Born to Shop: Hong Kong
Born to Shop: Italy
Born to Shop: New York
Born to Shop: Paris
Frommer's Britain's Best Bike Rides
The Civil War Trust's Official Guide
   to the Civil War Discovery Trail
Frommer's Caribbean Hideaways
Frommer's Europe's Greatest
   Driving Tours
Frommer's Food Lover's Companion
   to France
Frommer's Food Lover's Companion
   to Italy
Frommer's Gay & Lesbian Europe
Israel Past & Present

Monks' Guide to California
Monks' Guide to New York City
The Moon
New York City with Kids
Unforgettable Weekends
Outside Magazine's Guide
   to Family Vacations
Places Rated Almanac
Retirement Places Rated
Road Atlas Britain
Road Atlas Europe
Washington, D.C., with Kids
Wonderful Weekends from Boston
Wonderful Weekends from
   New York City
Wonderful Weekends from San Francisco
Wonderful Weekends from Los Angeles